INSIDE THE HARVARD BUSINESS SCHOOL

I N S I D E

THE HARVARD BUSINESS SCHOOL

STRATEGIES AND LESSONS OF AMERICA'S LEADING SCHOOL OF BUSINESS

DAVID W. EWING

TIMES 🅣 BOOKS

RANDOM HOUSE

Grateful acknowledgment is made to *The New York Times* for permission to reprint
an excerpt from "Gatsby at the B School" by Robert Coles from the October 25,
1987, issue of *The New York Times*. Copyright © 1987 by The New York Times
Company. Reprinted by permission.

LIBRARY OF CONGRESS CATALOGING-IN-PUBLICATION DATA
Ewing, David W.
Inside the Harvard Business School : strategies and lessons of
America's leading school of business / by David W. Ewing.
    p.   cm.
ISBN 0-8129-1827-4
1. Harvard University. Graduate School of Business
Administration—Curricula. 2. Harvard University. Graduate School
of Business Administration—Alumni—Interviews. I. Title.
HF1134.H4E95 1990
650'.071'1074461—dc20   89-40188

Designed by Beth Tondreau Design/Jane Treuhaft
Manufactured in the United States of America
9 8 7 6 5 4 3 2
FIRST EDITION

TO

those students and alumni
who gave me some of their time
and made this book possible

CONTENTS

INSIDE THE HARVARD BUSINESS SCHOOL

THE CATHEDRAL
OF MANAGEMENT

The Harvard Business School is probably the most powerful private institution in the world. Its ideas change the operations and standards of corporations, nonprofit organizations, and governments. Its fifty thousand graduates wield enormous economic and political clout. It stands chin-high in money, taking in millions more every year than it spends. Its educational influence is second to none.

The ability of the B-school, as it is often called, to change the way organizations do things is legendary. In marketing, it first championed the concept of the marketing mix, a potent tool that links a company's product, pricing, distribution, and communications policies into a unified whole. In employee relations it launched the philosophies of the informal group, participative management, and power sharing. In production and operations it tied what goes on in the factory and office to the organization's overall success, making them a key to strategy. In finance it pioneered the concept of discounting future cash flows to their present value. In managerial economics it developed such techniques as decision trees, preference curves, and quantitative risk analysis. In business ethics it seeks to make ethical awareness a part of *all* management decisions.

In these and hundreds of other ways the B-school has altered management practices forever. Some of these practices are now so familiar that we take them for granted—they are part of the management woodwork, so to speak. Many others are in the stage of becoming widely accepted standards.

What about the economic and political power of B-school alumni? The story is spectacular. More alums head companies in the Fortune 500 than do grads of any other institution; close to one-third of the top officers in these companies are HBS alums. In medium-size and small firms, the alumni directory is top-heavy with men and women in policymaking positions, many of them just a few years out of Boston. In addition, numerous alums are top executives of nonprofit organizations; many have amassed great political power; and a startling number have played key roles in dramatic technological revolutions with worldwide consequences.

Here is a tiny sample of B-school alums who have made it to the top:

- William Agee '63 heads Morris Knudsen Corporation, a construction and engineering firm in Boise with sales of $2 billion.
- Warren Batts '63 is chief executive of Premark International, an Illinois producer of household products with sales of about $2 billion.
- Roy Bostock '64 is president of D'Arcy, Masius, Benton & Bowles, a New York advertising agency with $1.3 billion in billings.
- Robert Cizik '58 is chairman of Cooper Industries, a manufacturer of engines, turbines, pumps, and other equipment with $3 billion sales worldwide.
- Marshall Cogan '62 heads Knoll International Holdings in New York, one of the largest privately held businesses in the United States.

- Louis Gerstner '65 is chief executive of RJR Nabisco, which has revenues of $16 billion.
- Robert Haas '68 is chief executive of Levi Straus & Company, with sales of $2.7 billion.
- Robert Hauptfuhrer '57 is CEO of Sun Exploration & Production Company, a $4.8 billion division of Sun.
- Richard Jenrette '57 is chairman of Equitable Life Assurance Society in New York, with sales of $5.7 billion.
- Victor Kiam II '51 heads Remington Products and owns the New England Patriots.
- Frank Lorenzo '63 heads Texas Air Corporation, with sales of $8.5 billion.
- Vernon Loucks, Jr., '63 heads Baxter International, a health-care company with worldwide sales exceeding $6 billion and rated one of the best-managed companies in the United States.
- Robert Malott '50 heads FMC Corporation in Chicago, with sales of $3.1 billion.
- Joseph McKinney '57 is CEO of Tyler Corporation in Dallas, a manufacturer with sales of $1.1 billion.
- Jerry Perlman '62 is CEO of Zenith Electronics Corporation in Illinois, with sales of $2.4 billion.
- James Robinson '61 is chairman of American Express, which has worldwide revenues of $18 billion.
- John Rollwagen '64 heads Cray Research, Inc., the Minneapolis-based corporation that has dominated the super-computer industry for more than a decade.
- Richard Thomson '57 heads Toronto Dominion Bank, ranked the fifth most powerful business in Canada.
- William Timken '62 is board chairman of the Timken Company in Akron, a steel company with sales of $1.2 billion; and Joseph Toot '61 is president of the organization.

In Washington, Nicholas Brady '54 heads the Treasury Department, and Richard Darman '67 directs the influential Office of Management and Budget. John Shad '49, former chairman of the Securities and Exchange Commission, is U.S. ambassador to the

Netherlands. Congressmen include R. L. Coughlin, Jr., '54 and Willis Gradison '51; Herbert Kohl '58 is the junior U.S. senator from Wisconsin.

In state capitols, W. Booth Gardner '63 is governor of Washington, Robert Orr '42 is governor of Indiana, and Charles Roemer III '67 is governor of Louisiana.

Including graduates of executive programs such as Advanced Management, nearly ten thousand alums work in more than 120 foreign countries. One is Peter Lougheed '54, the famous premier of Alberta, Canada, for fourteen years; another is James Ongpin '62, finance minister in Corazon Aquino's cabinet in the Philippines and a leader in the revolution against Ferdinand Marcos. Corporate leaders include Diego Bush '71, who heads a large integrated textile and apparel company in Brazil; George Pappas '71, who heads the top-rated consulting firm in Australia; and Christopher Hogg '62, who heads Courtaulds PLC, Britain's largest textile and chemical group.

In cash flow, bottom line, and alumni giving, HBS is the envy of almost all graduate schools and colleges. Its annual budget is about $100 million, its endowment has grown to $250 million, and it is engaged in a capital spending program of about $400 million. The renovation of one building alone, Morgan Hall, due to start in the summer of 1990, is expected to cost $22 million. The school rejects practically all government funding.

The annual take from alums is mind-boggling. For instance, the annual fund drive completed in June 1988 and headed by Carl S. Sloane '60, chief executive of Temple, Barker & Sloane in Lexington, Massachusetts, was carried out by about one thousand alums who raised more than $14 million for the school (an especially impressive figure in view of the stock market crash partway through that fund-raising year). In 1989 about $15 million was raised.

The most publicized gift to the school has been John Shad's grant of $20 million in 1987 for the study and advancement of business ethics. Dean John McArthur expects other givers to add $10 million more in the near future.

As for educational influence, the Harvard Business School conceived and refined the business case method, which has revolutionized management education all over the globe, and also conceived and refined the section system, a far-reaching innovation in learning. The school places enormous emphasis on excellence in teaching; its quality control of instruction has no equal and has become a gospel to educators elsewhere. In addition, every year the school sends reprints of several million cases and articles to training groups all over the world.

The importance of the school, however, must not be measured only in quantitative terms. In recent years it has become essential to the United States' welfare and survival as a world-class power. As the flagship of management education, it has become as important to the United States economically as West Point, Annapolis, Colorado Springs, and other fine academies are militarily.

Why is this so? What does HBS do that is unique? As one who has seen the school from the inside out for four decades, personally known most of its leaders, taught, and had a hand in many of its struggles, I shall try to answer such questions from an insider's viewpoint. My views differ a great deal from those of other writers. Of the various books that have been written about the B-school in recent years, three have come from students, including Fran Henry's fine account, *Toughing It Out at Harvard,* and the rest have come from outsiders. It is time to look at the school from the perspective of one who has lived a good part of its life with it.

THE HBS–UNITED STATES CONNECTION

The Harvard Business School occupies sixty-one acres on the south side of the Charles River in Boston, opposite Harvard College. On this campus stand more than two dozen well-cared-for buildings, most of them built of red brick and in the Georgian style, many with chimneys and one with a white cupola on top, most with ivy-covered walls and white-trim windows. The buildings are surrounded by spacious lawns that are as green as golf fairways. Hundreds of beautiful trees grow on campus along with elegant bushes and beds of colorful flowers. Here and there, a fine piece of sculpture ornaments the grounds.

The beauty is enhanced by the river. In spring the river reflects the green of the trees lining it; in fall, reds and yellows. Scullers and crews with their coxswains barking stroke up and down by day, and sometimes the domes of the college houses glow in the blackness. Visitors remember the sight for a long time.

But when HBS began in 1908, it was humble. Professors taught in several makeshift rooms in Harvard Yard, and it was far from certain that the school would survive. Fortune has been kind to the school. The faculty, staff, and students have taken advantage of many breaks, and what began in a tentative way has now become a permanent fixture.

When the B-school was conceived, the aim was to introduce more professionalism into U.S. business. The need was great but it wasn't urgent. The economy needed good managers just as the law needs good lawyers and medicine needs good doctors, but the supply wasn't critical to national survival. Now that situation has changed drastically. The school—and with it, of course, a number of other fine management schools, such as those at Dartmouth, Yale, New York, North Carolina, Virginia, Pennsylvania, Chicago, Northwestern, Stanford, and California—has become one of the country's keys to economic survival.

For more than a quarter of a century, the U.S. economy has been slipping in global competition. In industry after industry, American leadership has fallen away, as if our industrial forces were a big, fat, inefficient army that smaller, leaner, hungrier foreign armies could defeat in skirmishes and small battles. Three decades ago our economic legions dominated the world economy. Now some of these legions have been decimated, others have withdrawn, and many are fighting for their lives.

The consequences have been appalling. Hundreds of thousands of jobs have disappeared. Enormous deficits plague us. We can no longer afford the domestic programs required to deal adequately with hunger, homelessness, drugs, AIDS, and a host of other domestic problems. The crisis has been well publicized. But who can do anything about it? Few can really step in and make a difference. Legislators have passed some helpful laws but no politician can manage a computer factory or market auto parts. (Hubert Humphrey once quipped that the U.S. Senate couldn't even manage the Senate restaurant.) Economists can come up with revealing statistics, consultants can prescribe solutions for others to implement, and so on—but none of these useful services meets the number-one need, which is for people who can take charge and win.

In global economic competition, as in warfare, an industry has to have top-notch leaders. This wasn't always the case in the past because other nations didn't know how to compete. For several decades now, however, the West Germans, Japanese, Koreans, and others have been formidable rivals. No longer can American businesses match the competition without the guidance of fine top executives.

Without first-rate leaders, industry can no more hold its own against foreign enterprises than our armed forces could win without officers from West Point, Annapolis, Colorado Springs, and New London. In both cases, "naturals" and "rough diamonds" find their way to the top without formal training and become valuable parts of the picture, but the trained leaders are the core that we bet on. We bet on HBS and schools like it because we know they can help the nation win.

POWER TO CHANGE

What do Harvard Business School students learn that equips them to be leaders?

If you have any doubt that the school influences students—and not only influences but in a real sense transforms them—you need only compare what comes in with what goes out. At a recent opening-day ceremony for first-year students I was impressed with the brightness, energy, ability, and looks of the young men and women, most of them in their mid- to late twenties, some in their thirties. But after talking and listening to them I realized that this incoming group was no more sophisticated about management than any other group of bright, energetic kids their age might be. Their naïveté about business—and about their own powers—was colossal.

Two years later, however, these same kids possessed a remarkable understanding of profit and nonprofit organizations large and small, had an astonishing ability to put their arms about complex management problems and analyze them, were able to make decisions with imperfect information with great skill, possessed penetrating insights into their own strengths, weaknesses, and aims in life. I envied them. If some of their starting salaries (the *average* was between $55,000 and $60,000) humbled many of us on the faculty, I could find no fault with the system of supply and demand. The recruiters, who had descended on the B-school in hordes the previous winter, knew what they were doing.

What did the B-school do to these young men and women to make this progress possible? What equipped them to leave the starting gates so fast?

John Russell '59, now a senior professor at Boston University's School of Management and a former instructor at HBS, told me, "Harvard does one thing better than any other school that I know of: it *changes* students." For nearly four decades I have seen this happen—over and over and over again. In the early first-year classes in September, I have seen students deal with cases in an amateurish way, missing the point, pontificating, applying glib rules of thumb, and making every other mistake that a group of bright but wet-behind-the-ears people might be expected to make. They would be so sure of themselves that it was frightening. By early winter, however, the bloom would be off the rose and the sureness would have given way to grave doubts and wholesale despair.

Yet in class and study groups subtle but profound changes would be occurring in the quality of discussion and analysis. By spring wondrous new abilities would be showing, and during the second year a true blossoming would take place as the young men and women began to understand both the opportunities before them and the complexity of doing business.

In interviewing and listening to alumni I have been struck by the indelible impression made by the two years at Harvard Business School. Most MBAs say they will never forget the experience; almost all can recall details that influenced them; a surprisingly large number feel more indebted to the B-school for their outlook and skills than to any other school they attended. The HBS experience, said James D. Robinson '61, "was like lighting a bunch of lights in the room that I never knew existed."

In addition to the business know-how and savvy gained by Harvard MBAs, I have been impressed by the school's impact on personal beliefs. This could be the most important effect of all. For instance, students learn that they can do a lot more than they had thought. R. Lee Buechler '78, president of Phamis, a technology company in Seattle, told me, "The school changed my personal expectations about what I achieve in my career, about what I do with my life. It put a monkey on my back that probably I'll never shake, the idea that I can achieve a whole lot more than I have so far. I attribute the awakening of that belief to my experience at the business school. I'm not sure whether that's good or bad, but it's a fact."

What does the B-school do to bring such changes about?

Some critics attribute the strong track records of graduates not to anything that happens at the school but to other factors. Without question, alums have a lot of things going for them. There can be no doubt, for example, that just the fact of being able to say "I graduated from the Harvard Business School" is a real plus. When Lester Colbert '61 was chairman of Xidex Corporation in Sunnyvale, California, he noted that "the degree is like a Good Housekeeping Seal of Approval." Thousands of graduates have received a visible or invisible push from this association. On the other hand, it is going much too far to say, as Ralph Nader told an HBS audience recently, that "you come out of the school with a brand name, and all you have to say to people all of your life is that 'I graduated from Harvard Business School,' and they give you the benefit of a doubt." That simply is not true, as thousands of alums can attest.

Yet, countless grads have taken advantage of a strong alumni network. Including graduates of the Advanced Management and small company programs, about fifty thousand alums, the largest graduate business school group in the country, provide an extremely supportive club. Each graduating class adds to the flow—the class of 1990, with more than 750 members, is the biggest graduate business school class in the country. Alums hold meetings in countless places. They help one another. They organize workshops. The lift that such a powerful network can give an aspiring student or a graduate who is at sixes and sevens in his or her career should never be underestimated.

Also, alumni often give each other valuable contacts and assistance in reaching a business goal. Thus, John Wheeler '69 says that he got help from four powerful HBS alums at critical junctures in his campaign to establish a Vietnam Veterans Memorial—the beautiful monument that now graces the Mall in Washington, D.C.

Nor is this vast network confined to the United States. Alums occupy influential posts in countries all over the world—about ten thousand of them (including graduates of executive programs) working in more than 120 foreign countries. "There is certainly a tremendous personal reward," I was told by William B. R. Hobbs '75, chief executive of Bridon American Corporation, "when you walk into the boardroom of Samsung Industries in Seoul, the second-largest city in Korea, to discuss a license agreement and find your section mate Chong-Sang Ahn sitting across the table as director of the corporate planning division."

It is also true that the admission standards at HBS preselect students who are talented and ambitious. In fact, only about one-eighth of applicants are chosen. In a sense, therefore, success is built into the alumni body. One alum I know remembers Professor Milton Brown, a well-known marketing professor, telling a group of students gathered around his desk after class, "You guys are so good that we could teach you Greek here and you'd still go out and succeed."

Nonetheless, it remains clear that two years in the MBA program changes students quite a bit, stretching their native ability further, putting a sharper edge on it, channeling it. This extra power goes a long way to making Harvard MBAs the elite group they are. For two years they rub elbows with other extra-talented people, and that is part of HBS's secret. Their classes, study groups, and teams have a powerful effect on them *because* of this unusual chemistry.

EDUCATIONAL STRATEGY

Now let us look at how the school accomplishes its magic on students. What enables this "cathedral of American business management," as *Business Week* called it in a cover story on the school, to turn raw talent into management ability with such success? The faculty and administration have a conscious strategy of education. To encapsulate the main features of their strategy:

They have a sense of mission. They believe fervently that good management is important to the country. At faculty lunch tables I have again and again sensed the outrage and indignation felt by professors over incidents of mismanagement in the news. The students are their way of doing something about the situation.

I have found two major causes of jubilation among professors. One is a class that has gone well, especially a class expected to be difficult. The second is learning that a former student is setting the world on fire by taking the management reins successfully. I heard Professor Earl Sasser, a popular southerner with steel-rimmed glasses and a mustache, tell an incoming class recently that the school hopes "to get you to leadership positions by the year 2010."

I am told that this single-minded dedication sets the Harvard B-school apart from many educational institutions that have amorphous goals and whose teachers can't agree on what they are trying to do.

The B-school emphasizes learning over teaching. This may sound like word play but it isn't. What a student learns is not always what a professor teaches, and what a professor teaches is not always what a student learns.

At HBS students are not taught in the way generally practiced by universities and training programs—that is, by lectures and reading. Rather, they learn by discussing cases that lack simple answers and making up their minds themselves. The B-school promotes the idea that students—at least, able and mature students—learn (a) more realistically if presented with concrete problems from organizational experience, and (b) more thoroughly if they are forced to distill the lessons of those experiences themselves rather than be spoon-fed management principles.

The B-school relies on the case method of teaching. It doesn't rely on the case method exclusively—in every course there is background reading, professors often give a two-minute summation of a class at the end, and second-year students may spend up to a fifth of their time on so-called field studies (firsthand investigations of situations in organizations). But the case method is the warp and woof of the school's approach and underlies the teaching philosophy.

In the next chapter I will describe the case method in detail. The method, built around analysis of actual business and organizational situations, has been basic to the school for nearly seven decades. Once the late professor William Abernathy winked at me and said, "I tell my students that a tenured professor here can be fired for two reasons—immorality and lecturing. And you aren't fired for immorality anymore."

The case method is HBS's "baby." The school pioneered it, mothers it, spends large sums of money on it every year, and sends out more than 2 million cases a year (2.5 million in 1988–1989) to schools and training groups around the world.

Compared to graduate school as we generally think of it, HBS puts relatively little emphasis on memorizing facts. Attending class, you generally find few students scribbling notes (although most have made notes before class on the case assigned). The point is that management is not a body of knowledge but a discipline, an approach to complexity.

The school stresses class participation—speaking out on the case or problem at hand. Some students are more vocal than others, but no student is excused from sharing his or her opinions out loud. In consequence, classes are lively and students learn a great deal about the art of contributing orally to a discussion, an important activity in management. In turn, readers can learn a great deal from what *they* learn, and I shall describe some of these "lessons" in a later chapter.

In the first year, the crucial and traumatic year for students, HBS uses the section system. Each student has all classes in one room with the ninety or so other students in his or her section—from September to May. Although some students complain about this system, comparing it to life in a submarine or prison, I think it is crucial to the astonishing growth that takes place in first-years.

The B-school is the only school in the world I know of that practices the section system to such an extreme. A few other schools use it but for more limited periods.

B-school students typically work very long hours, especially during the first year. In my observation, most students work from 7:00 or 7:30 in the morning to an hour or two past midnight—and even then they can't get all the work done. "I didn't know I could work so hard," one student told me. I have heard that opinion echoed in all my talks and interviews.

You may say that it is unhealthy to put young people under so much pressure, but the fact is that B-school students weather the ordeal quite well. It forces students to collaborate in ways they wouldn't otherwise. They learn a few things about living under stress that should be interesting and valuable to us all. Also, students graduate and go into the management world with a standard of hard, arduous work that is extremely important if they are to manage with excellence.

Every part of the school reinforces the other parts. I know of no organization that does better in this respect. Practically every major activity of the school reinforces the other functions, resulting in a synergistic whole with remarkable resilience and powers of communication. The neo-Georgian buildings remind students of their links with tradition; the huge library, the admissions office, the main MBA program plus the executive programs, the alumni relations offices and houses, the student clubs—these and other activities all combine to say, "This is the Harvard Business School. This is the way to success."

HBS accepts and indeed celebrates capitalism. Professors may believe that this institution or that might perform better if such-and-such were done, and students personally may be for or against certain social programs and institutions in the news, but the common assumption is that you take the economic system as it is and try to make it work better. In short, the B-school does not, as some of its critics wish it would, hold up a daring new vision of economic America and society.

Early in the 1980s the students put on a lively spring musicale, a joyous parody of life at the school and in the business world. In the theme song sung by the chorus, one line was: "We love the system, we don't like to buck it." That says it all.

Later in this book we will look at some ideas emphasized in class and ranging from marketing to finance. But as a senior professor told me, "The substance of what we teach here is not all that different from what can be learned at some other schools." To be sure, there are some distinctions in curriculum between HBS and other top management schools, but they are small stuff compared to the distinctions in process. HBS students acquire no magic formula or technique that enables them to manage successfully. The tricks of the trade they learn are instrumental to their later success but are not what makes their education unique.

WHAT STUDENTS LEARN

WHY WISDOM
ISN'T TOLD

In the fall of 1988,
the class of 1963, marking its twenty-fifth reunion at the school,
gave HBS a record-breaking gift of $5 million. "The gift," said
Charles Ellis '63, chairman of the campaign, "will support what
we think is the most important part of the school: its commitment
to case-method teaching." The class wanted the donation to un-
derwrite a program headed by Professor C. Roland Christensen
to help teachers develop skills for teaching by the case method.
Ellis, the founder and head of a sizable financial services firm in
Greenwich, Connecticut, spoke with fervor about his allegiance
to the Harvard Business School.

The event shows how greatly alums value the case approach.
When they were students, it may have given them fits, especially
during the first year, but once they became used to it, it became
a way of thinking that changed their lives. "It's a little like the
lawyer's or doctor's way of thinking, but it's also different from
them," I remember Professor Fritz Roethlisberger explaining
once. Roethlisberger was one of the pioneers in the study of

employee behavior. "And it means you take people as they are, not as you think they should be."

The Harvard Business School conceived and launched the management case method. Its annual investment in the case method is greater today than it ever was. The faculty is likely to develop more than 300 cases per year from firsthand investigation of companies of all types. If you go through the school's MBA program, you are likely to study about 900 cases in the two years, each one calling for two or three hours of preparation. Cases will dominate much of your conversations with others, perhaps even enter your dreams.

In addition, the school spends a great deal of time and money on case-method training programs for instructors. For instance, films show how an instructor and class interact in real-life situations, and written cases raise provocative questions about an instructor's approach and style.

What is a case? It is a description of an actual situation. It is never made up, it is never synthesized, it is never hypothetical. In ten to thirty single-spaced typewritten pages plus exhibits, the case describes a management problem. In all probability the case was written by a professor or by a staff assistant under professorial supervision.

Studying the case, you begin by trying to figure out what's going on. The situation is described clearly enough but there are numerous conflicting opinions and a welter of facts and data, some of them inconsistent—all as a manager experienced them. In my own experience—and that of most others with whom I have talked—this stage is likely to be the most difficult and time-consuming one.

Then you wonder how things got the way they are. What people and conditions share the credit or blame? Next, putting yourself in the shoes of the subject manager, you think about possible solutions or plans of action—what could you do if you were this man or woman? Finally, you decide what you think is the best way to proceed.

Unlike cases in law school, you don't find an answer or decision with precedential value at the end of an HBS case. Unlike cases in medical school, there's no objective way of finding out whether your diagnosis was right or your prescription a good one. However, reasoning is very important—perhaps more important because of these uncertainties. While there are no "right" answers, some answers are more persuasive than others because they take account of more facts and conditions.

As we shall see in more detail in a later chapter, most cases require an enormous amount of effort to develop and write. Always the subject organization has cooperated, opening its files, making key people available for interviews, reviewing the drafts, and, when all is done, releasing the case for class use.

THE MITEK CASE

Although cases vary enormously in substance, subject, style, and length, I will pick one for purposes of illustration. Its name is "Mitek Corporation." It is about four thousand words long plus about eighteen pages of exhibits. Although Mitek is a fictional company name and the names of the people in the case are fictional, the company and managers described are 100 percent real.

"Mitek" was written by Assistant Professor Evelyn Christiansen for use in the course now called Management Planning and Practice. Christiansen told me that the case had worked very well in that course—that is, students had responded to it, discussed it energetically, and, under the instructor's guidance, learned from it. One of the reasons "Mitek" was fun to teach, she said, was that it raised so many interesting issues.

The lead character in the case is a human dynamo named Robert Tweed, who is the president and prime mover. Five years ago, he and four other men founded Mitek, beginning in the proverbial garage and on a shoestring. At the time the case opens, Mitek is heading for the big time. It is pulling in $40 million a year in sales, is listed on the big board, operates labs and offices, and runs both a domestic and foreign sales force. However, it also has some morale problems. Mitek is a high-tech firm, meaning that it uses advanced technology and depends on talented engineers and new products.

Although Tweed has great abilities, he also is capable of driving his associates up the wall. One habit that drives them bananas is his impulsive hiring. In the past year or so he has hired three key people without consulting his colleagues. Also, he has gotten into the habit of writing and distributing important memos and reports without consulting others first.

Without telling anyone, he sent out a twenty-five-page-plus-exhibits statement on company goals and policies for the future. The statement went to about fifty people, including directors and top executives. Although he expected them to critique the statement with interest and send him their comments, only half have done so, and of that half, most responses have been critical. One, in fact, comes from a vice president and cofounder of Mitek who blasts Tweed's ideas and accuses him of contributing to the morale problems described in the statement.

Tweed is baffled. Holy cow, what's going on here? Instead of generating some interesting collegial discussion, which was his intention, he walked into a buzz saw! What should he do? What should the board of directors or anyone else do?

Of course, Christiansen didn't write the case glibly, as I have described it, but carefully and thoughtfully, as described to her by Mitek people. The company wouldn't have released it for teaching otherwise.

As Christiansen told me, instructors are likely to focus class discussion first on Tweed's strategy statement. What is such a statement supposed to do? How should it be written? Naturally, there is a division of opinion on this question. Some students see a strategy statement as a kind of blueprint, others as a mere catalyst. Some don't object to the way Tweed sent it out; others do. "Look," said one student in a class I attended, "this guy's the president, and the president doesn't have to go around asking for opinions if he doesn't want them." But another student said, "Hey, this isn't a one-man company anymore but a hundred people, and they're all in it together."

One student faulted Tweed for not having a retreat for his top people at some nice lodge in the mountains and thrashing over the goals and policy statement there. Another said, "This guy has no business writing this statement himself; he should be assigning others to write it. *Then* they should go to that retreat."

When the instructor asked about Tweed's leadership style, one student said, "Well, it's pretty autocratic, but this man has gotten results. If the others don't like it, they know what they can do." Others disagreed vehemently. "That style was okay when the company was young," opined one, "but now it's big and that's not gonna work anymore." Another said, "Furthermore, this guy isn't going to change."

The instructor then asked the last student to imagine himself for a minute as a member of the board. What would he recommend doing? "We're going to have to tell him to step down," said the student. "The leopard won't change his spots." The instructor nodded and asked who the student thought should take Tweed's place. The student cleared his throat and hemmed and hawed. He didn't know. A flurry of hands went up, wagging for attention.

The Mitek case makes students think hard. An autocratic management style has strengths but, especially as an organization grows, serious weaknesses. Strategic planning is a futile exercise if done unilaterally. The board of directors may have a crucial role to play in a growing organization, a role that goes much further than simply reviewing financial statements.

Later I will give other examples of cases. First, let's look into some general questions about the method. What does it do that other methods don't do? What are its strengths and limitations?

HOW DOES ONE FIT ANSWER TO FACT?

The very first case was used in an HBS classroom in 1912, just a few years after the school was started. Thanks to the missionary efforts of the tiny faculty, the method caught on, and more cases were collected. By 1924 the school was ready to announce that the case method was the primary method of instruction. I have seen some of those cases, and I am struck by how bland and quaint they seem by our standards now; also, they were much shorter. One was less than a page long.

From the very beginning the school seems to have known that it was on to a good thing in the case method. The classic exposition of the approach was written in 1940 for the *Harvard Alumni Bulletin* by Professor Charles Gragg. A bespectacled, reflective man who had done a lot of teaching, Gragg entitled his famous article "Because Wisdom Can't Be Told." In the short space of a couple of years, he wrote, graduate business students have "to achieve the transition from what may be described as a childlike dependence on parents and teachers to a state of what may be called dependable self-reliance." Up to that point, he explained, the students have been fed information and principles gleaned from the wisdom and accumulated experience of others. It might seem to make sense to go on doing that. In fact, however, it is fallacious to assume "that it is possible by a simple process of telling to pass on knowledge in a useful form. This is a stumbling block of the ages."

Gragg admitted that it would indeed be gratifying to pass on one's knowledge. But no matter how well one memorizes and communicates facts, the problem of applying the knowledge persists. Gragg quoted the limerick:

> *A student of business with tact*
> *Absorbed many answers he lacked.*
> *But acquiring a job,*
> *He said with a sob,*
> *How does one fit answer to fact?*

"For both teachers and students," wrote Gragg, "the disciplines of the case method of learning are severe. Sometimes the shock is devastating to students who previously have been dominated by patriarchal representatives and thus have been faced merely with the relatively simple task of more or less verbatim reception and repetition of facts and ideas." In the classroom where the case method is used, students deal democratically with equals whose criticisms must be faced and whose contributions must be comprehended and used. "The outstanding virtue of the case system is that it is suited to inspiring activity, under realistic conditions, on the part of students; it takes them out of the role of passive absorbers and makes them partners in the joint processes of learning and of furthering learning."

One of the first things students discover, observed Gragg, "is the inability of the individual to think of everything that his fellow students can think of." Gradually students learn "to draw more and more fully upon each other's ideas in the working out of problems. Competition for high academic standing grows more keen, to be sure, but the mutual giving and taking of assistance ceases to be a matter of secret anguish." Ideas and possible solutions come from everywhere, giving active listening an importance it could not have otherwise.

Gragg had no illusions about the risks of the case method. A badly taught case discussion is an academic horror, he acknowledged, with the case being perceived by students as a means of confusing and boring them. If the instructor is unskilled or believes that he or she knows what the class should think, the case method won't work and "the out-and-out lecture system is infinitely less costly and less straining to everyone concerned."

If Gragg were with us today, he might say that the case method teaches students three things.

1. OF COURSE YOU'RE NOT SURE, BUT YOU'RE IN CHARGE

In a good case discussion, said Gragg, students are put in the position of executives who must decide what to do on the basis of facts in their possession. One has to stick one's neck out, and there is no ducking of responsibility. "As Winston Churchill is reported to have remarked recently, there is a great deal of difference between being responsible for an order which may lose several valuable ships and expressing an opinion without such responsibility."

This is one of the most important features of the case method. I have interviewed many alums and talked with numerous students, and I have yet to find one who didn't learn the lesson— sometimes traumatically—that leaders have to make decisions based on the best information available. One witness is C. D.

Spangler, Jr., '56, president of the University of North Carolina. Spangler, who had to apply to the B-school twice before gaining admission, says that when he arrived at Soldiers Field out of the warm and hospitable South, the day was inhospitably cold and he was scared to death. Remembering the first week of classes, Spangler says:

"Tom Raymond, who was head of the course then known as Written Analysis of Cases, called on someone to open the case and explain what he would do. When the student responded by saying he needed more information before making a recommendation, Tom immediately turned to someone else. About ten minutes before the class was over, he came back to the first student he had called on, looked him straight in the eye, and told him very sternly, 'Don't you ever come to my class again without having made a decision. As a businessman, you will often be in a situation where you would like to have more information. That doesn't make any difference. You have to be able to act upon what's available at the time.' The lesson in decision making provided by that incident was one of the most important we would ever learn."

In the student newspaper *The Harbus News* several years ago, Thomas King '87, then a student, used an analogy to describe the case method:

"Instead of reading lofty texts, beginning art history students look at slides and discuss what they see. A painting goes up on the screen. The professor asks a student for analysis, the beginner mumbles a few random thoughts. Not satisfied, the professor probes. Is the time dawn or dusk? Is the setting past or present? Is the focus people or nature? Classmates offer chip shots. The student gropes aimlessly. No matter, because another painting flashes on the screen. More questions, more mumbling. Another painting follows, and another, and another. The process is painful."

After a while, however, King pointed out, patterns emerge. "Drawing on a new data base, the student begins to speak about clouds, light conditions, placement of figures, and a host of issues never considered before." The B-school's approach, he wrote, was similarly inductive. "Initial cases have no apparent rhyme or reason, and we grope to discuss flatware, blankets, and vineyards. But eventually patterns develop. . . ."

Since students notice patterns themselves, the lessons learned feel earned. The lessons have a vividness and durability that patterns pointed out just can't have.

2. THERE'S NO SWITCH TO FLIP FOR AN ANSWER

The subjectivity of management decisions is what makes them difficult for students. With no "right" answers to tie matters up with, students gradually come to feel abandoned, lost at sea, confused and bemused. "I feel as if I were trying to drink water with a fork," one first-year told me. Another chimed in, "Everything seems like a loose football." If only some professor would tell them what's right! Having to decide for themselves what they should do becomes terribly depressing, and at first morale declines steadily as the relentless tide of casework rolls on. Sometime around Christmas, spirits sink to a nadir, rising a little after exams in January.

In *Teaching with Cases at the Harvard Business School,* probably the best book on the subject, C. Roland Christensen quotes educator Nathaniel Cantor:

"To escape from the discomfort of struggle, to avoid the disagreeable feelings of uncertainty, inadequacy, and self-responsibility, we turn to the expert, the formula, the book, the superior or *the* verbal answer. Thus we think we avoid the heartache and headache of assuming responsibility for our decision. . . ."

There is no such escape at HBS, however, and in the winter of their discontent students' eyes may show a kind of desperation, like those of caged animals finding there is no way to freedom. This, it seems to me, is the common experience. Every winter you can sense the mood, exacerbated by the fact that most of these people have never experienced a serious academic setback before. Fortunately, it doesn't last forever—and when it is over, the student is a more mature person because of it.

Christensen emphasizes the difference in the instructor's role between discussion teaching and lecture teaching. In the former, he points out, the instructor "serves mainly as a facilitator of classroom discussion—rarely 'telling' students what they should know, but constantly probing, questioning, hypothesizing, challenging, and rephrasing their comments in an effort to help them analyze the case and understand its implications." In lecture teaching, by contrast, the instructor delivers a monologue, and students may be stifled.

Glancing at a case in the privacy of your room before class, you may find it depressing at first. Typically, it is written in lumbering prose, the beginning doesn't grab you, the middle is likely to be heavy going with slews of data and detail, and the finale may have the charm of a bowl of cold oatmeal. All this changes dramatically in the classroom, however; the case has been designed for teaching, not easy reading. In a class with a skilled instructor and bright students, the situation comes to life and participants may get quite worked up about it. What seemed lifeless the night before becomes vibrant. In fact, many times I have seen students get so fired up that they keep arguing with each other after the class has ended. Some will be upset by classmates' attitudes, others stimulated by a line of reasoning taken, others provoked by things overlooked.

If one thing becomes clear when the dust settles, it is that there is no one right answer to many management problems. The issues, stakes, and options can be identified, but no one can say with authority, "This is what should be done." The answer for a situation depends in part on the values and talents of whoever happens to be in charge, and what works best for one person or group may not work best for another. There is no scientific answer, in other words—no objective solution that can be verified under different circumstances as can the stress resistance of metal or the operation of a mathematical formula. The desires of the decision makers affect the outcome too much.

The range and scope of cases assigned to a class are amazing. During one two-week period last fall, according to my case assignment sheet, first-years argued the case of a printer of diaries who didn't know for sure how many copies would be sold, the case of a plastics manufacturer trying to decide which production process to use for polypropylene plastic strapping, a video of one executive's leadership style, a case on "social marketing" of family-planning products in Bangladesh, a computer exercise, and a far-ranging variety of other situations.

All this time students are taking in factual information as well as analyzing the managerial situation. The information comes out of the descriptions of the situations, and while much of it is forgotten, some, depending on the students' interests, sticks in their minds. How this company accounts for inventory, what procedure that company has for working with jobbers, the way such-and-such an executive uses computers, and so on. Professor Stephen Greyser once emphasized to me the importance of such information. "There's a kind of learning that MBA students get from cases that has nothing to do with analysis and decision making. I mean learning about business or government or other phenomena because of what's *in* the cases." During the course of the MBA program, one is exposed to all kinds of businesses and methods of operation.

3. LISTEN, YOU MIGHT HEAR SOMETHING

Let's go into a classroom and observe a first-year class.

Perhaps the first thing you will notice is the fluorescent light flooding down from the egg-crate ceiling. In this particular room, the walls and carpeting are beige, the desks are blond, the boards in front—three sets of them—are tan. You will see that the desks curve in semicircular rows, and the rows rise from the front, each a couple of steps above the other, a bit like six horseshoes ringing each other. Notice that in the rows, the desks are not separated except at the aisles; they curve in one piece, and each of the ninety-two students has the space in front of his or her seat.

The seats, upholstered in orange, blue, or some other color, are swivel seats, and they also bend back. Sitting in them, you can turn easily and see any other face in the room. Without raising your voice, you can be heard anywhere in the room.

There are no windows in this amphitheater. All sorts of comparisons have been made, most of them pejorative—the room is like an air-raid shelter, a soybean trading pit, a tomb, the inside of a submarine, and so on. Only a few students and alums have described the rooms to me with words like "cozy" or "warm."

Whatever you compare it to, the amphitheater is home for the students here. They stay in it for all classes every day, every week, every month, all the first year. Through the day the classes will change, and the master schedule itself may change every few weeks, but always the professors come to this room. This amphitheater is the playhouse, and the professors are like actors who enter, perform, and leave at appointed times.

The area down in front is called the "pit." This is the professor's base. In the middle of the pit is a table on which the professor spreads papers and notes. The first row is called the "wormdeck," and the highest row, the "skydeck."

In front of every student, in a slot that runs along the long curved desk, is his or her name card, a 4" × 14" card with a hand-lettered name, large enough to be readable from anywhere in the room. From where we stand, we can read any name in the farthest corner. The cards fleck the room like large snowflakes. During the course of the year they will collect graffiti, cartoons, doodles, smudges, and stains.

You will see that most students are dressed comfortably and informally. Khaki pants, jeans, cotton dresses, sport shirts and blouses, loafers, running shoes. Most students are healthy-looking. "The people at the business school," wrote Robert Massie, Jr., '86 in an article in *Manhattan* magazine describing his first year, "actually looked like the people in ads for Caribbean vacations or for expensive liquor; they looked like *winners.*"

The diversity of backgrounds in any first-year section is astounding. If you sat in this section you would learn that it includes a few who have worked as lawyers, a few consultants, several accountants, more than a dozen engineers, a couple of dozen bankers, nearly a dozen on leave from companies, an architect, a karate instructor, a veterinarian from New Zealand, a ministry official from Japan, an army officer from West Germany. All are highly motivated, ambitious, competitive.

Some students, you will see, have brought their personal computers so that if the case involves quantitative analysis, as it does in courses like finance and control, they can run off answers to "what if"–type questions. If you look into the dormitory rooms, you will see none without a personal computer lying around somewhere. All incoming students are required to use PCs, and hundreds of cases now contain exhibits in Lotus 1-2-3 spreadsheets. If your computer breaks down or you have trouble with some program, the school offers a variety of support services—a PC information hot line with a bank of four telephones, a repair center, and a walk-in information center.

When it is time for class to begin, the professor—let's say he is a man—walks in, glances around the amphitheater, drops a slew of papers on the table in the pit, and begins arranging his notes. He makes some perfunctory announcements. The class grows as silent as if in a Christian Science reading room because it knows what is coming next—his dreaded call to start the case discussion. If he calls on someone from his roster without letting him or her know in advance, the event is called a "cold call." Waiting for his cold call, the students seem to be holding their breath. It is early in the first year, and sooner or later all will get called on, but at this point each is hoping to be spared.

"Charley Shedd," the instructor announces, "would you open the Pizza Hut case?"

Charley stiffens as if electrocuted. A collective sigh of relief goes around the rest of the room from those who have won a reprieve. "Thank God it's not me," the others say under their breath. All eyes, including the professor's, fasten on Charley. He feels like some innocent singled out from a crowd to go to the wall and face the executioner's machine gun. His mouth is like sandpaper, the back of his neck is hot. Though he went over the case last night, and his study group discussed it and he made some notes, he feels hopelessly unprepared. The case is twenty-four single-spaced typewritten pages long; the exhibits and tables are bramble patches of numbers.

The situation is a complicated one, he says in a raspy voice. A franchisor wants its franchisees to introduce home delivery of pizzas to customers. The franchisor believes that stand-alone units should be set up for delivery while the franchisees, less enthusiastic about the whole concept, seem to prefer delivering from their existing restaurants. What should the franchisor do, and how? How can it accomplish what it wants while keeping the franchisees?

Paraphrasing his notes in a bumbling, halting fashion, Charley tries to describe the situation and how it was created. Reaching the end of his spiel, he outlines the action steps he thinks should be taken by the franchisor. When the others see he is about to conclude, they raise their hands. Charlie finds this very distracting. Has he been so unpersuasive, has he left so many loopholes in his presentation? As he drops his voice and stops talking, he is wet with perspiration.

The professor calls on others one by one. "How did this happen?" he asks one. "Do you really believe that?" he asks another. "What evidence do you have for that statement?" he demands of another. He paces back and forth in the pit. Often he runs to the boards to jot down ideas or numbers. Pretty soon the boards are so full of scribbling that he has to press the button and lower the top board. As it rumbles down, leaving a space above it, the class sees written there in large letters, "God is alive and well but failing Marketing." Everybody laughs. The professor quips, "Somebody must have used a ladder to get up there. That's closer to heaven than you usually get in this course." Loud guffawing.

The discussion grows heated. The professor keeps coaxing, cajoling. "Aw, c'mon," he tells one, "you don't think that's really possible, do you?" Of another he asks, "How do you reconcile your point with what Lois said?" To another he says, "Suppose that the situation were reversed and . . . ?" Over and over he keeps nagging about the need for a plan of action. "Yes, but what're you gonna *do?*" he asks.

When the class is over, Charley slumps in his seat and passes his hand over his eyes. You see a friend pat him on the shoulder. "It could have been worse," says the friend cheerfully. "It could have been me."

PLUSES AND MINUSES

For all its strengths, the case method is more effective in some classes than in others.

Sometimes the good old lecture method and straight-out exposition are hard to beat—for instance, when you're trying to tell students how to make and use a decision tree or a preference curve, as in managerial economics. Sometimes cases can't give you the scope you need, as when the history of a situation is long, complex, and extremely important to a government decision maker. Again, the instructor must have the qualities needed to teach cases, and the class must be motivated to study the cases and be ready to participate—two demanding conditions that do not always exist.

The variable format of a class, the potential explosiveness, the spontaneity—all these are wonderful if the instructor and class pull them off, but they intensify the pressure. John J. Nevin '52, chief executive of Zenith Radio Corporation and, later, Firestone Tire & Rubber Company, remembers the prowess of HBS instructors in leading the class along.

Those two years, he says, became "the most meaningful educational experience of my life. I was immediately confronted with superb professors like Steve Fuller, George Baker, and Ben Selekman who were pushing us to answer 'what if' questions, rather than looking for the straightforward solutions found in textbooks."

Another limitation is that a good case discussion depends on the "chemistry" of the class, and while that is surprisingly good in a surprisingly large percentage of instances at HBS, it is not right always. Sometimes you'll see an instructor leaving the classroom with the shaken look of someone who has lost heavily at Las Vegas. For inexplicable reasons the case didn't "go," the class was flat, even the best students had little to say. Although teaching at the B-school is more predictable than, say, fishing, it is less predictable than delivering a good lecture.

What some consider the severest shortcoming of the case method is that it presents a situation to students in secondhand form. The case writer masticates the situation for the student like a mother bird chewing up food before dropping it into the beak of the baby bird. Fortunately, good case writers do this well, reporting honestly and, like good baseball umpires, "calling 'em as they see 'em." But even so, the *form* in which students get the material is different from that in which they will digest situations in the future as managers. They read, and they may see and hear if all or part of the case is on video, but the situation is still programmed for them. Also, as Professor John Dearden once reminded me, fortunes and careers are not made or lost in the classroom, so the "game" is different.

To deal with part of this problem, the school is enlarging the role of field studies. The effort to give students a firsthand look at company situations began in 1956 when Professor Harry Hansen introduced a second-year course called Creative Marketing Strategy. A great success, the course emphasized on-site student examinations of company problems, followed by reports. "We don't want our students leaving here with green eyeshades," Hansen once told me.

The idea of field studies grew, and thirty years later, according to a student survey, a quarter of the second-year class worked on one or more such studies. During the term the field study courses were taken—always under the supervision of one or more professors—the student commitment was 150 hours, or about 10 hours per week. The situations studied ranged as widely as conventional written cases, from market and industry studies to an anti-drug campaign for Boston youngsters and a movie-production strategy for the TV program "Saturday Night Live."

Early in 1988 the faculty voted to expand field studies for second-years still more. The decision emerged from the work of several student committees working in tandem with a faculty committee, and the consensus was that the new policy was altering the nature of the second year for almost all students.

For all such qualifications, however, the case method at HBS has compelling virtues:

It forces students to accept responsibility for decision making. Excuses such as "We need more information" rarely fly.

It encourages an appreciation of the complexity of many management problems. Glib rules of thumb don't work. Situations that may look alike on the surface are different underneath. Professor Malcolm McNair used to say that a good case forces students to become "detectives," looking for the particular clues that are the key to the case in question.

It encourages students to listen actively to others. The instructor doesn't have the answers, the class does. Dissenters must be listened to if they make cogent arguments for their heretical viewpoints. When I asked alums for their favorite memories of HBS, Gregory Copenhefer '86, head of Castle Keepers in Louisville, recalled a case that made a strong impression on him.

The case involved "a man who was working with outmoded equipment for his small company but really knew the process. He knew his stuff inside out. According to the books, he couldn't possibly be successful with that old equipment. Reading the case, I remember thinking, This guy has really put it together, he's taking full advantage of his experience.

"I went to the study group thinking that. At the study group, however, everybody else wanted to modernize. They wanted to take out the old equipment and put in new stuff. Their arguments were good, but I wasn't convinced. I argued that this guy should keep on doing as he was doing. In class, students took the same attitude as the majority in my study group. I didn't go along with that. I argued for the enterprise, I talked about the beauty of the unusual knowledge this fellow had of his product and business, I said that he had found a way to work with what he had and make an unglamorous business successful and profitable, to succeed with what most people would consider 'residue.'

"I continue to believe that. I think there's a lot more business out there than we realize for those who can make it with 'residue' instead of the latest equipment."

In my interviews I was struck by the lasting impression made by the case method on alums' ways of thinking about what they see and hear. Here is R. Lee Buechler '78 again:

"It seems that whether I'm just shopping or visiting a prospect's site or reading about a situation, I find myself analyzing the organization and the viability of the business [as in case analysis at HBS]. Is this a good business to be in? What's important about it? Will it be able to succeed? All those sorts of things. This happens almost automatically with me. Even on vacation I'll find myself on a train of thought analyzing a group or company that I see. It's a kind of mind game, I guess. It's fun."

PREPARATION FOR COMBAT

Why does the case method make managers good "fighters" on economic battlefields?

Not only does it make a lasting impression but it alters one's way of thinking about an organization's problems. No more does the manager look for solutions in easy rules of thumb, an amateurish approach that has killed countless corporations in global competition. No more does the manager say, "I'll have eight managers reporting to me because that way worked in the last company," or "I'll centralize this operation because the books say that's best." He or she looks at the problem situationally—that is, in terms of what its own facts suggest.

Admittedly, this approach is more difficult, complex, and time-consuming. But it also works better. It recognizes that each situation, each group of people is a little different from any other. It helps to make management better attuned to *this* manufacturing situation and *that* selling need. It leads managers to investigate more, listen more closely, look *at* individuals and machines and relationships instead of past them. It brings out the creativity in people—a strong advantage for Americans because if nothing else we are a resourceful, innovative, inventive people. It tends to produce sounder decisions and to make managers accept the responsibility for their decisions: "The buck stops here."

Most important, it makes management more fun.

If the U.S. economy is to keep improving in global competition, these are huge advantages.

> ■ *I entered the battle of the case method unarmed. The routines and tools that had allowed me to survive years of schooling no longer helped me; my old study habits were useless—counterproductive, in fact.*
>
> —ROBIN HACKE, HBS student, quoted in C. Roland Christensen, *Teaching with Cases at the Harvard Business School*

2

THE FATEFUL
STRUGGLE FOR
AIRTIME

The Harvard Business School has a much-used counseling center where students often go with problems and complaints. The most common complaint, says Patricia Light, director of counseling services, is, "I can't speak in class."

I have talked with many people at HBS about this problem, and when I taught in the doctoral program I had some firsthand experience with it. All sorts of reasons are given for inability to speak out well. Some students say they don't like being the center of attention, as they are when they get the floor. Some are afraid they will look foolish, others that they don't think fast enough on their feet. An alum mentioned earlier, Richard Jenrette '57, one of the founders of Donaldson, Lufkin & Jenrette, says that for a long time as a student he was reluctant to speak because of self-consciousness about his southern accent.

Whatever the reasons, for most students "class participation," as speaking out is usually called, is a learning experience they will never forget. It has an enormous impact on what they take out of the school, helping them to contribute effectively to management discussions and thus advance their careers.

Speaking out in class also accounts single-handedly for one of the most vivid contrasts between B-school classes and classes at many other management schools. A few years ago two students from the Graduate School of Business at the University of Chicago, Jean Liu and Christine Dale, came to Boston and monitored several B-school classes. Writing about their impressions, they said:

"We agreed that this [speaking out] is the one characteristic that truly distinguishes Harvard students from those at the University of Chicago. At least half the class raised their hand following each question or remark made by the professor, and everyone who spoke did so eloquently and at length, demonstrating their preparedness."

Many professors are masters at encouraging, coaxing, prodding silent students to open up in class. Jenrette gave the credit to Professor Milton Brown for coaxing him out of his freeze. Some, on the other hand, take a fairly unsympathetic, impersonal attitude—"It's up to them whether they participate. They know how much it counts." If a student maintains his or her reticence, these instructors will probably mark the student low at the end of the term. One professor tells me that a student in her class came in to see her at midterm. "I said to him, 'You don't participate.' The student tried to explain—he raised his hand but I never saw him, he would be about to make a point when someone else in class would beat him to it. I said, 'I'm not interested in excuses. Either you participate or you don't.' The student never did break the pattern, and I gave him a category four [failing] at the end of the term."

Some famous people have failed to break the sound barrier at HBS and paid the price. For instance, Edson de Castro '63, founder and president of Data General, came to the school in 1961 and, as the year progressed, found class participation a real problem. In courses that put a major premium on speaking out and making a point persuasively, he was too quiet and shy. When the final grades came out at the end of the first year, too many low passes appeared next to his name, and so, in the vernacular, he "hit the screen"—he flunked out. He never came back to try again. The school finds it easy to forgive business successes, however, and in 1986 de Castro received HBS's Alumni Achievement Award.

Students refer to speaking in class as "airtime." With ninety or so students in a first-year class, it is not always easy for a person to get airtime. Yet the pressure to speak is intense. Many professors make it clear from the outset that a third or even half of a student's grade in their courses depends on class participation—period. If the student has a problem, he or she knows where to get help.

FEAR AND SALIVATION

Instructors feel that class participation is a learnable skill, and experience bears them out. Over and over again, students demonstrate amazing ability to learn this skill if they have to. "Also," Professor Charles Williams once told me, "since the school is a training ground for managers, and managers spend a great deal of their time talking to people, students need to learn to speak out." Maybe they can never learn to speak with the finesse of a Ronald Reagan, but they can learn to make themselves heard.

Instructors work hard to give students the maximum possible amount of airtime. "Every time I speak," one professor told me, "I take away time when students can speak. There are lots of ways that I can throw them the ball. Instead of correcting a student, I can turn to someone else and say, 'Sally, do you agree with that?' Or maybe the best thing's to let the argument build, so I'll look to people who look ready to support the case and lay it out. Only after a while do I call on somebody who I know will take the opposite position and show the fallacy."

An extreme illustration of professorial abstinence was given to me by the late Professor Joseph Bailey. "Come to my class on Thursday," he told me. "I want to show you something." I sat inconspicuously to one side. During the whole class he never once spoke. With his eyebrows, facial expressions, and hands he ran an animated discussion, and not until the end did he point out to the students that he hadn't uttered a word. They were amazed—they had been so engrossed in the case that they hadn't noticed. Actually, Bailey's point was different from mine here: he was proving the importance of "body language," which was relevant to his course on communication, not student control of airtime. But his effort also demonstrates how far an instructor could go in letting students talk.

Visiting classes, you will never see a professor grading a comment after it is made. Not only would this interrupt the dialogue but it would add to student self-consciousness. Naturally, professors remember a particularly cogent or helpful opinion, and they soon learn who the articulate class members are. Repeatedly I have been astounded at an instructor's ability to recall a class and mark down all students who contributed to it, whether in a big or a small way. Going over the roster is usually the first thing they do after departing the classroom and closing the door in their office.

Everyone who has gone through the HBS mill has witnessed the terror wreaked in some students by class participation. Weird things happen. Suddenly expected to talk, people with fine speaking voices have been known to begin rasping like a piece of chalk scratching a board in the wrong way. Once I saw a student forget to lower her hand when recognized by the professor; all the time she spoke, she kept waving her arm, and not until everyone began tittering did she realize what she was doing. I have seen other students sputter and forget what they were going to say.

RULES TO SPEAK BY

If class participation is important to one's success at the B-school, it is even more valuable in business and government. As a result of the lessons learned from class discussion, students-turned-alumni find that they can become better communicators in management, that what they absorbed in class in order to survive the rigors of B-school life stands them in good stead as executives.

Here are the main rules stressed by instructors and students in their talks with me.

CONFRONT YOUR SPEAKING PROBLEM.

Practically everyone, including many of the great speakers of all time, has a problem of some sort. Probably the most important thing you can do is identify your problem and face it squarely. Whether the difficulty is physical, emotional, or something else, admit that it exists and place it in the open.

For HBS students this may be a difficult step. William Bennett, once course head in Management Communications, told me, "They are people with a great deal of pride, their track records are impressive, and a great many of them are accustomed to being first without having serious problems to contend with. Now all of a sudden they are no better than anyone else and fighting for survival."

Like alcoholics, students can't deal with their problems until they first face up to them. Some go to the counseling service. Others hash their difficulties over with friends. Some are good at self-diagnosis. However they respond, *they act*—they don't lie defenseless like a patient on an operating table. That is their secret. Otherwise they may find themselves packing their bags to go home.

STAY ON THE TRAIL OF THE SUBJECT.

To stay on track requires thoughtful listening. It may seem strange to emphasize the ears in a discussion of the mouth, but HBS students soon learn how important this is. To speak well means speaking appropriately, and to speak appropriately means following the sense and drift of the discussion. As Assistant Professor Julie H. Hertenstein pointed out at a seminar in Burden Auditorium a couple of years ago, "A series of unrelated random comments do not constitute a discussion. . . . A discussion is people working together." She added that some of the best contributors in her classes didn't speak often, but when they spoke they said something significant. They didn't enter the dialogue like a hand grenade or leave their arguments dangling meaninglessly in midair.

Students become very sensitive about needless wastes of airtime. Steven Etter '77, who was chief executive officer of Bridge Atlantic Corporation, a Cincinnati holding company, when I spoke with him, remembers the day a student brought a fishing rod into class. The student attached the line to an object near the center of the amphitheater. When some talker went "fishing" for a rationalization for some fact or number, the student would jump up and cry, "Got another one!" Another occasion Etter remembers was when the people sitting in the back row brought large scorecards like those that judges flash at athletic contests. When a long-winded classmate finished a pointless speech, they would all raise their cards showing how they scored his or her performance.

Numerous alums have told me how useful this lesson has been in their careers. Lots of managers, they point out, don't focus well on the subject under discussion, and this limits their effectiveness as individuals as well as the effectiveness of the groups they work with.

LOOK AT SOMEONE ENCOURAGING.

This suggestion comes from Professor Benson Shapiro. It has helped many people to overcome their "participation blocks" as students, and later as managers, to talk more freely in problem-solving meetings.

When you talk, advises Shapiro, look at a particular person so that you don't talk into thin air. Don't, however, pick some glowering Medusa with a paralyzing look. Make eye contact with a friendly, encouraging face.

Once I was discussing this point in a doctoral seminar I taught. One of the students told me how the idea had helped him. As a second-year, he had had to report to the class on the findings of a student team he had worked with. The night before his report, he had become very apprehensive. He came through the experience with flying colors, however, because he picked out a particular person in class to talk to, delivering much of his report with his eyes on that person.

DON'T LET YOURSELF GET STEREOTYPED.

If your audience tags you as a clown, a conservative, or some other stereotype, says Shapiro, it may not listen to you after a while because it thinks it knows what you're going to say. Some people like such labels, but most of us prefer to be heard as independent thinkers who don't necessarily follow some "party line."

One alum I know remembers a classmate who, though a born comedian, saved his cracks and quips for outside of class, rarely enlivening a case discussion with a "funny" despite his ability to do that. The fellow didn't want the responsibility of having to be humorous all the time, which he would have had if he'd let himself get typed; and when he had something serious to say, he didn't want it discounted because people were looking for his humorous touch.

Students refer often to the roles they see their classmates in. In one section students referred to one of their number as "Nellie the Number Cruncher." I learned that Nell was cast in that role after she threw up her hands one night in late fall at the imprecision of the models presented in a case she was preparing, went to the computer room, ran her own regression, and presented the results the next day in class. Because the instructor was so impressed, she did the same thing later on another case. After that it was difficult for her to say anything that the class would accept on any subject other than numbers.

Another student in the section became stereotyped early in the year as "section C's answer to Lyndon LaRouche," all because he stuck to an ultraconservative position on a couple of cases where everyone else was more open-minded. This fellow took the joshing too easily and didn't realize in time how he was being typed, and when later he tried to take quite different positions, everyone read into his statements feelings that he didn't have.

After graduation, students find that the instinct to avoid typecasting is a useful career strategy. It helps them to see the business whole instead of seeing just one activity—looking "through a wide-angle lens," as one told me, "not a narrow lens."

PRACTICE WITH TRIAL RUNS.

Patricia Light suggests practicing your speaking with your study group or in front of a mirror. If you don't have a study group, a few friends or a "kitchen cabinet" should serve equally well. A mirror helps because it provides a sense of animation (or lack of it); you are not speaking into a vacuum and can see yourself as others see you.

Students also like the feedback gained. While he was an MBA student, Forest Reinhardt '87 told me that his three-person study group was extraordinarily helpful to him for this reason. The group met at 7:30 A.M. "Somebody would tell me that an idea I had about some case was nutty, and I would see that he was right. I felt a lot more comfortable going into class knowing that I wasn't going to present *that* thought. Much better to get shot down in front of two people than ninety!"

This approach, too, has been found valuable by alums, and they stress it often when discussing the tactics they believe to be important.

DEVELOP A STRATEGY FOR WHEN TO TALK.

Sometimes you're afraid to talk for fear of sounding like an idiot or suddenly forgetting the inspiring thought that came to mind. One approach that Shapiro says works for many is to speak up early in the discussion so that you can talk on the basis of your advance preparation. Then you'll have confidence in what you're going to say, whereas later on the discussion may veer in directions that require you to extemporize or think on your feet.

Some at the B-school go to the opposite extreme, feeling uncomfortable with prepared comments because of the rigidity and "canned" sound that they think is forced on them. They prefer to trust in their ability to extemporize, confident that moments will come for them to speak if they are patient. Gregory Copenhefer '86 told me, "You don't have unlimited chances to speak in class, so I developed a strategy for when I could speak effectively. In general, this meant waiting until many others had spoken first. It worked, and I have kept using this strategy since leaving the school."

In any case, say knowledgeable HBS instructors, don't follow rules such as, "Talk in every third class." In the first year such formulas are popular, and of course some business people also are slaves to rules: "I make it a point to talk at every operations meeting" or "I never say anything until the end of the meeting." Although such rules may have the virtue of forcing you out of your shell now and then, they may also lead you to talk when you shouldn't and not talk when you should.

DON'T TRY TO BE WHAT YOU'RE NOT.

Some people are born with silver tongues and can bluff their way out of almost any situation, but many of us can't. If we can't, the worst mistake is to delude ourselves into thinking that we can. A valuable lesson learned by many HBS students is that they don't have as many gifts as they wish they had. Michael Maguire '85, vice president of marketing at SGI in Warwick, Rhode Island, told me:

"One of the things I learned at the school is that I have to go into a discussion prepared. Some people can dance and BS their way around a situation (more often than they think, though, it shows)—but I can't.

"I particularly liked a second-year class on marketing implementation taught by Professor Tom Bonoma. Up to the last class of the year, anyway, I had always been prepared. I had opened class once and participated like crazy in most. But on that last day I had gone over the case only briefly. I said to myself, It's okay, the chances that I'll be called on are small. Unfortunately, Bonoma called on me to open the discussion. I said to myself, This is my chance to test myself and see if I can BS my way through. I wasn't going to tell him that I was unprepared, I was going to give it my best shot. So I opened, and my comments were scrambled and didn't make any sense. I tried to make things better by telling some jokes. It was a disaster."

SET YOUR MIND ON MODEST IMPROVEMENTS.

Don't try to become a good speaker in one fell swoop but improve yourself gradually—*incrementally,* to use business-school
jargon. Light urges setting modest goals and raising the hurdle
a little every time a goal is reached.

One student I knew set himself first on just speaking. Whether
he did it well or not, he determined to pitch in and make himself
heard. After doing that a few times, he made his goal the expression of rational and relevant thoughts, a difficult task for him
because he froze when recognized and forgot what he had been
going to say. Gradually he gained confidence. Near the end of the
two years he was working on his voice and manner of speaking.
The last I knew, years later, he was billed as the keynote speaker
at a business convention.

TAKE RISKS, BE PART OF THE GAME.

B-school students learn that there is no way they can sound wise
and sagacious all the time. Now and then they're going to make
inane statements. The only way to prevent it is not to say anything at all—and that, of course, defeats everything.

Off and on through the years, the student newspaper has enter-
tained its audience by publishing lists of gaffes and bloopers committed in classroom discussions—"the carrot at the end of the
rainbow," "This company isn't giving employees enough French
benefits," "Wild ducks don't go out to pasture and become cash
cows," and so on. Sometimes a section will even give awards for
the worst mixed metaphor or most ridiculous statement made by
a student. All this is done in fun, and so far as I can tell, none of
the gaffers mind much that tin cans are hung on them.

Beyond such slips of the tongue, students get used to the idea
that whole opinions may strike others as absurd. In the second-
year course on money and banking, Hugh Graham, Jr., '58, now
chief executive officer of Albuquerque Federal Savings & Loan
Association, tried unsuccessfully to sway the class about a solution
to a problem in a case. He wanted to convince the others that

offering customers green stamps as a bonus for new accounts made sense for banks opening offices in areas where there was a lot of competition. "I'll never forget the reaction," he told the *HBS Bulletin* years later. "I went out on a limb and the whole class sawed me off." (Actually, Graham's point was wrong only for the late 1950s. By the early 1980s, the American public was beginning to see through the mystique of money and recognize it for the commodity it was—witness the advent of money market mutual funds.)

Naturally, most students resist going out on a limb that may be sawed off, especially in the first year, when they feel insecure. By the time they are in the second year, however, many have gotten used to the idea. Professors encourage them to take the risk by drawing them out and not letting them waffle or hedge. Laurie Leonard '77, at the time president and general manager of Station WMTV in Madison, Wisconsin, told me:

"You learn at the school that if you say the wrong thing or make the wrong decision on a problem, it's not the end of the world. You can go back later. You get over your fear because there are always eighty-five or ninety bright, aggressive people listening, waiting to debate you no matter what you say—every day."

KEEP YOUR EGO UNDER CONTROL.

Particularly when debates and negotiations heat up, there is a dangerous tendency for egos to take over. Your claims and arguments grow extreme and distorted, and instead of sounding overpowering, as you intend, you make yourself very vulnerable. Forest Reinhardt described this incident to me:

"In an early class in human resources management a union-management negotiation was simulated. The professor was Dick Walton. Teams of five students represented the union, while teams of five represented management. Before negotiations, each team went to a carrel in Aldrich to work out its approach.

"It happened that I was designated chairman of one union negotiating team. In our group were four of the most talkative, assertive students in the section. It seemed to us that the management team we were to deal with was okay, but we thought it didn't include many of the class luminaries. This happened in November, so that we thought we had a pretty good idea of who in the section was sharp and who wasn't.

"In the carrel we told ourselves, 'We can take these guys without much of a problem.' We wanted to beat them. We wanted to extract from them all the concessions we could possibly get. We made the mistake of letting our egos get deeply involved."

In their meeting, says Reinhardt, they escalated their claims beyond all reason. "As a result, when we met with the other team to negotiate, we couldn't compromise on some issues where, if we had only been more reasonable and less egotistical, we could easily have reached agreement."

In sum, the training B-school students get in class participation prepares them well for management. They learn to listen. They develop an instinct for timing—when to speak, when to shut up. They acquire that wonderful ability that comes only with practice to think on their feet and to present a viewpoint cogently. Most important, they begin to learn and practice some fundamentals of the art of communication, which is so crucial in management. More organizations screw up because of communication failures, many thoughtful observers believe, than because of any other failure. Good communications are a "must" for U.S. organizations competing with the top enterprises of Asia, Europe, and other continents.

People often wonder why Harvard MBAs advance so fast in large organizations and do so well as entrepreneurs. The ability to contribute to a policy or problem-solving discussion is certainly one of the main reasons.

■ *You're not just asking a rhetorical question—you want me to open the case, right?*

—Panicked first-year student to professor in Managerial Economics class

■ *They didn't open their mouths, and the longer they closed them, the less confident they became, until they reached almost a point of no return about Christmas.*

—Student quoted in Charles Orth, *Social Structure and Learning Climate at the Harvard Business School*

3

FUN WAYS
TO COPE WITH
STRESS

Late in 1989 an $18 million building was completed and opened on the B-school grounds. It took more than two years to build, received constant and personal attention from the dean during its construction, and was financed out of B-school funds, a symbol of HBS's financial power. The building does not meet the need for faculty and staff office space. It does not house books, computer terminals, or rooms for special functions. Rather, it is an exercise center.

Why did the school choose to devote the new building, named after John Shad '49, to basketball, squash, racquetball, a track for joggers, aerobics, sauna and steam rooms, showers, lockers, and a snack bar instead of to other purposes? Because of the pressure students are under. The exercise center symbolizes the need for regular breaks from study if students are to take stress in stride.

The new fitness center is official recognition of the fact that the school is, as it has been dubbed, a kind of boot camp—albeit a high-class one for aspiring young capitalists but a boot camp nonetheless. For sixty-five years the faculty and administration have known this. They have recognized that part of the trick of coping with heavy work loads is for students to be able to break away from academic routines and do something physical, do something that expresses body and feeling. The new fitness center is the school's way of saying, "We're doing our part to enable you to do this."

Visiting the HBS campus, you might wonder why the place is called a boot camp or why students ever refer to the experience as an ordeal. The men and women generally look happy and energetic. Nobody orders them around. Classes may be punctuated with bursts of laughter. In the main dining room in Kresge the air is filled with busy talk, and in the Pub, the fast-foods center, there is camaraderie and joshing. But after you have been around the place for a while, you sense that a lot is going on under the surface. Especially in the first year, the majority of students worry intensely about whether they are going to make it through.

Early in the 1980s the faculty realized that the student work load had crept up to nearly 10,000 pages of reading per year, much of it in the form of cases. "We reached a point where the pressure had forced students into gaming strategies—the quick thirty-second answer that would get them off the hook," said Professor Thomas Piper, senior associate dean for educational programs. So in 1982 the faculty kindly rolled the reading load back to about 7,000 pages. In the mid-1980s, Piper was able to announce that students were doing no less work and were coming to class better prepared.

Of course, the reading load *per se* does not create the pressure felt by students. The culprit, according to many students, is the forced grading curve. In every first-year section, somewhere around 3 percent to 5 percent of the students must fail. It doesn't matter if everyone in section A is a genius and everyone in section B is a moron, or vice versa; in each group of ninety-plus students, a few must hit the dreaded screen. The sad result, they claim, is excessive anxiety, overemphasis on competitiveness, and morbid workaholism.

One reflective alum I know believes there is another reason. "Harvard takes these high-flying students it gets and knocks them down to size," Steve Etter '77 told me. "It doesn't do this so much by pressure, because everyone's been under pressure and performed well, but by lack of feedback. In the past they had positive feedback. Therefore they think they don't need it. Well, when they don't get it, they get really frustrated. I saw people who actually felt that they weren't going to make it, though in fact they wound up doing well."

On the other hand, many professors I know believe that the real source of stress is not the forced grading curve, not the work load, not the number of classes per week, but the students themselves. "I think students put a lot of pressure on each other because of the kind of people we admit," Dean John McArthur told the student newspaper. "They're hard-driving, have high standards and a lot of energy. . . ."

Moreover, the prevailing philosophy of the school is that pressure is not necessarily a bad thing. If these young men and women are to become top executives, they are going to feel a lot of heat in the business world. That being the case, it is best for them to get used to it and learn how best to cope with it. How they do that is up to them—no professor will attempt to tell them, for the answers vary with the individual. But in learning to do it, they will acquire an extremely important piece of know-how for succeeding as top executives.

In this chapter I will focus on what students learn about coping with pressure. Judging from everything I know, practicing this learning over and over again gives students great confidence as alums. They know that if necessary they can work eighteen-hour days—and not once or twice but for weeks and months at a time. They know that whatever stresses they run up against in business, they can meet the test. Time after time, alums tell me, the reason they didn't buckle when the economic battle got tough was that they knew how to deal with stress and applied what they knew out of habit. The habit, they acknowledge, was developed at HBS.

What do students learn about survival in the boot camp of capitalism, and how does this insight help them later in their management careers? I shall focus on three basic approaches to dealing with stress. These are: (1) using the power of succor, (2) breaking away from the daily grind, and (3) staying in control.

USING THE POWER OF SUCCOR

In the early weeks at Harvard students may feel too proud and individualistic to reach out to others for help. After a while, however, the pressure brings them to their knees. They open themselves gladly to the warmth and kinship of friends and colleagues.

Most students have three groups they can turn to—small study groups of three to eight people, bands of close friends, and those in their section with whom they can feel empathy and concern. The personal bonds formed with people in these groups may last for years after graduation.

Early in his career Thornton Bradshaw '42 was an assistant professor at HBS, teaching in the Control course. He told me, "I don't know many B-schoolers who are loners. They don't fight the good fight by themselves. That isn't their nature. They don't say that loners are bad, mind you; they just don't think they could survive the first year without the help of friends." Although a fine teacher, Bradshaw left the school for industry in the 1950s and later became chief executive, first, of Atlantic Richfield and, second, of RCA. Before his death in 1988 he was widely recognized as one of the great leaders in U.S. industry. He used to confide that his confidence in his capacity to work hard was born at HBS.

Study groups. Many B-school people will tell you that the study group is the most important source of bonding and succor in the first year. In the second year, study groups generally become obsolete, and students turn more to friends and classmates. I know many alums who make sure that in every business situation they have the equivalent of a study group for hashing over problems and questions. "It's one of the best stress-preventives I know," an alum told me.

A few years ago I sat in on one study group. Its custom was to meet every night on the dot at 8:30. It had six members. All were members of the same section but they lived in different living halls, so they took turns hosting. Their sessions lasted for an hour or two and were devoted to going over the cases assigned for the next day; usually that meant three cases. One person would "open" as if he or she were doing so in class; the rest would chip in with comments or furiously make notes. Always one or more personal computers were at hand.

"We call it our study group," the host told me, "but it's more than that. It's our support group." He meant that because of the study groups, members didn't feel they were alone when they faced class.

This particular study group never met except to discuss cases. Several members told me that their best friends were people outside the group. However, some study groups become social centers as well. Howard Glass '83 describes his study group in a student newspaper article that appeared before he graduated:

"The roles formed. Most important for me was Mike—my extra professor. We had a numbers person, marketing, way-out ideas, and touchy-feely. Oh yeah, some partiers also. Something happened. There was more than just academics. We started having dinner before the nightly meeting. Then it was a Saturday night get-together.

"I had a problem (you know, girlfriend problems). I knew whom to call. The numbers of my study group were on my desk. I made the call. I had a friend. I had five friends. We were growing close, closer than we knew at the time. . . ."

Countless HBS alums later adapt the study-group technique to help them cope with crises in management. In an informal survey of alums, I found that the great majority used this approach.

Friendships. Although B-school students are young capitalists at heart, they find that competitiveness and materialism are not sufficient to get them through. Turning to friends, they find the camaraderie that they need to have. "They become father-confessors to each other," one professor told me. Another, Jeffrey Sonnenfeld, at the time an associate professor, told me, "They develop informal groups of friends for mutual support."

In an interview, Michael Maguire '85, then marketing head of *Sports Graphics* magazine, told me about an incident in the first term of his first year. He had made a good friend, and they helped each other often. At the midterm exam in Managerial Economics, the students were confronted with a horrendous problem requiring decision-tree analysis. About half an hour into the exam, Maguire saw that his friend, sitting nearby, was overwhelmed. "He couldn't find the handle on the case, and time was ticking away." To his dismay, he then saw the friend rise suddenly, throw down his pen, and leave the exam room. Dropping his computations, Maguire ran after the young man. He caught up with him in the men's room down the hall. He grabbed him around the shoulders and urged him not to give up. "Take a deep breath and you'll be fine." Maguire prevailed, the two of them returned to the exam room, and both ended up passing.

Here is a story told to me by Thomas Fontana '83, president of Acme Visible Records in Crozet, Virginia:

"On the very first day of my second year I was with my wife in the hospital where she was having a tumor removed from her thyroid. Fortunately, it was benign. After the surgery was pronounced a success and I had comforted my wife, I hurried up to the business school by plane, grabbed my two-foot-thick stack of cases, and ran off to the first class in Agribusiness.

"I was able to read the first nine pages of the case walking through the hall before class began. Unfortunately, the professor selected me to start discussion on the case, but before I was able to explain why I hadn't prepared the case, he spent ten minutes discussing what the course would be about. He specifically emphasized the need to be prepared for class or not attend at all.

"I had the good fortune to be sitting next to a former first-year section mate who had been raised on a farm, and I had had a dairy client which was the subject of the case. In a true spirit of cooperation and support, my friend handed me his notes—done with all the excruciating detail of an expert on the subject, interested in the case. I read these notes at a furious pace, and at the end of the ten minutes, when it was my turn to begin the discussion, I had a brilliant opening. It got me off on the right foot, and

I ended up getting an excellent grade in the course. I owe my fine start to my friend."

One reason alums recall experiences like this is that they have often duplicated them in management life, mindful of how valuable they were in Boston. "I have different kinds of friends now," one alum told me, "but I'm always reaching for people who can give me, and I them, comfort and reassurance like we gave each other at the school."

Empathy and concern. In many instances, reaching out has nothing to do with study groups or close friendships but happens simply because the students are classmates and understand what the others are going through. They are, so to speak, members of the same club, and as such extend helping hands to one another. This is an approach learned at HBS that is readily adopted in management life—clubs within clubs in churches, civic projects, athletic groups, and so on.

This delightful story was told to me by Lee Rodgers '84, now a partner in Trammell Crow Company in St. Louis:

"One of my friends was a Japanese student named 'Kaz' [fictional name]. He was very quiet and didn't speak English all that well. He was probably the smartest student at the school on the quantitative courses.

"Kaz had a real difficult time with Organizational Behavior and the 'touchy-feely' courses. He didn't believe in trying to manipulate and change people, as we do in the United States. Somehow he managed to pass the first third of the Organizational Behavior course—'OB I'—but he flunked the middle semester, called Human Resources Management. We would now go to the third part, called 'OB II.'

"Until then, Kaz had never flunked anything. The day he saw his failing grade, called then 'Low Pass,' he decided not to go to class anymore. He stayed up all night drinking saki. When we asked him about the trouble, he replied, 'OB does not exist.' He put it out of his mind.

"Sure enough, he didn't show up in OB II classes anymore. When the instructor arrived, Kaz would walk out the door. The instructor would ask, 'Kaz, where are you going?' and he would tell her, 'OB does not exist.'

"We had a little group project that everyone in the course had to do, and then make a presentation. Kaz just didn't do it. When asked, he replied, 'OB does not exist.'

"Weeks went by and it came time for the final. We went to him and said, 'Kaz, you're planning on taking the final, aren't you?' He shook his head and said, 'OB does not exist.' We warned him that if he didn't take the final, the penalty could be very severe, worse than for getting a failing grade because he wouldn't even get credit for the course. 'Just take it,' we urged him.

"The night before the final, we sat with him for an hour. We told him, 'Kaz, you've got at least to write something down. Pride is one thing, but you can't just allow that instructor (she was young, not very good, and did not have tenure) to do something awful to you because you have embarrassed her.

"The next day, Kaz walked into the final. He stayed there about two hours—about half the time allowed. We all felt proud of him. 'Congratulations,' we told him when we saw him after the exam. 'You'll really feel better that you did this. You did the right thing. How many bluebooks did you write?' 'Two,' he answered. That was less than normal, but it meant that he would get credit for the course.

"I said, 'That's great. Now OB really doesn't exist.' As I walked out of the room, he called after me, 'I wrote it *in Japanese.*'"

BREAKING AWAY

"At first," one professor told me, "the students think they can do anything. After a while they find out they can't. That's when they decide to manage the pressure." Discarding the notion that they can be 100 percent thorough and carry the burden by themselves, they begin talking with other students, finding to their relief that others are as sorely pressed as they are. They end up saying, "I can't beat the system by taking it head-on, so instead of trying to beat it, I'll try to live with it. One thing I'll do is break away. I won't do it as a reward but as a survival technique. I won't think, There now, I've done everything, and so I'll reward myself, but, I've got to break free *in order to* come back and face this work load." Almost always they find one or more others to break free with.

Advancing into the executive suite, alums find they can do the same sort of thing, with similar results. They can have an outing with the family, go on an impromptu vacation to Ireland, or spend a long weekend at a hunting lodge in Montana. "I *had* to learn to do it at the B-school," a bank executive told me. "I kept doing it when I went into business."

Some students have told me about their adventures in such rugged activities as skydiving, hang gliding, rock climbing, white-water rafting, backpacking, camping, skiing, and flying. During spring break a couple of years ago, a group of students went to sun-drenched Aruba, off the Venezuelan coast, to swim, surfboard, and cook out. In the fall, a bunch of first- and second-years went to the woods of New Hampshire to stage a mock combat with hand-held paint pellet guns. Andrew Tobias '72 remembers joining a student group one wintry February day to fly to Florida and see mogul Glenn Turner's cosmetics factories, with the host footing the bill for the three-day jaunt.

Many students run. In a recent year, in fact, fifty first- and second-years ran in the famed Boston Marathon. Others organize lacrosse, soccer, basketball, swim, rugby, and other types of athletic teams that compete with teams from other schools.

But there is another, completely different way of disengaging from the system. Reminiscing on his HBS days, Kevin Jenkins '85, group vice president and chief financial officer of PWA Corporation (best known to Americans for its subsidiary, Canadian Airlines International in Calgary), told me:

"During both years of business school, three other students and I got together one morning each week for Bible study and discussion. It helped us to retain our faith and to support each other. With time so tight, it was a big sacrifice to take an hour or hour and a half to do this, but it was very important to us. We have carried on, the four of us. We have reunions. Those three men and their wives are among my closest friends, even though we are far separated geographically now.

"We were very open with each other in those sessions. We didn't have to pretend that we didn't have weaknesses and insecurities. Our faith played an important role in getting us through the first year. We could focus in that time on things eternal, on praise, looking for the good—on all the things that God has done for us.

"I didn't expect to find this at the Harvard Business School. It is one of my fondest memories of the place."

Imaginative students do not overlook the possibilities of nocturnal outings. For example, one warm spring evening a couple of years ago, an enterprising group organized the first annual "nudie tennis night." Locale: the HBS tennis courts next to Morgan Hall. This three-hour event took place under cover of darkness—the only cover, apparently. "Even some shady characters present," I was told gleefully by one participant, "let it all hang out."

Probably the most erotic outing is the famous—or infamous—annual suitcase party sponsored by the student-run Southeastern Club. Tickets are sold to fantasy-minded students for about $15. The sponsors buy two plane tickets to an exotic island in the Bahamas, Virgin Islands, or some other tantalizing place, and reserve a scrumptious suite in the hotel there for a long weekend at the beginning of spring break. On the night the plane is to take off, a raffle is held at some designated place. Neither snow nor sleet nor rain deters these carousers from their appointed rounds—the time I peeked in, it was sleeting outside. Sporting sunglasses, fruity sport shirts, bermuda shorts, and even bikinis, with a packed suitcase and a date at the ready, the hopefuls become boisterous as the evening and raffle progress. At the center of their attention is a large glass bowl. One by one, tickets are removed from the bowl until, shortly before departure time, only one ticket is left. That is the ticket of the winner. After being showered with beer and raucous wishes, the lucky couple is handed the plane tickets, given several hundred dollars in cash, and packed into a waiting limousine, which speeds them to Logan Airport.

A few years ago, the destination was St. Thomas in the Virgin Islands. The bash was wishfully entitled the "Sleep on a Virgin (Island) Party." The promotion for raffle tickets urged, "Bring your toothbrush!"

STAYING IN CONTROL

One time at the faculty lunch table, a young professor described an event in his second-year class. It was the last class for students before a long weekend, and the instructor had determined to cover both the case and a topic that he had prepared a minilecture on—a topic that he felt was important to the integrity of the course. He decided to cut the case discussion short—to forty minutes—and use the second half of the class for his minilecture. Just as he wound up the discussion and prepared to deliver the lecture, however, the students rose en masse from their seats and stopped him from going on. He didn't know what to think. Were they going to shout at him and march out? Much to his surprise, however, they all sang "Happy Birthday." Before he knew what was going on, some students came in with a temporary table that they put next to his table in the pit, others threw a festive table spread over the tables, and others broke out a huge birthday cake, ice cream packages, soft drinks, and plastic spoons.

"Of course I played along with it," he said. "It was my birthday, though how they found out, I don't know. But I couldn't give the minilecture."

A retired prof happened to be sitting near us. As the young man narrated his story, the older gentleman listened in amusement. He said, "Hell, Sam, they were just asserting control."

What he knew—what all instructors soon learn—is that B-school students have to assert themselves from time to time. This is necessary to their self-image as people who control their destiny. It is also important to their ability to cope with stress, for it enables them to say, "Stop the world, I want to get off for a few minutes." By demonstrating that they don't always have to lie down in front of the system and take it without protest, but can rise up and take over the reins of control when they feel like it, they make it easier for themselves to cope. As alums, they keep applying the lesson with similar results.

In my interviews with alums, I asked for remembrances of B-school days. Sometimes the most vivid incidents etched in memory were these assertions of student power. One grad, Keith Van Sickle '85, product manager for KLA Instruments Corporation, Santa Clara, recalled a time shortly before Christmas break:

"We had a 'secret Santa' setup whereby everyone drew names out of a hat. You would be the 'secret Santa' for the person whose name you drew. During the week, you gave them small gifts, and on the last day of the week gave them a final gift and revealed yourself by sitting in their seat and imitating them for the day. Some of the characterizations were very funny, some maybe a little too sharp and needling. I played the part of another person in the section just like everyone else did.

"The case discussions fell apart quickly. Our profs were good-natured about it all. About halfway through the last class we walked out, went to the other classrooms, and began Christmas caroling. The caroling arose spontaneously. It expanded from just our classroom at first to a roving band of carolers disrupting classrooms throughout the building. Some of the professors were angry, but we had an awfully good time.

"Professor Stephen Fuller—a great man—later referred to our section as 'laughing its way through the Harvard Business School.' We used that quote on our section-B sweatshirt."

Another grad, Gregory Copenhefer, recalled his first year at the B-school. It was 1985, the first year the Business Game was played with personal computers: "Every student had been given a hard-wired computer connection for the game. We were to use that as our 'corporate office' and send our moves over the computer to the mainframe computer.

"Our group of people decided that the Business Game should be fun. We decided to move our 'corporate headquarters' to Cape Cod. One of our team members got a suite of rooms at the hotel on the Cape that also had a conference room. The hotel was about one hundred miles away. We set a fee for joining our group there. 'If you're going to be in the group, we're going to play from the Cape,' we said, 'and if you want to come, you have to pay so much money—about $50 for the hotel for the four days we'll be there, an open bar in one of the rooms, and the long-distance phone line that we have dedicated for our computers from the Cape hotel back to the mainframe at HBS.'

"We left a note on a bottle of beer in our designated room at the school—our 'headquarters'—for the professor in case he came by and wanted to talk with us. The note told him the name of our hotel, that we'd be there all week, and if he wanted to talk with us, what number to call.

"From our point of view the game was a rousing success. Most of the time when we weren't engaged in the game, making our moves and planning our strategy, we were on the beach or going bowling or playing miniature golf or just wandering among the curio shops on the Cape. The weather was cold but it was beautiful. It was great not to be stuck in some room in the basement of a Harvard Business School building."

The team didn't win the game but met all the deadlines for moves and finished respectably.

One might be tempted to call such actions pranks—and sometimes indeed that is all they are. But often another thing is taking place: students' insistence that they are not helpless, not completely victims of the system. The development and practice of this attitude at the school makes it so much a part of behavior that they use it in the management world. Experiencing intense pressure from a supplier, subordinates, or the community, they don't let it victimize them. Instead, they may stand up and thumb their noses. "To hell with it, I'm going to the golf course."

THE POTENTIAL OF SELF-MANAGEMENT

The three ways of handling pressure—using the power of succor, breaking away from the daily grind, and keeping control—are not completely effective for every B-school student. Here and there a coke-snorter can be found; some dropouts leave because of the pressure; and so on. But the three ways enable the great majority to survive and, while surviving, grow stronger. They find that they can work a lot harder and longer than they expected—*if* they manage stress. They find that the long, hard hours of work can be rewarding—*if* they meet nature's requirement of a soul group, regular disengagement from the gears of the system, and keeping the feeling of being in control of their lives. The impression made is a lasting one.

From the standpoint of society and the country, this is an important thing to take away from Boston. In fact, it is hard to think of anything more important. Strong leadership in today's economic world is not a nine-to-five job. The demands on executives are growing, not lessening. To take on the best enterprises from the Asians, West Germans, and others calls for a form of commitment that cannot be met without leading a very stressful life. What the B-school says, in effect, is: "This is the way it is. You can take it or leave it. If you take it, it doesn't have to kill you. Find ways to handle it."

You might think that B-school students, being the kind they are, would become ever more competitive and individualistic while at the school. In some ways, perhaps they do. But these are not the personal qualities that enable them to survive. That is the fascinating thing. The qualities that enable them to survive are the "soft" ones of caring, nurturing, reaching out, finding succor. I have no illusion that the average B-school student can say "Screw you" as well as anyone, but he or she does not get through by virtue of taking this attitude. What gets the student through is the discovery that competitiveness, materialism, and individualism can take you only so far. For the rest of the way you must depend on a philosophy that is more communal than competitive.

- *[HBS] is like that bastard chemistry teacher in high school whom everyone hated but whom you secretly loved because he pushed you to the limits of your mental and emotional capabilities.*

—Student "Gang of Nine" in *The Harbus News*

4

THE MYSTERIOUS
AND MAGICAL
POWER OF
A SECTION

If the Harvard Business School has a secret power, it is the section system. A first-year section has a life of its own, bigger than any student, more powerful than any instructor. It is not apolitical. It could not operate in any setting, only in a democratic setting. Just as a potter's oven bakes color and design into a bowl or vase, so the HBS section system "bakes" into the educational process such principles as freedom of inquiry, checks and balances on power, and dissent. Note that these principles are not capitalist but American. Thus, the B-school is not truly the "boot camp of capitalism" but the boot camp of *American* capitalism. It has built into it America's weaknesses, but it also capitalizes on America's strengths. Its alumni, to the extent that they are true to the B-school, personify the best that *American* management training can offer.

Strictly speaking, the section consists of the ninety or so first-year students in the room. You can list these people and describe them on paper. But you don't really describe the section when you do that. The section is like another person looming in the back of the room, now grinning, now shaking its head, now pointing a finger. Its impact is greater than any person's or group's.

All first-year instructors I know agree about the awesome power of the section. They may not like the way it works in all cases—who does?—yet it drives B-school students to learn, influencing them in countless ways. I have known some instructors who tried to tame the power of a section, thinking mistakenly that if they only did the right thing, they could neutralize this mysterious force so that they would be free to teach what and as they wished. All failed miserably. "You've got to go with it," Professor William White once explained to me. Since we were both golfers, he made an analogy. "You've got to allow for it, like hitting a ball in a wind." White did not mean to say that instructors are powerless. They can and often do alter the shape of this invisible giant—at least, a little.

In this chapter I will focus on the impact of the section on learning. It is my conviction that the transformation that comes over students in their two years at the B-school—the change from naïve, unsophisticated kids to young managers with awesome powers—is the work in large part of the section system. It wouldn't work as it does without conditions, especially the case method, bright and highly motivated students, and expert instructors. But, given these conditions, it works with extraordinary power.

It is remarkable that so few observers have attempted to describe section power. Nearly three decades ago Professor Charles Orth studied aspects of the system and wrote up his findings in a careful treatise for scholars. Most other mentions have been incidental or passing in nature. Yet here is a uniquely American invention of great potential that is affecting our fortunes in economic competition.

CLASSROOMS "OWNED" BY STUDENTS

Before attempting to explain what goes on in a section, let me mention a few historical facts and comparisons for the sake of perspective.

Most HBS students never notice a bronze plaque on the lobby wall in Aldrich. The plaque states that the building is the gift of John Davison Rockefeller, Jr., in 1953. At the time the amphitheaters (sixteen then, eighteen now) were called "revolutionary." They no longer are, for they have been imitated in so many places, but the use to which they are put is indeed revolutionary.

Aldrich Hall exemplifies the power of architecture to shape behavior. In no way could education be the same in classrooms of conventional design and number. Before Aldrich, classes were held in Baker Library, and the classrooms there were not unusual. Classes were taught by the same teachers who went to Aldrich when it was completed, and the rooms were filled by the same students, but the difference in quality of education was immediate and magical. One reason was the ease of class discussion; as noted earlier, Aldrich classrooms were designed specifically for the case method. A more important reason was that the number and design of the classrooms made possible the section system as the school knows it today. Nine rooms in Aldrich could be "owned" by first-year students and become the "home turf" of sections A through I for a whole school year.

The design of the Aldrich classrooms was masterminded by a faculty building committee headed by Professor John G. McLean. McLean, who possessed a mind like a computer and an elephantine memory, later was lured into industry because of a unique study of the oil industry he made with a junior colleague, Robert Haigh. In industry he became the chief executive of Continental Oil Company.

A few other business schools have section systems and mention them in their catalogs. For instance, at the Darden Graduate School of Business Administration at the University of Virginia, whose program is like HBS's in many respects, the four sections are rearranged at the beginning of the second semester so that a student sits with an entirely different group of classmates during the second half of the year. At Dartmouth's Amos Tuck School, the three sections are re-formed each quarter. The Anderson Graduate School of Management at the University of California, Los Angeles, also rearranges its sections each quarter. These three schools are similar to HBS in approach, but their systems are different from Harvard's in an important respect: In none of them does a section "own" a classroom long enough for students to know and influence each other the way they do at Harvard.

Before 1953 HBS had a conventional section system. That is, a student belonged to the same section for all classes for nine months, but since there were not enough classrooms for a section to "own" one, the students had to pick up and leave when a class was through so that another class could file in and take their seats.

It is significant that the first year takes nine months, for in a real sense this is a gestation period. Suppose you are a student. The classroom that you and your section mates live in becomes more than a physical space; it becomes a kind of womb in which nurturing and growth take place. Psychologically and intellectually, if not physically, you grow very fast.

In the second year the section system is dropped, though students habitually refer to themselves as "old A" or "old I" to distinguish themselves from first-years, who are "new A" or "new I." Since most courses are elective, it is impossible to hold students in constant groups and in one place anymore.

HERDLIKE LEARNING

Learning at HBS has a herdlike quality. Focusing on each other because there are no windows to look out of and because the professor won't let them focus on him or her, the members of the herd move forward, ever forward, perhaps not as fast as the professor and some others might wish, but always in the direction of the prize, the golden passport to management and power.

None of the members could make it alone, or by tying themselves to the instructors, or even in small groups. They might learn some things this way, but not the big things. They could not become MBAs in the sense the B-school wants. Let me use another analogy.

Most good baseball players begin playing on sandlots. Here they learn the most important things that will make them fine hitters, fielders, and pitchers—how to time a pitch, how to gauge a fly ball, how to fool a hitter, and so on. Few of these players profit much from how-to books. They watch baseball on TV, and this gives them a useful feel for the game and some ideas, but they don't improve their playing abilities much by watching.

How, then, do they learn? By playing with and against others who have potential. By trial and error. By succeeding and failing in competition. In short, by participating in what behaviorists call a peer group.

In a section room in Aldrich much the same process takes place. You watch Joe, you listen to Mary. You raise your hand and speak to the problem yourself, or maybe you get cold-called. You don't do very well the first time. Muttering to yourself, you watch Joe some more, you listen to Mary again. Sam gets called on and does no better than you did. You see him biting his lips and know just what he feels like. The next day he tries again and does better. You determine to try again, too, and so you do.

This process goes on hour after hour, day after day, week after week, month after month. You imitate. You find that this works but that doesn't. You do all right and get elated, you fail and feel miserable. All the time you have company—ninety-plus others not so different from you who are going through the same thing.

Much of the time you're unaware that anything is happening to you. That's partly because it all happens so slowly, partly because the others, who are your standard and reference point, are changing at about the same rate you are, like passengers on a train on the next track going in the same direction you are. Over and over again you try to get a handle on a case and test yourself in class. You measure yourself by your peers, you try to keep up with them, you feel in the swim of things with them. In effect, you're part of a self-propelled learning group.

What do you learn?

The most important thing is what no instructor or writer can teach you successfully in a lecture or book: how to get your arms around a large and complicated management problem. In September you may have been no better at this than anybody else. But by the end of winter you are approaching big problems such as a busy airport's logistics or a sizable company's marketing troubles with savvy, knowing instinctively how to get a grip on them. You may not be able to explain your approach to others—why you moved in this direction rather than that, why you singled out this fact rather than that—but you do it. You proceed intuitively, like Ted Williams swinging at a pitch.

Then, too, you pick up a lot of facts about companies and industries that catch your attention, and you learn a lot of practical knowledge about concepts—how to interpret a balance sheet, how to organize a quality control program, what to expect from a market research project, and so on. Because of the testing, comparing, and trial and error constantly going on with your classmates, however, you will learn such things in a very different way from the way you would learn them by yourself from a textbook or lecture.

You also learn a lot about yourself—how you stack up against others, your strengths and limitations, how best to present yourself. Spending hour after hour in that windowless amphitheater, you may come to think of yourself quite differently from the way you used to, and, with luck, you will develop a greater appreciation of what others can do.

TWO-EDGED SWORD

The section system is not an unmitigated blessing. It possesses some of the weaknesses that our American system of government has.

Every section has a different profile or personality. Often you can see the difference simply by glancing at the bulletin boards and paraphernalia on the walls. Now and then a section will come along that exacts more conformity from its members than most sections do, that punishes those who differ too much from the average. (The punishment may take the form of cold silence, hissing, or subtly ostracizing the offender in social activities.) A professor told me this story:

He wanted to lead his class to a certain recognition of a widespread accounting failure in U.S. business. But when the time came, the student he was counting on most to speak up was silent. Several times he hinted that he would like to hear the woman's view, but she never broke her silence. Not long afterward he happened to meet her on the sidewalk, and they talked for several minutes. He realized that the words he had wanted her to say were on her lips in that class but she had known that they would sound too precocious to the others. She didn't want to be penalized for being a "star." That was why she had remained mum. "It wouldn't have happened that way in other sections," the professor added. "Only in section C."

The *potential* for mediocrity exists in every first-year section by virtue of student "ownership" of the dialogue. The section soon becomes something of an extended family, and as in every family, members lose little time in finding out about the others. My guess is that the best-read publication in the first year is not *The Wall Street Journal, Fortune,* or even *The Harbus News* but the *Prospectus,* or "face book," which profiles students in the section. Attending a class early in the year, I am sure to see students feeling for the pamphlets under their desks, sneaking peeks in order to find out a little more about the individual holding forth on the Fieldcrest Blankets case or the Dominion Motors case.

Mercy Jiménez '83, president and founder of Trade Mission, Inc., operating out of Tampa, told me in an interview:

"The fact that the room is as large as it is gives you the feeling of being a tiny cell in a big organism. It's much like the feeling you have in a corporation—you're part of a larger whole. Operating with the same group for such a long time, you get to feel camaraderie, tolerance, competitiveness, also a sense of appreciation that would be impossible in a setting where you see the people on and off. You get to know the others in the section very well."

Sometimes a section develops such strong standards of behavior that it can be extremely tough on any instructors who don't fall in step with it. Reflecting on this point, John Wheeler '69, a West Pointer who went from HBS to the jungles of Vietnam, then organized and chaired the campaign to build a Vietnam Veterans Memorial on the Mall in Washington, D.C., told me:

"The section system gave the students a lot of power. It could be awesome for teachers, especially young teachers, to go into a section and establish themselves, make their peace with the section norms, preserve their purposes and standards as teachers. It was tough. . . ."

On balance, however, the sections do well. They have a positive effect on learning. They also have a positive effect on behavior, setting out-of-bounds markers that even the most arrogant people are forced to observe. Reminiscing on her B-school experience, Laurie Leonard '77 told me:

"People in my section found one man obnoxious. He seemed to us pompous and self-righteous, and he frequently aggravated us.

"One day when he was talking the people felt that he was too condescending to bear. They rolled up pieces of paper and threw them at him as he talked. He was bombarded with a hail of paper.

"This really shocked him. It seemed to sink in and make him realize how disturbing he was to people. After that he became much less arrogant."

How many times had this egregious person been advised in more conventional ways to watch himself, all to no avail? But the section had the power to make him change.

A PARTICULAR TYPE OF LEADER

To understand the B-school, first understand its section system. This is the multiplier that gives the case method, class participation, and the instructor added power. It is the booster rocket that thrusts students farther toward the objective of grasping difficult management problems and finding workable ways to deal with them. This quality is crucial to success in economic warfare today.

The B-school's section system also tells us something about America. Unlike much training that goes on in this country, which is really pretty totalitarian in nature, with the instructor having complete control of what knowledge is dispensed, the section system sets students up as "owners" of the classroom and what goes on in it. What and how they learn is as much a function of their whims and desires as of the professor's.

Under the case method, students have this power regardless of how they are organized. What the section system does is give them more power. Students find it quite natural to exercise this power to the hilt.

Years ago a student in a first-year section told me, "You know, Mr. Ewing, I have to live with these people. I can't just walk out." The significance of what this fellow was saying eluded me then, but over the years it has become clearer. He was saying that much of what he learned at the B-school depended on the section, and therefore it behooved him to pay close attention to his relationships with the others. When they learned, he would learn; when they didn't, he probably wouldn't. Learning wasn't symbolized by him sitting on one end of a log and the instructor on the other, that venerable analogy often used by educators; it was more like a square dance with the instructor doing the calling but the section members doing the dancing.

Return with me to a class I recently attended and see what I saw. In many ways it was a typical first-year class. To professors and management trainers brought up in the old school, however, it would have seemed chaotic:

The instructor, who was a slender and bespectacled young man, didn't begin with the case, as he usually did, but with a student summation. The section—like the other eight sections in the first year, which were doing the same thing that day—had come to the end of a miniseries, or module, of cases. Therefore the instructor wanted to devote the first few minutes of class time to reviewing the ground covered.

At 8:32, precisely two minutes after class started, the professor took his jacket off and moved out of the way so that two young women could take over. Turning on an overhead projector, which they had checked before class to be sure it was in operating order, they showed the main lessons of a series of cases just completed. For all I and they knew, their summary of the module was quite different from that of the summarizers in the other eight first-year sections. Although the case material covered would have been the same, the summarizers for the nine sections didn't know each other or coordinate with each other, nor did they show their summaries in advance to their professors.

The class listened attentively. A young man near me sipped from a styrofoam cup of coffee, another twisted the ends of his mustache, a young woman sitting near me was taking notes furiously. Product life cycles, market research, test marketing—lessons from these and other topics were described, each tied to one or more cases discussed. One case involved a poultry farm, another a contact lens manufacturer, another a giant pharmaceutical company.

Altogether, eight graphs were shown on the screen, and the presentation took five minutes. At the end the class applauded.

Then the professor called on a student to open, and the discussion of a case—the first case in a new module—began. About thirty students, a third of the section, talked. When the class was over, a student copied down everything written on the boards. That student, called a "scribe," would make photocopies of his sheet and distribute them to everyone in the class at the next meeting. A different scribe worked each time; he or she was the person who had opened the previous class.

Several facts about this class are striking:

First, the summation by the two women might not have agreed at all with the professor's. He never let on by facial expressions or comments. In fact, when I asked him later, he refused to say whether the lessons they culled were the ones he'd hoped they would. It was his way of saying, I suppose, that the students "owned" the discussion, not he.

Second, the section members who were sitting didn't necessarily agree with the presentation of the two women.

Third, the scribe copied down notations on the board that might or might not have made sense to others in the class. "A lot of garbage goes up on that board," a student told me once. "The prof writes down things to organize the discussion, not because they're good points."

Fourth, this particular professor had quite a bit of influence on the class, guiding and moving it ahead skillfully. But he had that influence because he took the section as it was, not as he thought it should be. He was somewhat like the circus man who runs the lions through their act knowing that he must adapt his ways to theirs or pandemonium will result.

■ ■ ■

In sum, the B-school's section system has many of the weaknesses that Congress or a state legislature has. The system forces
the gifted people to live with the less gifted, and the sensitive
people with the jerks, giving all of them equal airtime, with all
that means for compromising the best solution the class can produce. A B-school class is not like a class in mathematics where you
can measure results and prove theorems.

At the same time, given the right conditions, this democratic,
egalitarian system is very potent in an educational setting. It
accounts for a good part of the ability that B-school grads acquire
to grasp the reins of economic leadership.

> ■ *The business school experience was the
> most intense experience I ever had. I look for
> that intensity now in my work life. It was
> almost like a drug. We got used to having it,
> to feeding off each other's excitement.*
>
> —Member of the class of 1985, recalling the two
> years in Boston

WHAT PROFESSORS TEACH

5

THE VIEW FROM
THE PEAK

What do B-school professors believe about business? What knowledge and ideas do they think students should possess in order to become economic leaders?

In the chapters that follow I will sample the faculty's views in a half-dozen vital areas. First we will look at general management, including a way of thinking about corporate strategy that has taken the management world by storm. Then we will look at production and operations management, a crucial area in this era of global economic competition. Next, what the B-school teaches about leadership and the management of employees, followed by a look at the interesting and innovative courses in marketing. The fascinating world of entrepreneurs and small companies comes next, then the quantitative, down-to-earth courses in finance and managerial economics. To conclude this section, we will run through some of the guidelines for decision making that students learn.

Although, as noted earlier, the B-school stresses learning over teaching, we should not think for a moment that the views of the faculty don't matter. They are very important. Not only do the professors communicate these views in the classroom by the way they ask questions and lead the discussion, and in reading materials such as course notes that give students background for cases; they communicate them also by their choice of cases for a course. For every case that is used in an HBS course there are dozens discarded. When the course faculty agrees to use this case, that one, and that one to start off, and these three for the next section, those five for the next section, and so on, it is in effect saying, "These cases pose the problems and convey the material that we think is most important." Its view of the world is represented in that lineup—not its complete view, of course, but the most important parts, in its opinion, for students.

Thus, if the professors who teach Organizational Behavior choose a case describing a company that practices participative management, they are saying that this style of management is something students should know about. Students may conclude that the approach of People's Express or Donnelly Corporation is for the birds, but at least they get exposed to that style and know it exists. If the professors who teach Production and Operations choose a case on a maverick steel corporation in Texas, they are saying that this company's system deserves attention in an industry that has lost a lot of ground to foreign competitors. If the Control faculty believes that the dispute between practitioners and academics over the efficiency of markets is something every student should know about, it will choose a case such as "Kennett Mills" for the lineup; and if it wants students to know how far from reality a company's capital investment figures can be if they don't take into account the true value of money, it may choose a case such as "Super Project." If the finance faculty wants a good case showing why corporations pay dividends, it may choose a case such as "SCM Corporation." If the marketing faculty wants students to know what goes into pricing a bid on a desired piece of business, it may select a case such as "Computron," and if it wants them versed in marketing communications, it may choose a case such as "Ciba-Geigy Agricultural Division."

So while the case method throws the responsibility for decision making on students, and the section system makes them the "owners" of the discussion, the faculty's views still come through. The faculty is like the cook who decides what dishes to serve at the dinner party and how to cook them. The cook's decision may be lost in the festivity but it is crucial, underlying everyone's enjoyment or nonenjoyment of the meal. No one should ever think that these professors don't influence students' thinking a great deal—and not only influence it but channel it in desired directions.

BIG PICTURES

The first and most important emphasis of the B-school is on the general management point of view. The faculty does not say that specialized techniques in manufacturing, labor relations, personnel, financial, training, and other activities are unimportant, only that the first task of a top executive is to understand how the functions fit together. HBS's emphasis throughout is on the whole enterprise, not on the individual pieces.

Integrating skill is what top executives must have if they are to lead corporations successfully in global competition. If they lack the skill, the organizations may fail even though they have some top-notch people and departments. This has been true of almost every major corporate failure in recent decades. Harvester, Eastern, Kresge—all had some superb people and groups on their staffs.

What I am trying to describe is often referred to as "the big picture." Think of a pyramid. If you are halfway up one side, you have an expert, close-up view of that section of the structure. You can see in detail how broad the side is, how tall, what it is made of, and so forth. You can see the land directly below. However, if you go to the top, your view becomes quite different. Now you see all four sides. You see their comparative widths, the seams or corners where they join, the landscape all around. The pyramid as a whole and its setting in relation to the countryside now become your concerns rather than any one aspect.

This is the view that HBS wants its students to be able to grasp.

It is a difficult view to understand because the interrelationships become more important than the substance of any one department or division, and interrelationships often tend to be fuzzy, changeable, quixotic. You do not enjoy the stability and order in top-management thinking that you have in, say, sales management or research, which have their own professional disciplines.

A few years ago Professor Benson Shapiro persuaded the faculty to establish a new second-year course to be called Integrative Product Line Management. Now, Shapiro is a marketing man, and so one might expect his course to focus on the problems of marketing a successful product line. Not so. As Shapiro saw the course, it was to show students what impact a product line has on *other* company functions, and what impact *they* have on product line management. "What I'm fascinated with," he told me, "is that no single function in a company controls what the company has to offer customers. Manufacturing is important but not the whole thing; finance is important but not the whole thing; sales and marketing are important but they, too, are not everything. It's all of these activities *together* that decide what you can offer. But how often do you see a company that recognizes that? Or that has a system so people from different departments can talk with each other about their common problems?"

In hundreds of cases, this view of the enterprise as a whole is the one students wrestle with. Let us visit a couple of first-year classrooms to see for ourselves. One of these episodes took place a decade ago, the other recently, but except for the personnel, either could have happened half a century ago—or presumably half a century hence—for in some respects the school does not change.

We visit a class in Control taught by Professor John Dearden. The Control course, one of the building-block courses of the first year, deals with financial reporting, accounting, accountability, and other aspects of directing an organization so that it does what top management wants it to do. A trim, athletic man with steel-rimmed glasses and a quick smile, Dearden has taught at HBS for more than twenty years; before coming to the school, he was an

executive at Ford Motor Company. His teaching style is not
flashy. He is a no-nonsense guy who loves his subject; students
respond to his sincerity and sense of commitment.

The case assignment is "The Galvor Company." Galvor is an
electronics company that has just been acquired by Universal
Electric. Universal has imposed its fairly tight control system on
Galvor, and many employees at Galvor are screaming. They
think the thirteen accounting statements now required by Universal call for much too much detail and represent staff interfer-
ence in Galvor's operations.

Many students are inclined to take Galvor's side. A wiry, red-
faced fellow says that Galvor is being turned into a bureauc-
racy—forty-two people have to be employed in the controller's
department "to get out this laundry list," and that's close to 6
percent of the company's employees. Others want to argue
whether a single rate should be used to allocate factory overhead
for all operations, instead of individual rates tailored to each
operation's relationship, or whether transfer prices (that is, a
charge on something made for one division by another) should
be applied to in-house transactions. A woman whom the class has
obviously learned to listen closely to—you can tell by the close
attention paid when she speaks—argues that the reams of detail
required in the reports are going to focus Galvor managers' attention on short-term results. "That would be a tragedy, because
this was a family-run firm that looked ahead," she says. She com-
pares this case with one recently discussed, where the control
system was the work of accountants, not management, with disastrous results.

But Dearden keeps swinging the discussion to Universal's
standpoint. "Let's look at these criticisms," he says, going to the
board. "Jean, exactly what reports does Universal want?" As she
lists the thirteen, he writes them on the board—preliminary net
income, changes in retained earnings, analysis of receivables, and
so on. Over the column he writes "Report." Then he starts a
second column on the board, entitled "Use." He asks Jean, "What
does Universal want to use these reports *for?*" One by one, Jean
and others give him the answers—consolidation, control, management. "If you were at Universal," asks Dearden when the lists

are complete, "which of these reports would you eliminate?" Begrudgingly, even the opponents of the system have to agree that none can be eliminated because each has a useful purpose for headquarters, if not Galvor.

Then Dearden asks about the price Universal has to pay for such a tight control system. "What about the side effects?" he asks. Discussion heats up as the opponents get a new lease on life. The system will dampen Galvor's initiative, say some; others, harking back to Jean's earlier point, think that the system will encourage short-term action, that is, acts that will produce immediate results at the possible cost of longer-run benefits to the companies. A good many, however, are now on the side of Universal. "Look," says one, finally getting the floor, "if Universal is really using this system, it's going to tell them early if Galvor goes off the track. . . ."

When the period ends, there is no class agreement on whether the control system is too tight, but students are arguing the pros and cons from the standpoint of the whole company, not one division or department. "Continued Thursday," says Dearden with a grin.

We visit Professor David Mullins's finance class, where the case assignment is "O. M. Scott & Sons Company." Mullins's style is different from Dearden's. A genial, balding, bespectacled man (now on loan to the U.S. Treasury Department at the request of the White House), he paces back and forth in the pit and up and down the aisles with bursts of nervous energy. He breaks piece after piece of chalk as he hurries to the board to write a point down, and he is so intent on the dialogue that he just drops the broken chalk pieces on the floor, letting them roll, and grabs fresh pieces to write with. Gifted with an instant sense of humor, he makes the class laugh repeatedly as the discussion progresses.

At the time the case opens, Scott has encouraged retail dealers to stock up on its lawn and garden products by extending generous credit terms to dealers. From a sales standpoint, the program is a whopping success. From a financial standpoint, too, the program has been great; profits have been impressive, and the stock is selling at a high (32 times earnings). "So everything's great, is it?" asks Mullins, and immediately hands fly up. It turns out that Scott has been "selling" to dealers much faster than dealers have been selling to users, and many dealers must already be tripping over Scott products. In a year or two or three, dealers surely are going to have to cut down on their orders from Scott—not a little but drastically.

"So what should Scott do?" asks Mullins. The class bombards him with answers—price cuts, extra advertising, more publicity and contacts with financial analysts, changes in the trust receipts (legal documents controlling the company's rights until dealers pay for goods received), and so on. Any one of these activities will produce results, he recognizes, but he keeps throwing the ball back. It dawns on the class that they, putting themselves in top management's shoes, should be thinking not of the individual interests of stockholders, production, *or* sales people but of the overall interest of all three in the enterprise. That puts a different twist on the ball, and as time runs out the class is in high argument over the best course to take.

A business is like an ecosystem, in other words. All of its parts interact, and the quality of interaction has a great deal to do with the success of the enterprise. Watching over that quality is top management's job; it must keep the functions in some sort of creative interplay. In a sense, balance is as important to the enterprise as it is to the parts of a mobile.

COMPETITIVE STRATEGY

Earlier I used the pyramid analogy to explain the top management viewpoint emphasized at the B-school. Now suppose that your pyramid and many others, representing other companies in your industry, are mounted on wheels and are moving. How are you going to assure that your pyramid doesn't end up in a crunch? Or, if it does collide with others, that you come out of the fray in good shape? Questions like these are crucial to top management. All the people at levels below you on the pyramid, in fact, depend on you to steer a sound course, for only you can see around and ahead.

Not surprisingly, HBS pays a lot of attention to strategy. Although there are no courses on long-range or short-range planning, strategy comes up again and again in first- and second-year courses. It is an inseparable part of a top executive's job. On this skill depends the future not only of the enterprise but of part of the economy.

For quite some time HBS has emphasized strategy, and over the years various concepts and approaches have found their way into the classroom. The doctrine that has prevailed for several years builds on a lot of thinking that went before, and many faculty people are enriching and adding on to it. Perhaps the best-known spokesperson for the doctrine is Michael Porter, author of *Competitive Strategy* (now in its seventeenth printing) and *Competitive Advantage.* Also, Porter is one of the instructors whom alums remember best for his stimulating teaching and insight.

In his early forties, athletic-looking, always wearing large horn-rimmed glasses, Porter is a man of many talents. Trained at Princeton as an aeronautical engineer, he did his graduate work in economics, not business administration, but has done almost all his teaching at HBS. He is a crack golfer and, among many other things, manages a rock band called Reckless.

Porter believes that the answers to five questions hold the key to an organization's business strategy (it makes little difference, he once told me, whether the organization is a big company, a small company, a nonprofit enterprise, or something else). A notable thing about these questions is that they recognize how a company's welfare may be affected not only by direct competitors within its industry but also by the actions of competitors *in other industries.*

1. How great is the threat of new entrants if your part of the industry is profitable—or may soon become profitable? If competitors are likely to come in and set up shop in droves the minute you demonstrate that profits can be made, you are in a far different position from a company that for one reason or another (e.g., a unique product that can be made by no one else) has a monopoly-type hold on the industry. In the first case, your hope is going to be lower costs, for you will not be able to compete successfully with many rivals if your costs are high; in the second, keeping that monopoly-type hold so that you continue to dominate.

2. How subject are your company and industry sector to the power of suppliers? In many courses at HBS, cases illustrate different situations concerning suppliers. At one extreme is the firm that can tell a supplier good-bye with ease and get another one equally good; at the other, the firm that is so dependent on one supplier that the latter can virtually dictate prices and terms.

3. How subject are your company and industry to the power of strong customers? Sometimes a customer company can dangle you like a puppet, as when, say, it is your main outlet and can, if it pleases, turn you off and on like a spigot.

4. How vulnerable is your organization to competitors marketing substitute products and services? If you sell a general-purpose pain reliever in a market full of pain relievers, your competitive position is far different from that of the marketer of the only known relief for back pain, holding a perfect patent. If you sell a hard-to-make sun screen such as Koolshade, you are less vulnerable than a manufacturer of an ordinary screen whose competitors can, let us say, readily copy its product.

5. What is the state of your industry for competitors? In some industries, competition is ferocious and intense and always has been; in others, competition *could* be intense but newcomers are shut out and old-timers have learned to respect certain rules of coexistence. Why some industries are subject to dog-eat-dog competition while others are "gentlemanly" may have something to do with ease of entry and product substitution, but it is likely to be a result of history, happenstance, "industry culture," and other factors as well.

■ ■ ■

With the answers to these questions in hand, Porter believes that you can gain competitive advantage in one of two ways: by putting out your product or service at lower cost or by delivering a better product or service than competitors can, thus being able to command a premium price. (*Differentiation* is the term B-schoolers and many business people use for the latter approach.) Your strategic position, as indicated by your answers to the five questions, tells you which way to go or which combination of ways to take.

To understand your position better, look at the *activities* your firm performs—not at the systems or functions, as we know them from textbooks, but the tangible, everyday things such as buying, selling, designing, making, assembling, packaging, advertising, and so on. See how they are linked to each other and to your markets by what they do. What does your firm do better or cheaper? What does it do that perhaps no one else does? Porter calls these activities the *value chain.*

With information like this, says Porter, you can create a sound strategy. Then, implementing the strategy by investing more here, trimming there, restructuring there, and so on—Porter has a lot to say about such efforts—you can launch your organization on a good course.

Porter's approach is appealing because it seems to explain numerous ups and downs in corporate fortunes that aren't easily explained by simpler types of analysis. Also, it shows U.S. business a realistic way of deciding operationally where and how it will compete with strong rivals from Asia, Europe, and other continents. Whether you use Porter's term for the relationships of your organization's various marketing and production activities or some other term, it makes a lot of sense to look hard at what different groups are doing in your organization and how their work contributes to the enterprise's success or lack of it in the market. The approach promises to make U.S. companies leaner and smarter in economic warfare.

One time Porter was talking to a group of faculty about the differences between his approach and others:

"Look, for a long time diversification was the magic word. Buying up unrelated companies was supposed to be the secret of success. What happened? Company after company went through humiliating periods of selling off failed acquisitions. Gulf + Western, Borden, Cummins, Scovill, Continental Group—scores of them!

"Why did diversification fail so often? The answer is simple: because it was done in the name of portfolio management. The companies saw their job as allocating capital—lots of money to this division because it's a 'star,' not so much to that one because it's a 'cash cow.' Instead of cooperating, business units in diversified firms were often led to compete.

"It doesn't work that way. The most important thing is the links. Make the most of the links—that's what corporate strategy should be about. The trouble with portfolio management is that it says nothing about this."

In short, see the whole thing, the "big picture," including the links and connections between the key activities performed by your company, and then exploit the linkages.

Note that relationships are the focus of top-management thought, not the substance of the individual activities. The substance is terribly important, but that job is for department and division heads, not headquarters. This approach to strategy, therefore, is adapted to the B-school's emphasis on general management.

A CASE IN POINT: INFORMATION TECHNOLOGY

Many professors believe that an important source of competitive advantage for a firm may be computerized information—or, to use the buzzword, *information technology.* For instance, Professors William Bruns, James Cash, and Warren McFarlan point to a few imaginative companies that are harnessing the speed and flexibility of low-cost data-processing and information systems to enable managers to make quicker and better decisions. "Managers used to have to wait for days or weeks for crucial facts from production and sales," McFarlan explained to me. "No more. Information technology means that now you can get key data from the farthest operations in an instant. If inventory turnover is slowing in a plant in South Korea, if sales are spurting in the south-central territory—you can get that presented to you right away and in whatever form you want."

Writing in the *Harvard Business Review,* Bruns and McFarlan cite the example of a passenger elevator company. To shaft competitors, management gave excellent service and trouble-spotting to company customers. Using a new data-processing system instead of the old monthly sales-call reports that reached management late or not at all, managers were able to zero in quickly on trouble spots. They discovered, for instance, that certain elevators had been breaking down between eighteen and thirty times a quarter, a situation that had existed for years but been buried in field office files. The situation was written up in a case taught at the school.

For a few years, write Cash and McFarlan, the premier examples of competitive advantage gained from computer systems were United and American Airlines. Their computerized reservation systems, Apollo and Sabre, so linked travel agencies with them that they had a leg up—wing up, perhaps we should say—when agents around the country made reservations for passengers. In fact, a small airline, Frontier, went to the Civil Aeronautics Board alleging unfair competition because of the way travel agents were biased.

In terms of Porter's scheme, this was a superb example of exploiting linkage. However, such an advantage may also incur a cost, in his scheme: too much dependence on a supplier. For example, McFarlan cites the case of an aerospace company that required its suppliers to link up with its computer-aided design system; this gave it a competitive edge by reducing the costs of design changes but also made it more difficult for management to change suppliers, thus increasing its vulnerability.

■ *If the strategy is challenging . . . a band of people casually gathered to work for a livelihood can be made into an institution embodying values, creating loyalty, and providing nonmaterial rewards, to say nothing of profiting from efficient or first-class performance.*

—PROFESSOR KENNETH ANDREWS

6

THE COMEBACK
TRAIL FOR
PRODUCTION AND
OPERATIONS

One of the most no-
ticeable changes in curriculum at the B-school during the past
decade has been the resurgence of Production and Operations
Management (POM). It shows in the strengthening of first- and
second-year courses on the subject, in rising faculty output of
books and articles on POM topics, and in growing student interest in starting their careers in POM. The resurgence is a direct
reflection of the B-school's concern over U.S. losses on the economic front. It symbolizes the faculty's conviction that if the
school is to train economic leaders, it must instill the idea that
production and operations are crucial parts of corporate strategy.
In a great many cases, competitive advantage begins on the shop
floor.

Significantly, the change also shows in a subtle metamorphosis
in student values. Students don't seem as horrified as they used
to be over getting their hands dirty on a job after graduation.
There is a gradually growing sense that it is no disgrace to get

grime under your fingernails, especially in the first few years of a position. Among would-be entrepreneurs in particular the conviction is rising that it can be a good thing to run a machine for a while or drive a truck with a B-school diploma in your hip pocket. "I was the black sheep of the business school when I graduated," says Michael Bergman '77. "I went into a supermarket, which was really looked down on, and then, horror of horrors, I decided to open a bakery restaurant and work in it myself, making muffins and sweeping floors. It was not the thing to do." Bergman has since become the subject of a case at HBS, for what he began modestly as a shop grew into a seventy-one-outlet chain grossing many millions of dollars. His example appeals to a growing portion of students.

In POM cases and classes you find much emphasis on technical details—the calculation of setup costs, inventory size, learning curves, variable cost analysis, materials requirements planning, and so on. Let me describe several views and attitudes of the POM faculty that show the direction the school is heading in and its belief that a comeback for production and operations is important to a comeback for U.S. industry.

For clarification, let me add that, at the B-school, POM covers the production of services as well as manufacturing. Traditionally, manufacturing was the focus of the course; in fact, students nicknamed it "Nuts and Bolts." In the 1970s, however, the purview was broadened and operations was injected into the course title. Today you will find classes discussing cases in fields like electric power, insurance, food service, and airport logistics as well as manufacturing.

PROGRESS: THE TORTOISE OR THE HARE?

A half-dozen years ago Professor Robert Hayes told me about an analogy he had made to explain how organizations try to move forward.

He divided businesses into two species: hares and tortoises.

Most companies were hybrids, he said, but American firms tended to be more like hares than their counterparts in, say, West Germany and Japan. They were more like hares in that they depended for their success on strategic leaps such as the radical redesign of products, or an investment in a new manufacturing technology, or a move to a different part of the country with cheaper workers. In between such leaps, they made only minor improvements in operations. In contrast, companies in West Germany and Japan were more like tortoises in that they counted more on lots of little improvements made continually, great efforts in recruiting and training operators, and so on.

Both the hare and tortoise take risks, said Hayes. The great risk for the tortoise is that it will be leaped over by a hare as when, for instance, transistors replaced vacuum tubes, jet engines surpassed propeller engines, or New England mills moved south to take advantage of lower wages. On the other hand, the hare runs the risk that the tortoise's slow but steady progress will win in the end. There may come a point when, seeing the tortoise catching up, the hare says, "Let's take another leap forward," but strategists reach into their hats for help and find nothing there.

The upshot, said Hayes, is that in the marketplace, as in the fable, the tortoise often wins the race.

What the POM faculty wants to impress on students is that in global competition today there is no substitute for plugging away at shop-floor excellence. Design, new facilities, relocation, and other such leaps are fine, but it is a fateful mistake to think they can take the place of workaday improvements.

The POM faculty—and the school generally, for that matter—feel that a lot of damage was done in years past by strategic notions that emphasized portfolio analysis at the expense of excellence in production and operations. Before his untimely death from cancer, Professor William Abernathy lectured me on the fallacies of classifying an organization's businesses as mature or immature, stars or nonstars—the current fad in strategic thinking. The error too often made by otherwise sophisticated managements, he said, was to manage their manufacturing operations like Thoroughbred horses—according to their stage of maturity. Operations with technological promise were selected and nurtured through extensive investment like proud young stallions. Later in the stage of full development they were run at peak efficiency to get the most out of them. "Then, when headquarters thinks they are past their peak they are put out to pasture, so to speak," Abernathy explained. "Headquarters takes away their opportunities for renewal, slashes their cash resources, turns its back on them." The money made by these "has-been" divisions was channeled into the businesses felt to be the new up-and-coming stars.

The whole way of thinking was potholed, he thought. "With their profits siphoned off to somebody else, of course they became static!" It rarely occurred to top management that by betting a little imagination and money on the operations it might make winners of them again. The notion of comparing businesses to racehorses or any other form of biological life was ridiculous.

In POM there is considerable discontent with discounted cash flow analysis, a tool commonly used in financial analysis. This is a tool for discounting the projected future earnings of an enterprise to their present value, that is, to the dollar amount today that would grow at some interest rate to the sum projected in the future year. The farther in the future an annual earnings figure occurs, the more it is reduced because it is discounted more. The tool is widely used in business because it has such obvious value—for instance, enabling management to make quantitative comparisons of proposed investments with varying periods of return.

The reason for POM discontent with the technique is that it biases managers in favor of investments with short-term payoffs rather than long-term payoffs. If it is true, as commonly alleged, that American management is overly preoccupied with profits in the next couple of years instead of over a longer period, then such a bias must share part of the blame.

POM instructors also see too many U.S. executives using the discounted cash flow technique rigidly, as a yes-or-no decision rule for evaluating investment proposals instead of one factor among many that should be considered.

INVOLVE ALL EMPLOYEES IN QUALITY CONTROL

Professor Kim Clark, who sometimes can be seen teaching class in a sport shirt with one hand pointing to a diagram on the board and the other to a student, like a football coach rehearsing his team on plays, has spent many hours observing Japanese factories. He sees a profound irony in the lackluster performance of many U.S. manufacturers as compared to the high achievers in Japan. One time in our *Harvard Business Review* offices he gave this example:

In 1912 and 1913, the factory gate at Ford had become a revolving door, with workers coming and leaving in droves. Management responded by creating the famous "Five-Dollar Day," profit participation, communication programs on values and standards, committees to review discharges, and other measures. The efforts were fabulously successful in both economic and industrial relations terms. After World War I, management dropped these measures and became infamously heavy-handed, with severe effects on the company's production and competitive status. Today, Ford management is once again paying top-priority attention to the vital role of production employees in improving quality—with very positive results.

Too often U.S. firms have stubbornly resisted learning from our own history. Few things have been done abroad that weren't done here years ago.

But quality control is more than a technique, say POM instructors. Our very values as managers should be questioned. Speaking of a recent tour through Japanese factories, Clark told several of us:

"We came away convinced that the status symbols of American management often get in the way of first-class operations. We realized that if you define jobs narrowly, you're likely to waste valuable human talent. We saw that adversarial relationships between workers and managers aren't an inescapable fact of life. I'm not saying that Japanese workers have unbounded on-the-job happiness. I'm saying that the Japanese deliberately treat their work force as a key point of competitive leverage, which gives them an edge in manufacturing.

"I know that this has its costs. For example, workers face the same grueling pressures that managers do—they can't daydream on the job, they've got to be thinking all the time. But what an advantage this gives you! One senior Japanese manager said to us, 'As an individual you may be smarter than I am. But once I begin to work with my fellow workers, I am unbeatable.'"

FIX IT NOW AND FOR GOOD

More than two decades ago Professor Wickham Skinner began sounding the alarm about the disastrous impact of poor manufacturing management. He would stop me on the sidewalk and ask me how I liked my new car or refrigerator, and we would commiserate about the problems we had with equipment quality. Skinner had a mission: to wake up top management to the fact that production was an important weapon in its strategic arsenal and shouldn't be relegated to the status of poor cousin. For a long time his alarms fell on deaf ears. It was not until we realized that the Japanese "miracle" was for real and that American industry had, in fact, fallen behind that we saw the importance of what he was teaching.

One of Skinner's protégés today is Professor David Garvin. Garvin criticizes the tendency of American executives to rely on the "quick fix." In his studies of the air-conditioning industry and others, comparing output in this country to manufacturing abroad, he has seen this tendency too often. In his view, the quick fix is no solution to anything for very long. The only solution is for top management to commit itself to quality just as it commits itself to sales increases, profit growth, and other aims. This commitment would include working with suppliers, training and educating employees, setting quality goals, and working up better information systems showing quality trends.

Garvin is unimpressed by the plethora of fine words about quality. He sees many of them as slogans, gimmicks, and facile talk. Manufacturers may institute all sorts of quality programs, and the Commerce Department may present Malcolm Baldridge Awards to companies that have been most successful in quality improvement, but the fact is, he says, that most quality efforts in the United States are basically the same as they were twenty years ago.

In POM meetings, Garvin emphasizes that American managers often delude themselves into thinking that they can solve quality problems by dropping a new unit in place, as you do in an assembly operation. For instance, they will hire a new vice president for quality, or install more robots, or make certain that their engineers and designers map out a quality control plan before the production process starts. In his opinion, such efforts, however nobly intentioned, are poor solutions. They can't substitute for quality management, which means, among other things, learning what customers want and building those features into product design—*before* anything is produced.

DON'T THROW MONEY AT IT—FIX IT

Some companies' version of the quick fix is to spend a lot of money on new equipment. There is nothing wrong with new equipment, Hayes emphasizes, but it's a second-stage solution, not a first-stage answer. "Fix your production problems first, then invest," he says. In a study he made with Clark, one finding was that companies without a lot of money often achieved faster rates of improvement than big spenders because they adopted approaches that didn't require much investment, concentrating on doing better with what they had.

Significantly, in some Asian regions the same highly trained engineers who design the product and develop the production process also make continuous small changes in product design, machinery, testing procedures, and other functions. In so doing, they learn a lot about the work in question. In a workshop at HBS in 1987, Robert Hayes and Clark estimated that in Japan about two-thirds of the improvement in factory productivity was due to the everyday learning that occurs as experience with producing the product grows.

One time in a discussion of POM problems I heard an instructor recount a parablelike story from a new book by Professors Hayes, Clark, and Steven Wheelwright. A vineyard owner told one of the authors that the cost of duplicating his small, terraced vineyard would amount to several million dollars. The professor reacted with astonishment. A similar piece of land could be purchased for a couple of hundred thousand dollars; also, the vineyard owner had made no major investments recently. "But you see, I didn't build this all at once," the owner explained. "My great-grandfather began it, and my grandfather and father after him. Now it's my turn. Every year I cover all my expenses and make a comfortable profit. Some of my time, and a little of that profit, goes back into repairing the damage that occurs during the year and into making further improvements. I have never been in debt; I make a good living, and every year my vineyard becomes more and more valuable."

The moral for manufacturers is that, contrary to what capital budgeting systems may show, it may be better to improve a vineyard stone by stone and vine by vine over a period of time than to buy someone else's vineyard or have a new one built.

LINKS WITH OTHER FUNCTIONS

What distinguishes the HBS gospel most of all is the faculty's refusal to compartmentalize POM. The faculty, POM professors included, do not see this function as a box unto itself on the organization chart. People in production and operations contribute to the firm; they are, in the strategic terms earlier mentioned, parts of the value chain.

This vision of the firm as a whole, with POM but one of its parts, is given to students in many ways and places. Here are just a few of them:

Don't produce something that you can't sell. Since a fine production effort can be wasted if the output isn't salable, POM has a large stake in good marketing, just as marketing has a stake in good production. In our interview about his HBS days, Lee Rodgers '84 told me about this case:

"I can't remember the name, but it always stuck in my mind. The case itself was actually rather boring. It took two or three hours of study because there were so many figures. A company was trying to decide whether to build another rayon plant or just add capacity. In the study group and in class we compared different cash flow projections, different scenarios, and so on. At the end of a long class the professor called for a show of hands—how many would build a new plant, how many favored just adding capacity, how many wouldn't do anything (only one hand), and so on. Then he told us that management had decided to build a new plant [not in the case]. He asked us how we thought it did. Most everyone guessed that it must have done pretty well. He told us that actually the new plant's performance was awful. 'When was the last time you saw someone in a rayon suit?' he asked.

"I have always remembered that case because it showed that marketing assumptions are most often the key. You can crunch numbers all day long, until you're blue in the face, but if your marketing assumptions aren't right, you don't succeed."

Encourage unions to cooperate rather than oppose. Production and operations workers often are organized. Represented by unions, they may feel a wide gulf between management and the workplace, and this gulf can have serious consequences for productivity and quality.

In some second-year courses as well as in the first year, students see the damage done to the enterprise by antilabor and antimanagement stances. They see also how the vicious cycle is being broken in some companies. For instance, in some organizations joint labor-management committees are finding ways to increase employee participation in decision making. Traditional adversarial attitudes are giving way to cooperation and mutual commitment to the enterprise. Students also find how spurious these new approaches can become if management and the union aren't sincere. In all cases joint committees have their pros and cons depending on the peculiar nature of the business, but the result generally is one of the most promising developments in American business.

Two B-school people who have been very articulate on the crucial connection between labor relations and POM are Professor Quinn Mills and Associate Professor Janice McCormick. Going back into history, they find an ironic twist between developments in West Germany and Japan versus England and the United States. At the end of World War II, they point out, the Allies imposed on West Germany and Japan reforms in their industrial relations that broke sharply with the past, such as the breaking up of the *zaibatsu,* or great trading companies, in Japan and, in West Germany, organizing unions about the companies represented instead of as national union organizations. Thus, Germany and Japan did not copy the patterns in England and the United States but improved on them, and these improvements, think Mills and McCormick, have had a lot to do with the postwar success of Japanese and German manufacturers.

In the United States, the unions were born in adversity, and when their strength rose in the 1930s and 1940s, they continued acting as opponents of management, creating webs of rules that often immobilized management and crippled productivity. Walter Reuther, the charismatic United Auto Workers leader, spoke of General Motors as a goose from which more and more fat would be cut for the workers. By the 1960s this antimanagement posture was beginning to boomerang on the unions as plants became less competitive in world markets and jobs were lost. By the 1970s and 1980s, traditional union attitudes were playing a major role in the declining fortunes of many American manufacturers. Reuther's union was so carving up the economic goose that the animal was being incapacitated.

Put accounting in step. According to Professor Robert Kaplan in a conference at the school, cost accounting has not helped top executives to see the light at the end of the POM tunnel. It has obscured many of the things a company needs to do to improve production. For instance, accounting systems are geared too much to direct labor content, which represents an ever-decreasing percentage of total manufacturing cost, instead of equipment and maintenance, which is growing in importance. Moreover, conventional accounting systems, good as they may be at reflecting cost changes, do not recognize fully human accomplishments, such as dramatic increases in manufacturing efficiency, greater capabilities in the work force, reductions to zero of work-in-process inventory, or greater flexibility as a result of computer-controlled production. Such limitations come to light in a variety of cases taught in the first and second years.

Don't forget POM in mergers and acquisitions. In the view of some faculty members, the takeover mania of the 1980s is an example of the American malaise. Obsessed by short-term financial criteria, new owners come in with little understanding of the organization's needs for steady improvements in operations. POM seems to be the last thing on their minds. "How often," I heard Professor Joseph Auerbach argue once, "do the acquirers know as much about what makes the enterprise work as the present managers do? Rarely! What they know is mostly financial."

Think of the United States as an enterprise. Instructors challenge students to think of nations as enterprises whose economies are giant production systems. If it is important to a corporation to have collaboration and sharing between different groups in production and operations, might it not also be important to the nation? Obviously, the analogy can be pushed too far, but the parallel is worth thinking about.

Two professors who have worked long and hard on national economic policy are George Lodge and Bruce Scott. They point out that the countries of East Asia have become formidable competitors by adopting national strategies for economic growth. Using incentives and penalties to encourage work, saving, and investment, they have overcome their lack of natural resources and eclipsed most European nations. The United States and many European countries have made themselves vulnerable by national policies emphasizing greater security for people and more equitable distribution of income. If the United States isn't willing to consider revising its policies, they think, it is going to end up in even deeper trouble than it is now.

For a long time almost single-handedly, though now with growing support, Lodge, who once ran for U.S. senator from Massachusetts on the Republican ticket, has insisted that one American trouble is its age-old attachment to individualism. Heretical as it may sound, he argues, the individualistic philosophies of John Locke and other thought leaders of centuries past are not well suited to the realities of modern global competition. The need is to put much more emphasis on what he calls *communitarian* values—teamwork between companies as well as within, and between companies and government agencies, so long as markets do not suffer because of the cooperation.

One example Lodge uses is the debate over antitrust policy. The economy benefits from joint ventures such as General Motors' collaboration with Toyota in Fremont, California, and from consortiums such as the Microelectronics and Computer Technology Corporation in Austin, a collective of major American electronics companies. Yet such tie-ups strike many traditional economists and government officials as collusion in violation of free markets, and so the ventures have been attacked.

"The U.S. is not fully mindful of what it is doing," Lodge told a colloquium at the B-school. "Even as U.S. institutions move in the direction of communitarianism, there is a tendency to sing the old hymns even more loudly. This ambivalence tends to inhibit change." He went on to explain that the country needs to put its preaching more in line with practice, play up the values and benefits of cooperation more, and stop acting as if competition and rivalry were the be-all and end-all.

Political leaders are recognizing how dependent their foreign policies are on the quality of individual corporate efforts. But the dependence works both ways, for the success of one corporation's POM may depend critically on the nation's policies.

YOU WIN MORE OFTEN WITH THE TORTOISE

If this book had been written a dozen years ago, POM might have been relegated to a minor place. Although it was a required first-year course, its critical role in world economic competition was just beginning to be recognized. Also, only a handful of professors saw it as a major element of corporate strategy.

Today the situation is dramatically different. Students see as they never could have before that an organization's policies toward POM alter its options in competition. Does it try to position itself in buyers' eyes as the producer of unique goods and services that no one else can offer? Of goods and services that are as good as those sold by competitors but lower-priced? Or some combination of these attractions?

In teaching classes and choosing cases, professors don't minimize the potential value of research, innovation, product redesign, and other ways of leapfrogging over competition. To use Hayes's analogy, the hare can still win the race. But the tortoise is going to win more often. Eschewing the quick fix, making small improvements every day, learning by doing, the tortoise is a formidable competitor. Recent history proves it.

The importance of this viewpoint is growing. Not long ago, American enterprises competed mainly with Japanese and West German firms. Now the competition is coming from many other quarters as well—Singapore, Hong Kong, Korea, Brazil, and Spain, to mention just a few. In most instances, when the Americans find themselves head to head against such foreign rivals, the outcome rests in large part on what is going on in the plants and offices. Our corporations are like warships battling other warships. How quickly can the engine rooms respond to commands from the bridge? How fast can the gun crews load the guns? How good are the shells and ammunition?

Let there be no illusion that all students who sally forth from HBS and comparable institutions are smitten with the new gospel. All have been exposed to it, but all are not sold. I have heard many say, after completing POM, "Thank heaven I don't have to think about *that* anymore!" Yet the current crowd of MBAs, no matter what their personal interests, are far more aware of how economic wars are won and lost than many of their predecessors were. Maybe there's more money to be made in financial wheeling and dealing, but POM is where, in the words of the old saying, the rubber hits the road.

- *The realization is finally taking hold that the design and production of high-quality goods and services is not just a quality manager's technical problem on the factory floor but a general manager's problem throughout the entire corporation. It leads everywhere and touches everything.*

—PROFESSOR EARL SASSER

7

PEOPLE ON THE
BOTTOM LINE

In many ways the Organizational Behavior department at the B-school, often called "OB," is the most intriguing part of the faculty. Although it consistently creates more controversy in almost every quarter than any other department, it has had a dramatic influence on the curriculum, on faculty thinking, on HBS alums, and on the ability of U.S. firms to compete with the world's best.

OB is the term for the school's "people course." It deals with the way managers and employees act in organizations because they are human beings with feelings, biases, prejudices, and personal aspirations. It covers aspects of leadership, subordinacy, what is popularly called human resources, what is often called human relations, personnel management, and related topics. It is part of every other course, and every other course is part of OB. For instance, OB cases frequently raise marketing and production issues, while marketing and production cases frequently raise OB questions.

Although Organizational Behavior has influenced the school

profoundly, it has not operated without internal problems and frictions. "I doubt," one member of the administration once confided in me, "that any group on the faculty has had more ups and downs or made more turnovers, as they say in basketball, than the OB group has." I am sure that no other faculty group has been the subject of so much furor. It has been cordially detested in the past by such influential professors as Malcolm McNair; today, too, it has enemies on high at the school. Only the steadying hands of strong deans and some capable departmental leaders have saved the day. It is significant, for instance, that OB professor Paul Lawrence was chosen to codirect the American team on the highly sensitive American-Soviet research project, this country's first clinical look into decision making in Russian firms, an assignment demanding a high degree of diplomacy as well as skill.

For all its troubles and setbacks, however, Organizational Behavior has taken hold and grown vigorously at the B-school. Ever since the pioneering work of Elton Mayo, Fritz Roethlisberger, and others during the 1940s, the department has had a burning sense of mission. It knows that the ability of U.S. firms to compete depends on the management of employees. Further, its impact on students is tremendous. If any first-year courses have produced 180-degree changes in student thinking, they are Organizational Behavior and Human Resources Management. What is more, their impact seems to last and, if anything, grow when students go into the business world. For instance:

- Peter McColough '49, the illustrious head of Xerox for two decades, says that the organizational behavior courses (then called Administrative Practices) made more difference in his life than any other course did. "For the first time I became aware of the sensitivities required in dealing with people."
- Robert Kirby '56, Westinghouse's fine chief executive during much of the 1970s and early 1980s, gives the B-school credit for making him realize how important it is for a manager to delegate authority, particularly in a large organization. "When I gave someone a job to do, I made it a point not to look over his shoulder. That way, he could make the daily

decisions himself and develop the ability to come up with his own ideas and put them into action. . . . I laid the groundwork for that process at the business school."

- Robert Waggoner '60, head of Burrelle's Information Services, told the *HBS Bulletin,* "I remember one of the human relations courses we had at HBS and our discussions of Theory X and Theory Y as appropriate management approaches. I felt, at the time, that human relations material could be ignored, that the 'hard' things you could quantify were more important. Now I look back and say, 'That was the most important stuff of all.' "

ORGANIZING AND FACILITATING INSTEAD OF DOING

Organizational behavior professors see the manager's job in a special way. The manager, in their opinion, is not personally a task accomplisher. Rather, he or she makes it possible for others to get the job done. Stated as a generality, this may seem like an obvious proposition, but in the teaching it calls for major changes in the attitudes of numerous students.

One reason this is so is the educational system. In school and college, students learn to work *solo.* In management, by contrast, administrators hardly ever get tasks done by themselves; instead, they see their job as organizing and facilitating the work of others.

Two obstacles keep many students from seeing the manager's job in this manner. First, it doesn't jibe with the value they have learned to put on personal performance. You get Nobel prizes for your own accomplishments, as a rule, not for helping others to accomplish. Second, the approach doesn't check with the philosophy of control that they believe is necessary for a manager. Professor Paul Lawrence once told me:

"It's not a matter of either/or, it's a matter of where your priorities are. Do you think of your duties primarily as checking up, delegating and following through, applying pressure when performance fails to measure up? Or do you think of them pri-

marily as facilitating communication and understanding between different people with different points of view—for example, between a staff engineering group and a production group
who do not see eye to eye on a change they are both involved
in?"

Lawrence does not question the need to check up, follow
through, and apply pressure *some* of the time. But more of the
time, in his opinion, managers should see themselves less as
controllers and more as *facilitators*—his term for people who
communicate skillfully, help others communicate, spread understanding, bring employees together. Managers should be watching closely for the messages that pass back and forth continually
as people discuss their work problems, the questions that are
always going on in their minds, such as "How will he accept
criticism?" "How much can I afford to tell him?" "Is he playing
games?" Lawrence says, "When the administrator concerns himself with these problems and acts to facilitate understanding,
there will be less logrolling and more sense of common purpose."

This view of the job is a far cry from what most of us are
accustomed to. It is not charismatic leadership in the sense that
numerous writers portray heads of business and political organizations. It has nothing to do with being a good figurehead, nor
does it have much to do with dramatic appeal or flashiness. In the
view of professors of organizational behavior and human resources, I suspect that the managers and administrators who are
most often seen as the heads of strong organizations and groups
are more like general Omar Bradley than George Patton, more
like Alfred Sloan than Henry Ford.

This view of the job also calls on resources that most of us aren't
taught to develop in school and college. This is what upsets students at first, and angers so many frustrated managers in business—the notion that the manager himself or herself may be
largely responsible for cultivating the contacts and wangling the
resources necessary to do a job. It won't do to blame somebody
else for not setting things up right. Professor John Kotter once
put it this way to a small group of us:

"Stop and think for a moment about the implicit message
about 'work' that gets drummed into students' heads from kin-

dergarten through graduate school. Working as a student means performing tasks largely by yourself, even though other people are around. So we grow technically better than we grow as leaders. We learn to focus on the substantive aspects of work. We do a great job there, but we blow the leadership function completely. When the project performs in a lackluster way, we blame it on Harry because he was late in producing a proposal, or on John who was too busy playing company politics, or on a dumb customer who couldn't make up his mind. Managers tell me, 'The problem is we aren't organized right. If they gave me formal authority commensurate with my responsibility, I could do the job just fine. As it is, my hands are tied.' I don't buy that."

Kotter and colleagues on the Organizational Behavior faculty feel that power doesn't depend on edict. It isn't gained or lost mechanically. The effective manager fashions alliances, finesses, finagles IOUs from people, cultivates impressions and images with groups, learns to use the light or heavy touch as needed. Also, as Professor Richard Hackman pointed out in a recent colloquium at the school, effective managers accept personal responsibility for the outcome of their work, continually monitor and correct their performance, and wangle the organizational resources they need rather than leave that often-messy task to others. They may have to manipulate groups, scheme with colleagues, contrive with key individuals, and plot rather than rely on logical analysis and report writing.

I don't know whether OB professors feel that managers *should* act as described or that the rules of power *should* be as they are. But this is the situation as they see it. Putting themselves in the role of realists rather than idealists, they see their job as guiding students in the ways of real-world management. This descriptive (rather than normative) view of Organizational Behavior's mission is one of the legacies of Roethlisberger.

PRESCRIPTION FOR PARTICIPATION

The Organizational Behavior faculty is sometimes criticized for favoritism. Professors are said to be partial to cases portraying the benefits of participative management—that is, leadership styles and systems that encourage subordinates to take a part in deciding how their groups will operate.

Knowing a number of OB instructors, I have no doubt that they are indeed biased. I also know that their bias goes back many years. Yet OB professors are pragmatic enough to know that the approaches they personally favor do not always work.

Sometimes participative management doesn't work simply because it doesn't have much of a chance: managers don't practice it with finesse or enthusiasm. One time I asked an OB professor to review a manuscript by a corporate head raving about participative management and its benefits for his company. After reading the article, the instructor informed me that he had spent a fair amount of time in that company and knew that participative management was rarely practiced. "The managers give a lot of lip service to it, but I didn't see much of it going on," he remarked wryly.

At other times, however, the Organizational Behavior faculty finds that participative management doesn't always work well even with the right conditions. Some time ago Professor Jay Lorsch and John Morse, then a doctoral student at HBS, made a study of four plants. They found that in one the managers were highly motivated and the plant productive despite a fairly authoritarian setting, while in another the managers were less well motivated and the plant was not very productive despite a participative style. In the other two plants, other contrasts occurred that could not be explained by the ideologies of management theory. Exploring the work and worker feelings at some length, they found an explanation: where there are good operating results, managers adapt their approaches not only to the kinds of tasks performed but also to the needs and desires of employees. This may or not mean participative management; by the same token, it may or may not mean a top-down style. In one situation, employees may want to be told, "Tell me what to do and let me do it, just don't bother me." In another, they may want a say in everything that goes on. In short, a participative approach can be at odds with the need as much as an autocratic one can be.

If employee participation is called for by the nature of the work and workers' feelings, what should the manager do to elicit collaboration, teamwork, and commitment? Professor Richard Walton, who has spent countless hours with companies of many different types, describes some of the most important steps:

1. *Create broader jobs for employees.* In particular, says Walton, try to create jobs where the people who do them will have a hand in planning their work as well as deciding how to implement the plans. For example, an OB case describes one large manufacturer who allowed a key assembly-line group to work out how it would get several tasks done instead of stand mindlessly at work stations, carry out specialized tasks, and get paced by the production line.

2. *As much as possible, make teams of employees, not individuals, accountable for performance.* One example is a case on an electronics firm. In one department in this firm, the manager let the employees themselves work out most of their working arrangements. The ensuing spaghettilike tangle of relationships and procedures was an industrial engineer's nightmare, and several horrified engineers told the manager this. But the manager made the department as a whole accountable for performance; he was convinced that this bunch knew better than anyone else how it should work *as a group.* The department's productivity soared under his direction.

3. *Let pay policies emphasize group achievement as much as possible.* This conclusion of Walton's is a corollary to the one just described and reinforces it. An example is a case on McDonald's where management was considering different possible schemes of paying the managers of hamburger-and-french-fry outlets. The schemes favored by students (and in the end by management) pay a manager a base salary based on the cost of living in his or her area plus a quarterly bonus reflecting the *outlet's* performance (sales volume, quality of service, cleanliness, employee training, and so on). Since the bonus is substantial, it gives the manager a strong incentive to have employees work as a team.

4. Set relatively high expectations. Walton likes to call them "stretch objectives." He says that in practice the expectations often are framed in terms of customers and sales, and always they emphasize continuous improvement. He contrasts the emphasis on continuous improvement with the relatively static measures of performance generally found in traditional organizations using the "control model." Many OB instructors believe that it is a mistake to increase expectations mechanically—say, by 10 percent per year. What the organization can reasonably be expected to do may be more or less than 10 percent. Sometimes, they tell me, the most ambitious annual goals come from the employees themselves and take managers by surprise.

5. Give a high priority to employment security. Not only does such a policy help morale but it makes sense economically. This doesn't mean a categorical no-layoff policy, only that serious managerial attempts will be made to avoid layoffs. In a recent study of IBM, Professor Quinn Mills reports the conviction of that company's executives that layoffs are expensive. As the newest employees are let go first, recruiting and training investments are lost and must be recouped, unemployment insurance costs paid by the company rise, and community relations suffer. The full costing of such intangibles, IBM management believes, should be weighed against the direct labor savings that come when pink slips are handed out.

6. Let employees speak out; protect them when they do. Walton doesn't want to have employees screaming for attention like traders in a pit—no one in his or her right mind does. On the other hand, a totalitarian atmosphere warning employees to keep their opinions to themselves is bad, too, for often those opinions should be expressed. A new study for HBS tells about the Employees Committee at Polaroid, which does many things including representing employees who believe they have been unfairly discriminated against for expressing opinions their bosses may not like. The industrial relations climate at nonunion Polaroid is very positive—both a cause and effect of the speech policy. In 1989, the Employees Committee gave management some valuable assistance in staving off a takeover attempt by the Shamrock organization.

FATEFUL CHANGES IN CLIMATE

The OB department feels that in its favoritism for participative management it is riding a wave. Although top-down, authoritarian management styles still are useful here and there, their usefulness is declining. Although participative styles are difficult for many managers to practice, their value is spreading. This is happening not only because of ubiquitous changes in mood in the workplace but also because of profound technological developments.

The new mood. Quinn Mills explains his finding, based on many surveys and a great deal of personal observation, that employees today want their work experience to be part of their whole life experience. Unlike their parents and grandparents, they don't want the two experiences segregated. "They are not content," he told us, "to have one personality at work and a different one at home."

Mills feels that managers are among those who are changing. At a B-school seminar several years ago, he talked about contemporary views of work. Managers whose attitudes were shaped by military experience in World War II, he said, are gradually being replaced by managers who don't follow the hierarchical military model. In the latter, management assumes unquestioning obedience to orders passed down a chain of command. Mills thinks that the military model is going out of date; increasingly, "adaptation is the greatest virtue" in organizations. In his talks with the new generation of managers he found them citing often their experiences as members of churches, political groups, clubs, professional organizations where clear lines of authority and unambiguous direction were rare. "What people remember most about their experiences in these groups is the feeling of belonging and of being an effective participant."

Technological change. This development springs from the rapid proliferation of employees who work more with their minds than with their hands. In one industry after another, the trend is for management to hire employees for what they know, not for the manual motions they can perform. A good case in point is modern information systems.

For a historical perspective, says Associate Professor Shoshana Zuboff, you need to look back to 1915 and Henry Ford's automation of the Highland Park assembly plant to find a development that has affected management and employees as profoundly as the computer has. However, there is a great difference in the two developments from a managerial standpoint. "Ford used a mechanized assembly process to supplant supervision—he increased control while increasing continuity," Zuboff told an editor of the *HBS Bulletin.* "But something very interesting happens when you take computer-based technology and apply it in the service of control and continuity in the way we have applied other generations of technology. What happens is that new information is also generated. At the same time that you are increasing control with computerization, you are also—almost as a by-product— creating new information. Workers now have thousands of additional facts available to them as a result of computers' capabilities. The new technology is not only suited to automate, it is also suited to do something that I define as 'informate,' that is, to turn objects and actions into information."

Yet Zuboff finds managers automating the new tasks in much the same way that they mechanized work earlier in the century, their objective being to reduce the number of employees and to minimize the skill requirements of those who remain. They let computers control work at the expense of worker discretion. The workers complain bitterly; but, more important to the enterprise, it loses much of the potential benefit of the new information. If it is to respond quickly and skillfully to what it learns, it must empower operators more than it has in the past. It is operators' minds, says Zuboff, not their manual skills, that must be brought into play.

Thus computerized information systems are fueling employees' desire to participate in decision making. The OB faculty points to cases showing some organizations improving their performance by capitalizing on this desire rather than suppressing it.

HOW TO BE AN EFFECTIVE EXECUTIVE

In a real sense, all courses at the B-school teach leadership. You see it in the cases—a case in the computerized information system course, for instance, referring to an executive's style of leadership. You also see it when alums talk about their impressions of the school. Repeatedly in my own interviews, grads told me about gleanings of leadership styles from marketing, finance, or production and operations.

In locating this section under the OB rubric, therefore, I am doing an injustice to the other courses, to say nothing of a second-year seminar dealing with leadership from a psychoanalytic viewpoint. The reason I have done this is that the Organizational Behavior and Human Resources courses tackle leadership questions more directly than other courses do; also, these courses have more cases focusing on leadership style than other courses do. Significantly, however, the ideas that follow are based on talks and teaching by professors in a variety of areas as well as on the memories of alums, which tend to fuse courses and eliminate boundaries between areas.

Know your industry intimately. In the B-school there is a growing conviction that most managers become good in certain types of industries. For the sake of clarity, let me first point out what the faculty does *not* believe. I know of no professors who fall for the myth, often propagated defensively by insecure insiders, that nobody can run operations in a certain business without growing up in that business. It may be true, as the insiders insist, that "our business is different," but there simply are too many cases—everywhere in U.S. industry—indicating that a good financial executive in, say, publishing can do a fine job in, say, a financial services firm, and vice versa, to allow the myth to stand.

However, neither does the B-school faculty believe in the notion of the all-purpose general manager who can parachute into a new job anywhere and make a success of it. Once upon a time some professors might have been tempted in this direction, but events during the past twenty years have made it clear that most managerial positions demand a firsthand understanding of the industry. Some managers' experience in other industries will make it easy for them to acquire this understanding; some managers' experience will make it difficult.

Many professors believe that the illusion of the all-purpose manager is an arrogant one that has done much damage to U.S. industry. They tell me that if a firm is to develop its competitive advantage, it needs managers who can work skillfully with employees to develop the company's strengths and work around its limitations. Usually this means managers who are well versed in the business.

Many studies and observations bear out this belief, which finds its way into many cases and classroom discussions. For instance, Professor John Gabarro made a lengthy study of fourteen executives who had taken over new positions. He found that the ones who were industry insiders (defined by him as people with five or more years of experience in the company's industry) took hold more quickly and were able to make twice as many important changes as the ones who were new to the industry (that is, who had four years or less experience in it). His findings are convincing because his study covered such a wide variety of personalities and managerial styles.

Don't get locked into one managerial style. HBS professors believe—and their cases show—that there is no such thing as *a* right style of leadership. Some successful managers are devotees of frequent consultations with subordinates, some are not; some use fear to motivate subordinates, some do not; some spend most of their time telling, some spend most of their time listening.

Most important, good managers are inconsistent in style. Two professors who have voiced this view lucidly are Earl Sasser and Wickham Skinner (now retired). The evidence they cite shows that effective managers typically vary their ways of working with subordinates, now operating in this manner, now operating in that. In contrast, they tell me, the evidence shows that managers who are rigid, more set in their ways, accomplish far less.

Encourage trust. In the Organizational Behavior department in particular, instructors find effective managers doing everything they can to maximize trust among employees in their organizations. Professor Louis Barnes offers this case example:

Manager Jones habitually pitted subordinates and colleagues against each other. He did this to avoid giving an appearance of weakness, about which he had had a phobia since youth. As Jones succeeded because of his reputation as an aggressive, two-fisted executive, he was almost always suspicious and skeptical of others. He became skillful at setting one faction of subordinates against another. Jones was a bright man, and his words had the ring of toughness and willingness to face up to reality, so at first he impressed superiors. After a while, however, the superiors saw how divisive his influence had become. Nobody in his department trusted anybody else, and teamwork was virtually impossible. After getting Jones out of the job, it took them more than five years to correct the situation in his department.

Setting subordinates and colleagues against one another is an old Machiavellian technique that works sometimes in the short run to solidify a manager's power. Instructors won't deny that—the record is clear. From the standpoint of building effective world-class *organizations,* however, trust is vital.

Convey vision. Most B-school instructors believe that corporate leadership is not so much charisma as a combination of vision and strategy for achieving the vision. Kotter thinks we must stop treating leadership "as mysterious and possibly unknowable" but as a tangible skill. Asking professors for examples of vision and strategy, I have been offered two that should be mentioned here:

- James Robinson '61, chief executive of American Express, talked to students late in 1987 and described several visions that he had for the company. One was to put major emphasis on marketing in Japan. He then outlined his business strategy for achieving the goal, including making a $50 million commitment of funds, annual gains of 20 percent in Japanese card holders, and the building of certain relationships with the Japanese government, business, customers, and other organizations. He communicated this vision to employees in many ways.

- W. R. Timken '62, chairman of the Timken Company, talks about the importance of telling employees in detail about what the company is trying to do and how it is faring in the marketplace. It is not an easy job, he says. "Employees do not like to hear bad news, yet the problems must be commonly understood before successful action can be undertaken. During these stressful periods, the employees' biggest concern often is whether or not the leaders know where they are headed."

Establish a power base. The importance of cultivating management power—that is, your ability as a manager to have others do what you want them to do—was mentioned earlier. But how do you accomplish this? Students see managers succeeding (or failing) in case after case and become very mindful of different techniques. John Kotter and other instructors point to four helpful steps for managers: (1) create a sense of obligation in others; (2) build your reputation as an expert in certain areas, for the more people believe in your know-how, the more they will defer to you; (3) encourage others to identify with you by behaving in ways they respect, making yourself visible by giving speeches about organizational goals and values, and so on; and (4) make others realize how dependent they are on you and how committed you are to protecting them.

What the OB faculty most wants students to realize is that managers don't gain power by being handed pieces of paper from top management. For instance, a long-celebrated case at the school is "Dashman Company," a very short case written more than forty years ago. Although it is not taught anymore, its point is as valid as ever. A new manager arrives in the company. He is put in charge of purchasing. Quickly he orders field agents, most of whom he hasn't yet met, to submit contracts to his office for approval. When none of them responds, he can't understand.

He has the power, doesn't he? Unfortunately, as students see during the discussion, he has relied on formal "paper power" only.

Professor Hugo Uyterhoeven finds that one of the secrets of success in middle management is willingness to go beyond the formal definitions of one's job. Managers who stick rigidly to their job descriptions, he told me, are likely to ignore critical tasks such as purchasing or getting a divisional conflict resolved. While there is always risk in reaching out in this manner, there is likely to be opportunity, too, and he finds effective middle managers willing to stick their necks out and take chances.

Share power. Because of the technologies that more and more companies are using as well as the growing savvy of employees, many professors feel that traditional notions of management control are outmoded. Richard Walton describes a case used in OB:

"It stems from the introduction of new technology, and it revolves around changes in a paper plant called Tiger Creek. The company develops a cost-monitoring system that provides the paper machine operators with cost information and equips them to make trade-off decisions. These are decisions not only about quality and production, which the operators traditionally made, but also decisions about cost. And the new cost information given to the operators is more than their supervisors had under the old system—and furthermore, it's all on an on-line basis [coming directly by computer rather than by staff compilation].

"In the case, then, we see management coming back and trying to take control of this decision support system. The students can appreciate the fact that while you've changed the nature of work for the operators, it has been at the cost—at least in the short term—of the meaning and status and power of the supervisors. It's a classic dilemma, and it raises the question, Can management let go of the functions that are challenged by a commitment strategy [employee commitment to goals because they participate in making them], by a high degree of delegation, by a high amount of employee voice?"

The pressure on managers to revise their notions of control is one of the greatest causes of stress and soul-searching in organizations today. One corporate vice president explained to Shoshana Zuboff:

"An issue that the technology is forcing us to face involves the loss of managerial control. . . . There is a legal definition that management is the steward for the owners of the enterprise. They are expected to be loyal and unswervingly dedicated to achieving the objectives of the owners. They are expected to not let the situation ever get out of control. . . . [However,] new information technology introduces some very new problems. Suddenly the folks who work with these systems are interfacing with a tremendous technological power—power to see all the functions of the operation. That is pretty scary to some managers."

OB instructors feel that managers who adopt more open control systems skillfully are likely to be rewarded. For instance, Walton reports that one convert, a top executive, remarked to him, "I've never had so much power since I started giving it away."

MAKING WAVES

Instructors in the courses on organizational behavior and human resources pride themselves on being pragmatic and clinical. The need for communication is a fact of life in organizations, so they talk about communication. The alienation and cynicism of employees who feel that they could participate in decision making but aren't asked to is a fact of life in organizations, so they talk about participation. The failure of work groups to be as productive as they could be is a fact of life, so they talk about that. The practical importance of power to a manager is a fact of life, so they talk about how power is gained or lost.

The OB courses may be dubbed "touchy-feely" by students, but in many ways they are more interlinked with Production and Operations Management—thought of as a "hard" course—than with any other part of the curriculum. And they have a crucial bearing on competitive advantage and strategy. The way groups and organizations function affects economic fortunes in significant ways.

Organizational Behavior can also be an upsetting course. Unlike Managerial Economics, which distresses many students because of its emphasis on quantitative techniques, OB creates turmoil because of its messages. For instance, it says that easy rules of thumb about management are mostly nonsense. If there are qualities, techniques, or styles that define good managers, the evidence doesn't show it. This secret may work for you as a departmental manager but not for me; this method may do wonders for me as a plant head but not for you.

In a word, the courses are *situational.* They say there are no magic formulas, shortcuts, or statements of wisdom that will help us become good managers; the only answer is skill, analysis, and hard work on a situation-by-situation basis.

Finally, Organizational Behavior and Human Resources Management might be called the most revolutionary courses at HBS. That is, they raise more philosophical questions and challenge more basic values of students than other courses do. "We want students," I was once told by Professor Michael Beer, then department chairman, "to confront their implicit assumptions about corporations, management, and the role of employees." He emphasized that OB does not provide the answers, only good reasons for asking the questions.

I attended a class where such questions were raised. An assigned case served as the vehicle for discussion. Did the students want to regard the shareholder as the primary stakeholder in the organization, asked the professor, or did they want management to be accountable to other stakeholders, too—employees, suppliers, and the surrounding community in particular? How a student answered the question affected his or her answer to the problem faced by management in the case.

In another class I heard students debate a company's purpose. Was it solely to make a profit, and was management to be judged primarily on the criterion of quarterly earnings? Or should account also be taken of the impact of management action on human and economic resources that would affect the organization's future? Here again, a student's view of the question made quite a difference to his or her interpretation of the problem and recommendations for action.

The fact that such questions are raised disturbs some business people. Let me tell you a story. I once praised a paper delivered to a southwestern audience by one of my favorite people on the faculty. In carefully couched legal and economic terms, it suggested that top management might no longer have a single accountability to shareholders but a dual accountability to shareholders and employees. "How did the audience take it?" I asked its author. The professor answered, "After my speech, one man in the audience, who was aghast at my point of view, asked, 'Do you teach that to students at the Harvard Business School?' I assured him, 'Of course not. I say this only to you people who are more experienced and mature.' "

> ■ *Once he [the manager] learns what he cannot do, he is ready to learn what little he can do. And what a tremendous difference to himself and to others the little that he can do—listening with understanding, for example—can make!*
>
> —PROFESSOR FRITZ ROETHLISBERGER

8

THE CUSTOMER
IS THE ONE
WITH THE MONEY

Marketing profes-
sors teach students what every smart executive knows: the customer comes first. Nothing an organization does makes sense
unless it wins and pleases its customers. Marketing's viewpoint is
hard-nosed and pragmatic. Production, employee relations, finance, strategy—none of them has much justification unless the
net result is profitable sales. Marketing has a viewpoint toward
its own functions that is equally hard-nosed. Success is not fine
sales management. It is not superb market research. It is not
advertising awards. It is not finesse in "push-pull" selling to retailers or wonderful relations with certain key buyers. Success in
marketing is meeting a need that customers are willing to pay
for. It shows up at the cash register for a gift store, in a high
renewal rate for a magazine, in the bottom line for a company
with complex activities and divisions.

In one sense the marketing concept is as ruthless as any military goal. It is: win. In another sense it is warm and invigorating,
one of the secrets of capitalism's crowd appeal.

In first- and second-year marketing classes, this general philosophy translates into a way of thinking about a business or operation. A business, you learn, is not so much products and services as a mutually satisfying relationship with customers. It is not barrels of oil but low-priced energy; not a certain airplane but swift, safe travel; not lawn-raking and -seeding but beauty and standing in the neighborhood. Today, yes, the market's needs may be met by certain products and services, but tomorrow the needs may be met with quite different offerings.

Russell Amick '65, president and owner of Floy Tag in Seattle, an international fishery tag and research firm, told me:

"What I remember most from Ted Levitt's marketing class is that the customer is number one. When I was at HBS there was a lot of talk and feeling about how you could program your company to make certain goals, and there was an awful lot of emphasis on the idea that if you didn't have goals, you weren't going to get there. . . . The whole message that Levitt was pitching was that the customer runs your business. That is the way I've tried to run mine. The customers are king. What really makes you a believer in this philosophy is when you look at the P and L at the end of the year. We say, 'We'll just keep doing what we're doing.' Every once in a while customers go overboard and screw up the order, and it's not really our fault, but even in those cases it's worth it to redo the order so they're satisfied. Every year as a result we keep adding customers to the base and keep growing."

Putting the customer first means focusing not on products but on needs. A customer's need may be not just for one thing but for a group of products and services that solve a problem. An example is Weight Watchers International. The company's main product is a particular type of meeting where customers learn what to do in a way that they enjoy and find meaningful. Charles Berger '60, chief executive officer of the company, explained as follows at his class's twenty-fifth reunion:

"The essence of this business is a good weight-loss program based on people meeting together with the right kind of leader conducting the session. We have thirteen thousand such meetings a week in the United States, and their format is not unlike a case discussion at HBS. The learning comes not from the lecturer or, in our case, the meeting leader, but from the synergy between the leader and the group, and among the group members themselves. That's the fundamental concept of the business; everything flows from that."

But management realized that customers wanted more than meetings—and were willing to pay for more. Although it was running classes in about twenty countries, it went further. It began marketing low-calorie frozen dinners, publishing its own magazine and best-selling cookbooks, and competing in the cable TV and video markets with videocassettes featuring Lynn Redgrave. With such offerings it was able to satisfy customers' needs better than it could have with a single product. It realized, in other words, that people wanted to lose weight but wished to do so with not one but several reinforcing activities.

As a school, HBS has been marketing-minded for more than seven decades. During that time it has traditionally had a strong marketing faculty keenly interested in teaching and case development. Marketing courses have always been stocked with strong, fresh, and interesting cases; in one recent year, I found a higher proportion of new cases in marketing than in any other first-year course. In the second year, marketing electives have been favorites of students year in and year out.

One of the appeals of marketing has been its close relation to corporate strategy. In fact, the very term *marketing* was invented in 1914 by the legendary Melvin ("Doc") Copeland, a twinkly-eyed professor who became associated with the school during its second year of existence and was active on campus until the early 1960s, as a way of emphasizing that more than salesmanship is involved in getting a firm's products and services sold. By definition, therefore, marketing calls for a lot of planning and collaboration in order to strengthen the value chain, as defined earlier, and give the firm competitive advantage.

MANAGING THE CUSTOMER

Let's visit a first-year marketing class.

The case for discussion concerns a company that has introduced a new line of dresses. The line is not selling well. Chagrined, the top executives give speeches and exhort sales people to try harder. The national sales managers urge regional sales managers to motivate their salespeople to "push the line." Contests and awards for sales success are devised. But the harder sales management tries, the more frustrated executives become with lagging results.

Does this situation sound familiar? It probably does if you are a sales manager with experience. "It's a common mistake," Professor Benson Shapiro told me. "Too often top management thinks that motivation is the answer. Motivate your salespeople! But it doesn't solve the problem because top management doesn't have a good marketing policy to begin with."

The class discusses how to right the situation in the case. Some think the compensation scheme should be revised, others opt for changes in recruiting salespeople. "If we had motivated salespeople," they say, "we wouldn't need clever pay schemes." Others think better training is the answer. "The trouble with this sales force is that they don't know how to sell."

The instructor, who has been writing furiously on the boards, now lowers a fresh board and directs the discussion onto a new plane. What's the purpose of sales management? "To generate loyal customers," one voice says. "Is that all?" asks the instructor. "Loyal customers *and sales,*" calls another voice. The instructor makes an appropriate addition. "No, that's still not all," says another student. "Those two things plus reasonable costs and *profits.*" Quickly the instructor rounds out the purpose.

The class begins to see how customers affect salespeople and how in turn salespeople affect marketing strategy, and vice versa. To have a good relation between the company and customers is more than a matter of skillful advertising and promotion, more than a matter of having good salespeople, more even than having the right product or combination of products; it is a matter of organizing everything the company does so that the combined effect is to produce a relationship that customers are willing to pay as much as possible for because they don't think they can get it anywhere else.

What does this mean in terms of how management deals with its salespeople? The instructor asks the class to consider four key questions, each of which becomes the subject of succeeding sessions:

1. What is the role of personal selling in a company's marketing strategy? This is a very interesting question because situations, costs, and effectiveness vary so widely. For instance, as students see in one case, advertising is relatively inexpensive in terms of people reached, but its impact is low. On the other hand, personal selling has a high impact in this company's experience, but its cost is great. A student with extensive selling experience points out that personal selling also has the advantage of two-way communication; the call reports salespeople sent to management in her company told a lot about problems, trends, preferences, and the competition.

Some companies, the case tells, have been de-emphasizing personal selling and passing the savings on to customers as price cuts. Discount stores, cash-and-carry wholesalers, and others have followed this route. So have some consumer goods manufacturers, who employ relatively small sales forces to call on wholesalers and retailers. (Well-known exceptions are Avon Products and Fuller Brush.)

2. How should management assign salespeople to different prospects, territories, and sales tasks? One case discussion reveals how hopeless it is sometimes for the salespeople on existing lines—even the best ones on the force—to add a new line to their wares. Contests, awards, and other motivational techniques simply don't cut the mustard; the salespeople know that if they are selling the existing products well, management won't touch them. Why make life more difficult than it already is? "It'll do no good to harangue this bunch," says one student. "They [management] better hire a new group."

The instructor distributes a sequel case showing that that was precisely what the company did. Management recruited and trained a different set of salespeople to call on the outlets that were good prospects for the new product. Sales began rising almost immediately.

3. How should existing and prospective accounts be managed? In a fascinating case involving a manufacturer of heavy equipment, students see that a company is selling not only to different groups with varying interests in a prospect firm but also to individuals whose needs and outlooks vary. The groups are somewhat predictable—for instance, manufacturing wants a machine that is state-of-the-art and will require little repair, purchasing is interested in total costs (including materials, depreciation, and installation), and so on. On the other hand, the individuals who will influence the prospective sale are less predictable. Salespeople need all the information on them they can get, from any source. There's a young and influential treasurer in the prospect firm who is trying to consolidate his power; there is a manufacturing honcho who is smarting over a rebuff by the chief engineer and seeks revenge.

In every such situation, the class sees, sales managers must work out the best approaches to building an ongoing *relationship* with the customer. This may mean understanding the buyer's needs so keenly that the seller gives up some sales along the way, realizing that they are not in the customer's long-run interest. (Shapiro calls such sales "Pyrrhic" because, if made, they will jeopardize the seller's continuing relationship with the buyer.) It may mean giving a salesperson authority to draw up specifications for what should be produced for the customer. It may mean assuring that the customer will be able to get, if necessary, fast delivery of spare parts from an emergency inventory.

4. What will the sales program cost—and can that cost be justified? Cases and class discussions bring out that for some companies making simple products or selling simple services to a mass audience, a low-powered sales force may be the answer. A salesperson's job is to "go out and sell it." The salesperson should be likable, deliveries should be on time, training in simple techniques of persuasion is important—but no unusual abilities are required.

For other companies, however, a highly talented sales force may be essential. The salesperson must be good at analysis and problem solving, alert to the psychology of different individuals influencing a sale, capable of tailoring expensive products and services to a prospect's needs. Summing up at the end of one class, the instructor offers as a maxim that the higher the profit earned by individual salespeople, the greater the company's ability to pay for a high-powered force.

"Obviously, the sales force is important," Shapiro once told me, "and obviously management should organize and direct it very carefully. But it's only a conduit to the customer, not the object itself. If you don't keep your priorities straight and remember the objective, you're heading for trouble." Even sales management, for all its prestige and power, is but a means to an end.

WHY SOME MARKETERS MAKE MORE MONEY

So you need to manage your relationships with customers, making your many selling activities the means, not the goal, and organizing your promotion to meet particular needs and desires—not yours, not the industry's, but the buyer's. Still, some companies seem to do much better at this than others. Why? By its choice of cases and tactics for leading class discussions, the marketing faculty shows some of the reasons.

MARKET FOCUS

For one thing, the top marketers do business in the markets where it is easiest for them to make good profits. Producers have a multitude of market choices, depending on their talents and resources, but instructors introduce a scheme for classifying markets that helps students see how to make the choices.

Conceptually, this scheme is quite simple. One time Shapiro drew it for me on a scratch pad. He sketched a diagram that he said his colleague Martin Marshall used to draw for students on the board. At one extreme was the commodity product—for instance, rock salt. At the other was the specialty product—for instance, the Polaroid camera (this was in the days before Kodak went on the market with instant cameras). The key term that describes the extremes is *differentiability,* a fancy name for how distinctive a company can make its product or service appear to customers as compared to other companies' offerings. It was easy to give the Polaroid camera differentiability; it wasn't easy to give rock salt this quality.

Product differentiability makes an enormous difference in market strategy. High differentiability makes it easier for marketers to make their product appealing to consumers and stand apart from other products; low differentiability makes it tough. High differentiability leads more often to high profits; low differentiability usually means medium or low profits.

Marketers of undifferentiated commodities need not despair, however. They can and often do succeed because of what they communicate to customers. In truth, the product itself is just one of the things a company sells. It sells reliability, delivery, service, perceptions of status ("I shop at Talbot's"; "I bought this hardware from Shattuck's"). If it can attract profitable customers because it succeeds in selling such "intangibles," it doesn't matter if its product or service is like a competitor's.

The fine art of market segmentation enters in here. Those customers for your products or services out there aren't all the same. Not only do they live in different regions with different cultures and have different incomes and tastes, but their motives for buying your product vary widely. Some want it for its function, others for its looks, others because the neighbor up the street has it. Except in unusual cases, you must make up your mind which group is your best bet and then produce, price, promote, and distribute your product or service so that it will appeal strongly to that group. In other words, you have got to focus. You cannot sell to everybody.

In a second-year course on industrial selling, instructors teach cases that dramatize the importance of various criteria for segmentation. Here are some of the most important criteria stressed by Shapiro and Professor Thomas Bonoma:

The type of industry. Companies selling paper, office equipment, industrial computers, and financial services go to a wide range of industries that may be quite different from one another. Hospitals have computer needs but not the same ones that retail stores do; banks buy paper in great quantities but have quite different specifications from publishers. In short, markets often can be segmented on the basis of what types of business customers are in.

Location. A manufacturer of heavy-duty pumps for the petrochemical industry knows how important it is to have plenty of salespeople and promotion along the Gulf Coast, where customers are concentrated, rather than in New England. A manufacturer of prestressed concrete has a problem because many customers are not nearby, a factor that is important in the economics of its distribution. Location thus is another criterion for segmentation for these companies.

Customer status. Two prospects may use gears in manufacturing, but one may use metal gears and the other, nylon gears. The fact that one has stuck to the traditional gear may mean that it looks at risk differently, or that it has different relationships with suppliers, or that it has yet to appreciate the values of nylon. Whatever the case, the two prospects may represent different market segments that should be approached in different ways and with different people.

Prospects' capabilities. These may affect their interests in new products and services. They may separate buyers as prospects and make one more attractive to a marketer than the other. Thus, for many years Digital Equipment Corporation specialized in selling its minicomputers to customers who were able to develop their own software, and Prime Computer has had a strategy of selling to business users who don't need the intensive support and "hand-holding" that IBM and other marketers give so well. The particular capabilities of customers led to useful ways for these companies to separate types of customers and seize on the type they could best appeal to.

ACTIVITY FOCUS

Another secret of the most successful marketers is their concentration on the activities that produce the most return, what Shapiro calls "leverage." They pay a lot of attention to two seemingly insignificant but profoundly important variables: degree of customization and run length (the number or dollar volume of identical products, services, or materials ordered at one time).

For example, if the product is fairly standard and the run length is short, the company must manage its distribution system very skillfully. Thus, Procter & Gamble spends a lot of money on advertising, which apparently is aimed at the consumer but actually helps to obtain strong retailer support for P & G products, a critical factor in the company's success. On the other hand, if the product is highly customized and the run length is long, as in the case of missiles for the military or a telephone system for a large customer, the company must have strong account managers and be very good at applications engineering in order to fit its product into the customer's system. The two sets of skills are quite different.

Thus, the amount of customization and run length you have affects the activities that are important in selling your product profitably. Your distribution systems may vary radically, depending on what is best in each case.

MARKETING CONSISTENCY

A third thing that the top marketers do especially well is develop consistency in their various marketing activities—and between marketing and such nonmarketing functions of the company as production and public relations. "They get all of their marketing horses to pull together in the same direction," Shapiro says. Product changes, price changes, communications campaigns, sales development—all these support and reinforce each other. The best analytical tool for making sure this is done is the *marketing mix*.

Early in marketing courses, students get introduced to this tool. It has helped many leading marketers unify their programs and make money. It has wide usefulness. For instance, I recall one discussion with marketing instructors about how differently cosmetics companies sold, yet how each related its various marketing efforts with great finesse. There was Avon with a sales force of several hundred thousand men and women calling directly on individual prospects; Charles of the Ritz and Estée Lauder using selective distribution through department stores; Cover Girl and Del Laboratories emphasizing chain drugstores and other mass merchandisers; Redken selling through beauticians; and Revlon using a variety of selling approaches. Yet each company management used—consciously or intuitively—the marketing mix, dovetailing its distribution tactics neatly with its other marketing choices. "The marketing mix," a director of one of these companies told me, "is our bible."

The marketing mix is one of the most powerful concepts ever developed for management. Since the early 1920s it has been the organizing theme of marketing courses at HBS, and it has become the key concept of innumerable corporate marketing plans. More than any other idea, it is the "tool kit" that successful marketers use to do their job. It has endured, marketing instructors tell me, because it is both effective and simple.

As a student you learn that the marketing mix consists of four elements: (1) product policy, (2) pricing, (3) communication, including advertising and personal selling, and (4) distribution. You learn that almost any marketing strategy can be described in terms of these elements and the particular market segment that management wants to reach. For instance, you might view Digital Equipment's strategy in terms of how it produces, prices, communicates, and distributes for computer customers who can develop their own software. Thus, you would be tying market segmentation to the marketing mix concept.

To illustrate in more detail: when IBM began selling personal computers, the market segment it targeted was managers and professionals. It decided it could sell best to this segment by:

- Producing PCs that were as good as or better than any other PC on the market (product policy);
- Selling PCs at reasonable prices—that is, prices high enough to yield healthy profits but not so high that an umbrella for competitors was created (pricing);
- Heavy advertising and demonstrations stressing the user-friendliness and broad value of the company's PCs (communication); and
- Reaching large customers personally through its powerful sales force and smaller customers through independent full-service dealers (distribution).

In similar fashion, says Shapiro, the four elements of the marketing mix can be used to describe the approach of a toothpaste manufacturer, a producer of coal-fed boilers, or almost any other marketer.

Using the concept to analyze corporate strategies, you learn to pay particular attention to how the pieces fit together. You see, for instance, how inconsistent and damaging to profitability it would be to sell a high-quality product through a low-quality retailer, or how valuable it would be if your price were high enough to allow heavy advertising expenditures designed to make your brand distinctive in customers' eyes.

MARKET RESEARCH

Another thing that separates the most profitable companies from others is market research. At the B-school, marketing students spend countless hours massaging data and poring over statistical relationships. They can't master the cases if they don't.

Nevertheless, it is fair to say that professors have reservations about marketing research. No matter how good it is, it cannot dictate management's decision. Executives cannot afford to sit back in their steel-and-glass towers and trust to the data alone; instinct, intuition, and hunch often prove to be as useful in every way as good data. Although the sixth sense possessed by some fine marketers appears to be God-given, a sound working sense of consumers, buyers, and market trends can be gained by frequent contact and personal observation. Research may be valuable in quantifying this knowledge and giving it breadth and depth.

Many firms spend large sums on market research in the effort to get good information about customers, and students wrestle with some of the questions raised by such undertakings. For many years, the "Quaker Oats Company Life Cereal" case was discussed in class. In the case, the brand manager for Life cereal is considering ways to increase Life's market share of the ready-to-eat cereal market. The manager reviews some of the research done—a motivation research study showing Life's appeal, several test market experiments, surveys, consumer panel studies, advertising campaigns, and other efforts. The case introduces students to the mind-boggling array of research procedures that may be employed.

Two of many terms added to the student lexicon are *experimental methods,* which refer to research where the firm itself is active in the marketplace and manipulating it in some way (e.g., through a price change or an advertising change), and *nonexperimental methods,* which do not involve the company in any direct action (e.g., using statistical data, collecting information from a panel where the firm's interest is disguised). The former are more costly but enable you to test any and every element of the marketing mix; the latter are more limited but don't run the risk of affecting the market.

Why, asks Professor Robert Dolan, do marketing managers use research so little? Most likely, the answer is that the information collected is not what they need. For instance, the research may analyze in beautiful detail what users like about a product when the question on managers' minds is how the product is used. Dolan's response is to urge managers to take a hand in directing research efforts. For instance, they can initiate the project, work with research specialists to define the problem, clarify how the information will be used, and review the proposed research design to see that potential benefits outweigh the costs.

APPROACHES TO GLOBAL MARKETING

For more and more companies, the ultimate marketing test is global. First- and second-year marketing courses give increasing emphasis to the fact that a company's territory is likely to be the world. World-class marketing calls for a sophisticated understanding of cultural differences, headquarters-region relationships, and competition. Also, although the marketing faculty does not say so, global marketers are creating webs of international trade and dependency that give an impressively growing number of nations a strong vested interest in peace.

Among global marketing experts, a major question has been, Have markets grown so homogenized as to allow fairly standard selling programs? Professor John Quelch's answer is no. Quelch's studies show without question that successful marketers distinguish themselves by paying close attention to the need for local authority and tailoring all or parts of a marketing campaign to local tastes. If you look at global marketing on a case-by-case basis, he says, you will find some companies, like Coca-Cola, that have standardized most of their programs but many, like Nestlé, that allow a great deal of diversity. In some ways it is the old question of centralization versus decentralization—but with some new wrinkles. Quelch offers this example:

Procter & Gamble developed a new sanitary napkin in the 1980s. P & G International designated certain countries in different geographic regions as test markets. In pragmatic ways it both standardized and customized. On the one hand, headquarters standardized globally the product, brand name, positioning (that is, the napkin's advantages vis-à-vis competing products, the segment of the market the promotion would appeal to, etc.), and package design. On the other hand, recognizing the need for local voices and decentralization, headquarters invited national managers to suggest how other elements of the marketing program should be varied to suit local preferences.

As a result, Quelch told me, top management approved important changes in several markets. In addition, local sales managers came up with some ideas about sampling, couponing, and other techniques that ended up being used in all countries, including the United States.

Examining the wide spectrum of approaches to global marketing, says Quelch, you find that many differences are due to understandable causes. For example, consumer products used in the kitchen, such as Nestlé's soups and frozen foods, are likely to be more culture-bound than items used for business purposes, such as personal computers, whose technical benefits are about the same to users everywhere. In contrast, some companies' approaches have historical bases and can't be rationalized in economic terms.

To executives of U.S. companies seeking to strengthen the bonds between national or regional sales managers and headquarters, Quelch makes five suggestions:

1. Encourage field managers in the different countries to generate ideas, and use their ideas, with appropriate recognition, in global marketing programs. Unilever's subsidiary in South Africa developed Impulse body spray; headquarters bought the idea and transformed it into a global brand.

2. Take a bottom-up rather than a top-down approach in formulating strategies for global brands, encouraging wide participation by field managers. CPC International, for instance, employed marketing and advertising staffs at headquarters that worked with field managers. Frequently the experts from headquarters visited the directors of national subsidiaries to discuss local problems and describe new concepts and techniques for marketing programs. These experts did not visit to criticize what field managers were doing but to coach them with the objective of improving their skills, finesse, and success.

3. If possible, allow local managers to market local brands as well as global brands. One company that does this well, says Quelch, is Seagram. By allocating funds to support local marketing efforts for the company's global brands, it keeps local manag-

ers working for those products, but at the same time it allows the managers to market local brands in their countries.

4. Allow country managers to control marketing budgets enough to respond to local demand and counter in-country competition. When British Airways launched its $18 million global advertising campaign, it left intact the $25 million of tactical advertising budgets that each country manager used to promote fares, destinations, and tour packages for the local market.

5. Emphasize the general responsibilities of country managers so that they spend time on manufacturing, industrial relations, and government affairs as well as on marketing. The tendency of sales executives is to concentrate on selling, whereas competitive strategy calls for building values for consumers, a broader task that may have to do as much with quality control and service as with promotion and salespeople.

THE NECESSITY FOR TOUGH-MINDEDNESS

Marketing is both strategy and execution. Both are likely to demand some extremely difficult choices. While business need not be a zero-sum game, it may involve a lot of head knocking and elbow twisting. What marketing teaches is that often there is no way of making a choice without hurting some group or interest in the organization. For example, as Dolan points out, the choice of channels of distribution involves a complex web of personal, economic, and legal relationships. Once the choice is made and the organization commits itself to a combination of channels, it is extremely difficult for managers to change the system. It would be easier, he notes, to cut an advertising budget in half than to drop half a firm's retailers as part of a decision to change company outlets. Yet change management must, if it is to keep the firm moving ahead, for the conditions—competitors' tactics, technical service needs, consumer familiarity with the product, and so on—that gave rise to its earlier decision are bound to change.

Another example of tough choices that impressed students in one section I visited some years ago is the Clairol case. As described, the sales director of the appliance division (hair dryers, makeup mirrors, etc.) is worried about poor product displays and so-so promotions in the stores where Clairol is sold. How can his salespeople light a fire under distributors?

Some students favor more "push marketing"—that is, trade promotions and other incentives to dealers to feature the product. They argue that retail servicing will lead to better displays, shelf space, and inventory control, which increase sales; in turn, better retail sales will make selling easier and encourage more distribution. (The case mentions that the company president, among others, apparently leans toward this approach.)

However, as the discussion progresses the class sees that this means that national advertising and other promotions—"pull" programs—are going to have to be cut back. If pull programs are favored, the same thing happens to push programs.

In short, whichever route management takes, people are going to get hurt. What course will do the most good at the expense of the least harm? How should it be carried out? The ability of the B-school to prepare young men and women for economic leadership depends in no small part on how well it prepares them to make such choices.

From the standpoint of the public at large, however, the end result of this internal pushing, shoving, and gnashing of teeth is beneficial. Consumers are enriched, national interdependencies and dialogues between people of different nations increase, world peace is enhanced.

Of course, this is one of the ways that economic competition differs from military competition, making any parallel between the two very limited. In the ebb and flow of global economic fortunes, competitors are destroyed, and this gives rise to analogies to warfare. But there are enormous differences. As world business grows, the stake in peace grows. Thus, economic competition—even what some people may loosely call economic warfare—leads to quite different results from military campaigns, benefiting mankind instead of jeopardizing it.

■ *Effective marketing programs continually stress the importance of congruence. When one or more of the elements are not synchronized with the others, marketing falters.*

—PROFESSOR BENSON SHAPIRO

■ *The rule on who should perform what functions is very simple. The most effective organization for the task should do it.*

—PROFESSOR ROBERT DOLAN

9

ENTREPRENEURS
WITH HOT HANDS

T he management of
fast-growing companies is the growth sector in the B-school's
curriculum. The faculty knows what a big role entrepreneurs
play in this country's economic dreams. Not only do entrepreneurs add to U.S. competitive power but they bring a zest, daring, and irreverence to business that appeals mightily to the
American spirit. The victory of David over Goliath is part of our
culture.

The school emphasizes new venture management in several
ways. It injects many cases on entrepreneurial firms into required courses, offers second-year elective courses focusing on
new enterprise management, and conducts a successful program
for small-company managers that is offered in three stages so that
the managers won't have to leave their enterprises too long.
Although these courses and programs have roots that go back to
the 1930s, during the past decade they have seized the imaginations of more students and faculty people than ever.

Significantly, Professor Howard Stevenson surveyed the careers of members of the class of 1972 and found that about one-third of them were self-employed. His survey showed that the entrepreneurial life is financially rewarding, too—only fifteen years after graduation, more than half of the respondents reported net worths above $1 million. Again, in my own contacts with alums, many of them from recent classes, I have found a surprisingly high proportion who are taking the small-enterprise route rather than going with a large company.

The emphasis on entrepreneurial management has had a profound and pervasive influence on the Harvard Business School. A quarter of a century and more ago, the prevailing image of a B-school graduate was of a professional manager in a large company. That is not true today. Many students want freedom from the constraints of large company bureaucracies. They don't want to be on Mahogany Row, they want to run their own shows and be their own bosses.

ARE YOU WILLING TO PAY THE PRICE?

Since the life of an entrepreneur is demanding, Stevenson believes that if you are interested in small-business management, the first thing you should do is assess yourself critically. "One of the key things that a person going into new ventures has to do," he said once, "is confront his or her own set of values and decide what he or she will or won't do in order to succeed." The price of success may be long hours, weekends away from the family, driving a beat-up car, living in an unfashionable neighborhood. It may mean making countless trips to banks, putting up with rudeness from investors, suffering endless turndowns, getting the cold shoulder from old friends. These and other possibilities are quite real. Are you willing to accept them? If not, entrepreneurial management isn't for you.

Instead of discouraging students, however, this reality challenges many. It excites them: they are willing to bleed for a while if there is a good chance the travail will be rewarded. In particular, they appear to welcome risks if they can put them on the table where they can see them and size them up. Instead of being a negative, therefore, the uncertain life can be a plus.

One time I listened to Irving Grousbeck '60, chairman and cofounder of Continental Cablevision and for several years a member of the entrepreneurial management faculty at HBS. Talking about the second-year course he taught, he said:

"We show them the dark side—the risks, give-ups, and trade-offs one makes in an entrepreneurial career. We talk in class about risk management and about our belief that it makes no sense to think in terms of risk avoidance. You need to think in terms of the necessity to assume some risk; therefore, be sure you *know* what risks you're assuming. Are they risks you feel are manageable and consistent with the potential rewards?"

Grousbeck emphasized, however, that at first in the course many students showed great naïveté about entrepreneurs. He said:

"I've found that most students have a stereotyped notion of the entrepreneur, and that stereotype seems to include such characteristics as 'unable to work in groups,' 'impetuous about taking risks,' 'flamboyant'—almost a circus-barker mentality, if you will. One of the real functions of our second-year course is to disabuse students of the notion that they have to have these characteristics in order to be successful."

Another thing that appeals to many students is the entrepreneur's emphasis on value instead of short-range financial performance. If you look at many small firms starting up, says Associate Professor William Sahlman, who teaches a second-year course on entrepreneurial finance, you find an approach to personal and financial risk that is very different from that typically taken nowadays by executives of non-entrepreneurial companies. At HBS the entrepreneur is taught to focus on cash flow and value rather than on short-term profitability or accounting profits.

Sahlman's second-year course is popular; about half of the class of 1989 signed up for it. He says that he approaches finance more as an enabling function than an opportunity-creating function; that is, he wants the class to concentrate, as he believes most good entrepreneurs do, more on company-building opportunities and their exploitation than on finance as a specialty per se. "If, as an entrepreneur, all you have is a sharp pencil, you'd better get a different kind of job. Sharp pencils are great, but they have nothing to do with determining the success or failure of business enterprises."

The course's caseload examines failures as well as successes, and the cases range from the startup of Lotus Development Corporation to the Passamaquoddy Indian tribe's purchase of a cement plant in Thomaston, Maine. Students find this range refreshing. One told me that he found it easier to identify with such situations than he did with most large-company problems.

In the field studies section of entrepreneurial management, where students develop proposals for new enterprises, John Van Slyke, at the time a lecturer, told me that student projects ranged all over the map, from ideas for starting up an airport limousine service to a new UHF television station. Van Slyke himself had founded one new company, American Management Company, and had worked with numerous new firms.

HOW TO TELL AN ENTREPRENEUR

Howard Stevenson returned to the B-school early in the 1980s to head up the entrepreneurial management courses. One of his contributions was seeing entrepreneurship not in economic but in human terms. This departure from tradition enabled the B-school to break away from the old concept of small companies employing less than a certain number of people and with sales volumes under a certain level, to an understanding based on what entrepreneurs do and how they act. Stevenson saw these people as change agents who may be found in businesses of all sorts and sizes—usually new enterprises but sometimes older, larger companies, too. The traits that distinguish entrepreneurs aren't neat and decisive, Stevenson once told a group of us. However, the traits show a special emphasis, he says, and you can see the difference by imagining a spectrum. At one end of the spectrum, imagine "promoter," and at the other end, "trustee." The promoter is the person with blue shoes and a diamond pinky ring who says brashly, "I can make it happen," and the trustee is the more staid person who says, "I must guard what I have." Entrepreneurs, says Stevenson, are much closer to the promoter end than to the trustee end. (As he emphasizes, however, bear in mind that entrepreneurs are not all brashness and chutzpah, just as trustee types are not always conservative.)

Using this imagined spectrum, Stevenson describes five traits or dimensions that distinguish entrepreneurs:

1. They are opportunity-driven. They say and think, "I will search for opportunity, and my main task, when I find it, is to get enough resources to pursue it." Often this means breaking new ground, but not necessarily. For example, entrepreneurs may come up with a fresh mix of old ideas or find new ways to apply old approaches. Because of this attitude, entrepreneurs are sometimes criticized as opportunistic—or lauded as creative and innovative. At the other end of the spectrum, says Stevenson, trustees focus more on conserving what they have, thinking, "I will prune my opportunity tree based on the resources I control. I will not try to leap very far beyond my current situation."

2. Entrepreneurs are willing and able to çhase opportunities. Stevenson says that they get off the mark quickly—no long periods of discussion and negotiation. "It is this willingness to get in and out quickly that has led to the entrepreneur's reputation as a gambler."

But they don't swing wildly for the fence, he cautions. They know the territories they will operate in. It is because of this knowledge, he believes, that entrepreneurs are good at recognizing new patterns and betting on trends. And it is because of their willingness to act that they stand separate from the armchair dreamers and blue-sky thinkers who never get anything done.

In 1985 Sandra Kurtzig, who five years earlier had attended the school's program in smaller-company management, was interviewed by the *HBS Bulletin.* She was then founder and head of ASK Computer Systems in Los Altos, described by *Inc.* magazine as one of America's one hundred fastest-growing firms. Reflecting on her experience as an entrepreneur, she said:

"At the beginning, I was really president, CEO, chairman, and everything else. I did everything myself: the financial work, the R and D, all the programming, and the sales. I collected the money, put it in a shoebox, and at the end of the month I'd pay the bills with whatever was in the shoebox. If there was still some money left, I knew I'd made a profit. In a two-million-dollar company, it doesn't matter if you have any or all of those titles. What does matter is that you're good at shooting from the hip and looking at the big picture."

At the opposite end of the spectrum, what Stevenson calls trustee types move so slowly and cautiously that it may appear that they are stationary, even frozen.

3. Entrepreneurs manage with less money. Although they commit themselves at each stage of growth (idea testing, marketing, new financing, increased production, etc.), they do so with limited funds, plant, and staff. Stevenson says that the real risks they take usually have more to do with the tension caused by their commitments versus limited resources than with anything else. If and when they succeed, they may remember the high points of the experience as being these crises when they placed their last chip on the table knowing that it might not be enough. Speaking from his own experience as a successful entrepreneur in real estate, Stevenson says:

"At one extreme—the Exxons of the world—a full-time secretary and a word-processing unit are needed to get a letter typed. As a good entrepreneur, however, I would write it myself. Somehow the letter would get out. Good entrepreneurial management requires you to learn to do a little more with a little less."

In contrast, trustee-type managers, after analyzing commitments and needs painstakingly, tend to make very large commitments of resources. Their attitude is, "Since my object is to use my resources, once I finally commit I will go in very heavy at the front end."

4. Entrepreneurs don't feel that they must own equipment, service groups, facilities, and other resources. Instead, their attitude is that if they can just *use* the resource—renting, leasing, borrowing, or otherwise getting their hands on it for a short time—that is enough. In contrast, trustee types feel they must own the resource or have it on their permanent payroll.

Once in a small group discussion, Stevenson gave us the example of a book publishing company. Most of the country's largest book publishers have numerous editors, production specialists, publicists, salespeople, and others. But many of today's young publishing ventures, he pointed out, consist of a handful of people who rely heavily on outside professionals and suppliers. When these people acquire a manuscript, they will often hire a free lance to make editorial improvements. Next they contract with a typesetting company to have the manuscript set in type, with a printing and binding concern to produce the volume, and with a public relations firm to promote the book. Finally, people who are the equivalent of manufacturers' reps sell the book to stores.

Entrepreneurs, said Stevenson, have several things going for them in this approach to control of resources. For example, by using instead of owning an expensive piece of equipment, they lower the cost of pulling out of a project.

Ironically, entrepreneurial management instructors tell me, success may change this approach. As the new firm grows and finds profits, its managers begin seeking more control. They find it tempting to take a large-company attitude and own resources. For instance, on reaching a certain level of sales volume, a producer of an electronic product decides that it can no longer run the risk of having a valuable component made by an outside supplier who may be subject to severe market or financial pressures. In so doing, managers edge across the spectrum toward the administrative-trustee viewpoint.

5. Entrepreneurs organize their businesses so that they can personally see and talk to the key people and feel how things are going. They don't want to work formally through channels, as does the trustee, who views organizational relationships in terms of rights, responsibilities, and authority. This bias leads entrepreneurs to favor flat organizations (as seen on an organization chart) rather than pyramidal ones with detailed hierarchies.

Stevenson also feels that entrepreneurs rely heavily on informal information networks because of their lack of control over services and facilities; they can't count on formal reporting systems, as trustee types do, to update them on the status of resources. Suppliers are an example. To make sure that the supplier is on the ball and will produce as directed, the entrepreneur stays in touch with the person and keeps his or her ears open to the opinions of others about suppliers.

Summing up, Stevenson emphasizes that these five qualities don't mean that entrepreneurs aren't good managers. Contrary to the common stereotype of entrepreneurs as egocentric and idiosyncratic, and thus unable to manage, they need and practice managerial skills as much as anyone does. However, they employ different skills from those used by trustee types and administrators in bureaucratic organizations. This is why they are often misunderstood by scholars, writers, and others.

QUESTIONS TO ASK IN PLANNING

In entrepreneurial management courses, instructors place a lot of emphasis on what might be called pre-start analysis—that is, sizing up an opportunity before deciding to go after it. They try to make students see the crucial importance of spotting a good opportunity, understanding the magnitude of the job of exploiting it, identifying the risks, and planning how to cope with the risks.

In the courses, professors create no illusions that a firm's plan will hold in any detail or that the future can be predicted. As Van Slyke used to point out, there is almost always a steep learning curve in an enterprising effort, and that is what smart entrepreneurs bank on. Making adjustments on the basis of feedback, learning from experience—these are the keys. This doesn't mean, though, that they don't sit down and analyze data. Just the opposite. Careful and systematic thinking helps entrepreneurs whether they put their business plans on paper or just think about plans. Also, as indicated earlier, careful analysis can help the owner-manager to impress bankers and investors.

To illustrate the range of questions that should be asked, here are six that instructors ask students to think hard about when assessing start-up ideas:

- What is the expected economic life of the opportunity?
- Is the profit potential great enough in view of the capital required, time required, amount of risk, and other needs?
- Will the firm be able to hold its own against powerful competitors, customers, and suppliers?
- Can specific customers or groups of customers be identified who will be willing and able to make the changes required?
- What do I bring to the enterprise in the way of needed skills, resources, contacts, or other advantages?
- Will we have sufficient reserves, alternatives, and/or other resources to weather crises and reverses?

Expected economic life. Every opportunity exists for a limited period, which may vary considerably from one field to another. In the music business, the opportunity to succeed with a new hit tune may last only a few months, whereas in real estate, the opportunity to buy a property may span several decades. During this economic life, moreover, the opportunity may be more valuable at some points than at others. The economic life of the opportunity for many types of fuel-saving equipment, for example, may be long, but the value of capitalizing on that opportunity may be tied to fuel crises occurring spasmodically.

Profit potential. In most cases, Van Slyke told me, opportunities that require lots of capital, long periods of time, and the taking of large risks make little sense for entrepreneurs. In the end valuable ventures may result—but not for the original risk takers. The numerous rounds of financing reduce their percent-age of ownership so much that when the payoff finally begins coming, they get only a small share of it.

In a good opportunity, he says, you should be able to create and sustain real values for the market (a new service, a new product that the customer wants, etc.) in three to five years. You should be able to obtain a gross margin of 40 percent or more on sales and an after-tax profit of 15 percent or more. Sales should grow steadily and rapidly during the first five to seven years.

In addition, you should be able to generate funds internally to finance and sustain part of your firm's growth; adding this source of money to the combination of equity and debt financing you can get, you should be able to meet your needs for more plant, equipment, people, services, and so on. The assets that you build up should have market value so that you can use them as collat-eral. Your earning power and cash flow should be enough to cover service charges on debt. The rate of return on your invest-ment after taxes should be 40 percent or more.

Competition. Essentially, this is the strategy issue discussed in Chapter 5. It is extremely important for entrepreneurs. Particu-larly if their firms are successful, students learn, they are going to face competition for the dollar. True, they may be blessed with a lead time where they have the field pretty much to themselves, if they come out with a new product or service. But as certain as death and taxes, competitors will emerge. The first ones may enter the market with what some instructors call a "copy and cut" strategy for pricing and production.

What measures can management take to renew itself, to dif-ferentiate its offering, to fortify its image in the marketplace, to create barriers to competitors? Perhaps costs can be cut. Perhaps patents or trade secrets can be exploited. Perhaps service and maintenance can be improved. In Van Slyke's opinion, failure to plan for this stage has hurt many entrepreneurial firms.

Powerful customers and suppliers will, of course, have an inter-est in keeping the firm going. This does not mean, however, that they won't try to put the company over a barrel. In a number of cases students see the high tolls that a large customer or crucial supplier tried to exact from a new company.

Customers' ability to change. This question is important not only in persuading lenders and investors but in planning distribution. As instructors point out, if you are an entrepreneur with a new product, process, or service, most of the time you are asking customers to change. You are asking them to do something differently, even to make important changes in their manufacturing or distribution. Ask yourself if the change you are trying to sell will be affordable to customers, what the incentives are for them to go to the trouble, and so on. Be as specific as you can, instructors urge, about the changes that specific customer groups will have to make.

One of the side benefits of asking such a question, Van Slyke once told a group of students, is that it helps you to become more aware of the power game that often goes on between you and key customers. "Becoming integrated into the customer's procedures," he said, "is often the most effective barrier to entry of competition; it is, however, often the major hurdle which a new product or process must overcome."

A good example comes from the *HBS Bulletin.* Randall Poliner '83 and Steven Bilodeau '83 were chief corporate officer and manufacturing head respectively of Macrodyne, a small young electronics company that produced a new type of signal-processing equipment. (Their interest in the firm began when they made a field study during their second year at HBS.) They described their market as 150 utilities that would be able, as a result of using the new product, to do a better job of measuring voltage, frequency of electricity, air patterns, and molten-lead speed. However, Poliner and Bilodeau also knew that customers who bought their product would have to change, both in their technology and in their management. And change, they told the alumni magazine, is always difficult to sell, particularly in an industry as conservative as utilities.

They also offered an interesting reflection on an enterprise's business plan:

"Basically, you put it all down on paper and let some smart

people look at it, shoot holes in it, and figure out where the good ideas are and where the bad ones are. Once it's put together and has some direction, the next step is to put the right people in place to make it work."

Personal assets. Rarely does one man or woman possess or control everything that the new firm will need. HBS students learn the importance of looking as objectively as possible at what they or someone else might add to the organization as well as the resources of the entrepreneurial team as a whole. The less the key people bring to the enterprise, the more fragile and vulnerable it will be; but the more they can bring that is unique, the more potent and durable the venture should be.

An unusual example is Rainbow Tropicals on Mauna Kea in the Hawaiian Islands. As mentioned earlier, Rainbow Tropicals is headed by Jules Gervais '63. The firm grows and exports orchids, heliconias, gingers, and anthuriums to many parts of the world. Before starting Rainbow Tropicals, now a firm employing thirty-five people, Gervais had worked with Standard Fruit Company's banana operation in Honduras, headed a company in Thailand that cooperated with local governments to provide services to U.S. forces, and managed United Fruit's Asia Pacific division. When, early in the 1970s, he started his enterprise, Gervais therefore brought valuable experience and skills to the operation.

Damage control. Obviously you can't plan for every potential reverse, but it is a good idea to plan for the most likely ones. Things will go wrong—and at the worst possible time for the enterprise. Van Slyke used to cite an old rule of thumb that new ventures can have variances of "three and two"—that is, require three times as much time and twice as much money as anticipated, or vice versa.

In times of financial distress, instructors point out, the "golden rule" takes effect: the party with the gold rules. If the venture has to be refinanced, often this must be done on a confiscatory basis ("down and dirty" financing), and those who come in with cash rarely show much mercy for those who are already trapped in the deal. The usual pattern is for the new financiers to demand that the old ones stay in and, in terms of legal priority, give up much or all of their control over the venture along with future opportunities to get out.

Consequently, instructors try to get students to see the need for a damage-control plan, not for the worst of all possible events, but for events that realistically could happen—the death of a key person, a dropoff in sales due to an economic glitch peculiar to the industry, a serious lawsuit, loss of a crucial trade secret, or whatever else has a reasonable chance of happening that would make the firm vulnerable. When such events happen, the entrepreneur who has what Van Slyke calls a "backup vision" will have a better chance of survival.

ENTREPRENEURS ARE WHERE YOU FIND THEM

The cases in entrepreneurial management don't always reflect "exciting" business situations. "It's important for the students to see that opportunity can come not only in rip-roaring, fast-growth industries but also in industries that one might otherwise say weren't very interesting," Stevenson says.

It is also significant that a few cases come from larger, older companies. "It's our belief," Irving Grousbeck stated several years ago, "that entrepreneurial management is a way of approaching the management of businesses of all sizes and ages, not just businesses one might start and not just small businesses." For example, one case concerns Hewlett-Packard, a large and well-established company by any measure, yet one that appears to nurture the entrepreneurial spark successfully. How does management keep such an outlook? The case shows some of the ways: setting money aside for new ventures, relieving the managers of bureaucratic constraints, and other strategies.

Instructors emphasize that entrepreneurs are not people with certain knowledge or MBA degrees from Harvard or California but people who can build organizations and enterprises. "There's an old saying in real estate that what matters is location, location,

location. In entrepreneurial firms it's people, people, people," a professor once told me. The school recognizes that it can't make entrepreneurs. However, it can take young people who have the right stuff and make them better entrepreneurs than they would be otherwise. It does what it can, in other words—and the difference, though little, can be significant.

Entrepreneurial ability is a potent ingredient in American economic leadership. It comes as close as anything to being this country's "secret weapon" in international trade. The more the B-school succeeds in sharpening the entrepreneurial edge in managers-to-be, the better our country's chances in global competition.

> ■ *I would rather invest in a B venture with an A person than an A venture with a B person.*
>
> —PROFESSOR GEORGES DORIOT

10

CRUNCHING
THE NUMBERS

Graduates from the B-school and other management schools are criticized for many things but not for inability to play with numbers. Even students who barely get by in the numbers courses may impress outsiders, when they become managers, as wizards of data analysis.

This is as it should be, for you can't lead a corporation, government organization, or nonprofit agency unless you have a working understanding of the quantitative reports on operations. Alfred Sloan, the famous head of General Motors for many years, once remarked that sooner or later everything a corporation does shows up on the bottom line.

As pointed out earlier, the whole B-school focuses on how managers and employees do behave rather than on how the faculty thinks they ought to behave. (In the lingo of decision theory, which covers quantitative analysis, the B-school's emphasis is descriptive rather than normative.) Professors in the "numbers courses"—finance, control, managerial economics—seem to do this more wholeheartedly than anyone else. They probe the weaknesses of accounting data, they examine the foibles of bankers and auditors, they look frankly at different attitudes toward risk. They do this not to show up decision makers but to clarify the realities that students will encounter when appraising a situation and seeking ways to improve it. In the words of Roger Sant '60, head and cofounder of Applied Energy Services in Virginia at the time of his class's twenty-fifth reunion: "I think one of the things Harvard, and the case method, gave me was a vicarious feeling of what it would be like to be in a real business situation."

When they first come to the B-school, students often are inclined to say that the only way for a dilemma or conflict in a case to be resolved is by changing the system. "This company needs a new control system" or "That company needs a new debt policy." They soon learn that such glib solutions are a cop-out— worse than that, most of the time impossible to carry out.

Once I visited a class in the Control course where the case under discussion involved a vice president who was caught in a difficult and unpleasant bidding situation. The mess he was in was not at first obvious, but when the situation became clear, it appeared that he couldn't do what he wanted to do without hurting another division in the company. "Well," said one student wisely, "the real problem is this company's control system. It's an accident waiting to happen." The student went on to explain that the system virtually invited this sort of disaster. Her explanation was convincing.

"Are you recommending, then," asked the instructor, nodding thoughtfully (the class couldn't see the gleam in her eye), "that the vice president order the system thrown out?" The student started to say yes, then caught herself and began hemming and hawing. She realized, as others in the section did, that this would be a tricky move because top management itself had put in the system and installed it.

The instructor asked the student to play the role of the vice president for a moment. "You're in the president's office," said the instructor. "What exactly would you tell him?" Every way the student tried sounded ridiculous. Each attempt sounded as if the vice president were pleading with the president: "I've got a problem down there that I wish I didn't have to solve, and I hope you'll throw out the system to relieve me of the responsibility for making a decision." The class got the message.

Control systems (that is, systems designed to make employees act in a certain desired way and show the financial costs and benefits of the action taken) are particularly vulnerable. Almost always they require trade-offs between opposing objectives, such as the desirability of allowing employees to use their discretion versus the desirability of making sure they act in the company's best interest, and by definition this choice means imperfection. "Sometimes," Professor John Dearden once told me, "the best that can be achieved is the least-worst system."

Also, as instructors in the courses indicate, systems go out of date as times and conditions change, and managers simply cannot keep updating them—the organization won't let them. Then, too, managers down the line must consider in-company politics. "If the chief executive wants to look only at a certain figure or look at the data in a certain way," says Dearden, "that's the way it's going to be."

In this brief chapter we will look at several samples of what professors teach and students learn in the "numbers courses." With a few possible exceptions, this taste of knowledge will be familiar to practicing executives, for it mirrors the real world that they operate in every day. My selection of ideas has to be arbitrary; also, I must overlook many techniques of analysis—decision trees, present value, and return on investment, to name a few—that become very important in the courses. We will touch on some methods that enable students to think through numbers, weaknesses of so-called hard numbers, lending and borrowing, rules for coping with financial analysis, and a few other topics.

SEEING THE FOREST DESPITE THE TREES

Before students can come to grips with the management problems in a case in finance, control, or quantitative analysis, they may have to cut through dense thickets of numbers. With class time limited, how is this done? Often students' first inclination, after glancing over a case, is to despair about being able to uncover the real issues.

First, instructors try to help students see that many of the numbers aren't central to the main problem—they are what the managers in the case saw, and they are relevant, but they are not pivotal. Just what types of numbers these are varies from case to case—instructors have to rely on students' innate skill for wrestling with facts and learning how to cope.

Second, instructors encourage a variety of tricks and shortcuts for number-crunching, as students may call it. By suggestion and example—most often when they are framing a problem and putting key numbers on the boards—instructors may communicate useful shortcuts to the section being taught.

The most articulate describer of such techniques whom I know is Roger Golde '59, a management consultant working out of Cambridge. Golde tells me that he didn't necessarily learn the methods at HBS but he put them to frequent use in analyzing cases and discussing them in class at HBS. Of the many he details, the ones I have seen used most often by instructors and students are the following:

- *Restating numbers in helpful ways.* For instance, a machine's monthly output might be restated as 960 units per month instead of (as in the case) 6 units per hour or 1 unit every 10 minutes.
- *Trying to visualize the reality behind a number.* For instance, suppose you are told the "average hourly wage" of employees. That may seem clear enough if you don't think about it, but suppose you try to visualize it. Immediately questions arise. Does the number include vacation time or sick pay or other fringe benefits? How is overtime pay handled in the average?
- *Looking at disparities between input and output.* The report may tell you, say, that 20 percent of a customer's customers account for 20 percent of sales volume. That may seem like a ho-hum fact, but suppose you look further and see that 80

percent of the profits come from 20 percent of the sales volume? You may then have a good lead for further analysis and action.

- *Rounding off numbers to make it easier to think about them.* Once, teaching a doctoral seminar, I reacted in awe when a student announced quickly that an additional $87,400 of earnings spread over the 4,278,000 outstanding shares in the case amounted to an increase of roughly 2¢ per share. Later I learned that the student wasn't an Einstein but simply had a technique: he noted that 43 (rounding of 4,278,000) went into 87 (rounding of 87,400) a little over two times—.02, when you adjust for the decimal places, or 2¢ directly if you think of the dollar sum in cents.

Technology also has made it easier to discuss numbers. Since 1987 first-year students have been able to run numbers past their section in easy-to-read fashion. In each of the nine classrooms there are large-screen video-computer display systems. These screens enable an instructor, student, or group to present numerical calculations on a ten-foot display for all to see. Personal computers, three-quarter-inch videos, and videocassette recorders can be used to transmit data or images from a seat to the ceiling projector and onto the screen.

Withal, more students probably get wet under the arms because of the numbers courses than because of others. Once the student newspaper carried a spoof column showing the wise answers of a sage named "J.B." to fictitious student inquiries (but inquiries that mirrored student concerns). "Dear J.B.," asked one student, "I've crunched so many numbers that last night I dreamt my roommate turned into a calculator. What do you advise? Sincerely, Dave Digit." The oracular J.B. replied, "Dear Dave Digit: Isn't it great to have a roommate you can count on?"

SOFT SPOTS IN HARD DATA

In all quantitative courses, class discussions focus repeatedly on possible illusions in data. The lesson is that no manager or analyst can blithely assume that the numbers given in a situation portray reality correctly. Let me mention just a few examples.

In a case taught in finance, students are asked to evaluate a garden apartment complex that is up for sale. Many features of the building are familiar to them, yet many students fall into a trap: taking annual return estimates as givens and thus failing to appreciate the importance of the judgments that lie behind the estimates. For instance, the projected cost of maintenance of the building is iffy because, while double the previous figure, it probably won't cover replacement costs of equipment in the apartments (disposals, air conditioners, etc.) after a few years. The case also brings home to students that the value of a property in resale rests less on its original cost or physical depreciation than on the cash flows it can continue to generate.

Instructors teach students to be wary of traps like this. In a number of cases in control and finance, students wrestle with the reality that financial accounting data are not as precise as the figures might indicate. For one thing, different accounting principles may be employed, and managers are not always objective in their choices, choosing the approach that provides the results they would like to see rather than the one that most accurately measures the event reported. For another, accountants have to measure the results of operations in dollars and, as one professor I know puts it, this is not unlike a carpenter trying to measure the length of a board with an elastic yardstick.

Also, when accountants measure specific past periods such as last year or last quarter, it is amazing how many predictions of the future may be contained in the measurements. For example, how long will a piece of equipment last (a longer or shorter time than the period it is amortized for)? How much credit will eventually prove uncollectible (not necessarily the ratio assumed)? How much will product warranties cost the company (not always the estimate given)? In many statements you could find thousands of such forecasts.

The book value figure in a financial statement may be illusory, too. Once in a financial seminar I heard Professors Thomas Piper, William Fruhan, and others discourse on what little insight book value frequently provides into the true value of a stock, and how disconcerting it was to see stocks called cheap or undervalued because they were selling at less than book value. For instance, one instructor pointed out, Boston Edison was caught in a hostile regulatory environment in which it was nearly impossible to earn a satisfactory return. Investors saw the company as a "cash trap" and priced its shares accordingly. Book value notwithstanding, the stock was not underpriced.

In short, since book value doesn't show what a company earns on capital—the latter being a much more significant measure, in the eyes of investors—it may be close to worthless. If a stock price is less than book value, students are urged to see if the company's financial performance doesn't explain the discrepancy.

Finance instructors and their cases also teach students about price-earnings ratios. The lesson is that these ratios are an old but potentially dangerous friend. Therefore, use them—but with crossed fingers. Several precautions can be taken. For instance, compare today's price-earnings with the average level of the past five or ten years for the company, and with price-earnings ratios for a fair sample of other companies; again, calculate what the company must earn during future years in order to justify the present ratio.

Some professors relate financial reporting to malaises that keep American industry from performing at its strategic best in global competition. For example, Professor Robert Kaplan and others believe that cost accounting and control systems are a major stumbling block to corporate progress. Most companies still use the same systems that management developed decades ago, when conditions were drastically different from what they are today.

Once I attended a class that brought this reality home to students. The case involved a division manager who inherited an organization that had enjoyed such greatly improved profitability that the previous head had been promoted into top management. The new manager found, however, that the division's market share had decreased, unit productivity had fallen, and costs had been reduced on the profit-and-loss statements by skimping on investments in new equipment and holding workers' pay down lower than it should have been. In other words, the numbers didn't show what damage had been done.

Kaplan has been developing a second-year course in which students design cost-management systems that truly reflect advances and declines in an operation in the light of its particular product mix, market, strategy, and production technology. He finds big differences, for instance, between fabrication-and-assembly businesses (e.g., automobiles and washers) and process industries that transform materials from one state to another (e.g., chemicals). He and many colleagues believe that accounting and financial reporting can't do their job if such differences are covered over.

BORROWERS AND LENDERS

Although the public often thinks of banks as cold-blooded, HBS students soon learn that bankers, beneath their computational covers, are as human and biased as anyone else.

For instance, finance professors love to refer to a venerable case concerning a cabinet producer. The producer has obtained a bank loan to finance a big increase in plant. Then, apparently carried away by an abundance of orders, the producer expanded more even than he had told the bank he would. But he didn't inform the bank officer about this; further, his ebullient action was in direct violation of a restrictive provision in his loan agreement. As the case opens, the producer asks the bank for more money; he wants the agreement rewritten and money for the additional expansion.

In a class I visited, most students, after discussing the pros and cons of the loan, favored the bank's making it. Although the ratio of debt to equity was high, and although the producer turned out a single product for an industry that was not yet mature and might be subject to sharp fluctuations, the producer's earnings record was good. In the discussion, more and more students spoke bullishly about the loan.

Then the professor distributed a brief sequel case and asked the section to examine it. The sequel reports that the loan was made but that the cabinet producer's business has become unhinged. After getting the loan, his orders have fallen off unexpectedly, throwing him into real trouble. He asks the bank to extend more credit so that he will have time and money to work out of his jam. Now the bank—especially the officer responsible for the loan—is in a fix as well as the borrower.

The situation is far from uncommon. In fact, it lies behind some of the failures and fiascos that have rocked the financial world in recent years. What do students learn from it? Finance professors tell me that they hope their classes will see such things as:

1. The foibles of lenders and investors. In particular, it should become clear how they can become ever more committed to a borrower, taking greater risks than they would consider if dealing rationally with the borrower for the first time or at arm's length. In the cabinet producer case, for example, few students would have the bank make the loan if they had foreknowledge of what would happen to the producer as reported in the sequel case. Nor would the bank officer go ahead with such foreknowledge. However, once a lender or investor commits money to a venture, it is very difficult to draw a firm line beyond which further help won't be given. Almost always there are some bright spots in the situation or earnings forecast that can be used to rationalize lending more money.

2. Recognition that if the borrower has a solid net worth, that can be valuable for creditors. In the sequel case of the cabinet producer, the man's balance sheet was in shambles, a far cry from what it had been in the first case. Nevertheless, the bank next tried to bail out the producer by making a further loan. When that money, too, failed to solve the producer's woes, the bank gave up and turned to liquidation of the borrower's company. In this effort it didn't do too badly because the firm's net worth was great enough to absorb heavy losses and attract a buyer.

3. The value to the investor or lender of taking a hard look at the industry and asking the unpopular "what if" questions. In the cabinet producer's case, for example, the company was awfully vulnerable to a dip in sales. John Nevin '52, erstwhile chief executive of Firestone Tire & Rubber (he sold it to Bridgestone in 1988 for many times more than it had been worth when he took over a decade before), remembered this part of his HBS training vividly when he was interviewed a few years ago. One with a euphoric view of a firm's future may come down to earth awfully fast when asked what would be the impact on earnings of this or that unhappy event.

4. The need to leave room for further lending. Lenders and investors should be given credit for one of their conservative instincts: the tendency not to loan up to the hilt but to invest less than the borrower's situation would seem to justify. This allows the possibility of further lending if necessary.

5. Recognition that the United States has a profit and loss economy. Many students today have become so accustomed to prosperity that they are willing, as one finance professor put it to me, "to loan almost anyone anything and greatly need to be jarred by a vicarious experience of failure."

Teachers want students to appreciate the lending officer's responsibility for a good relationship with borrowers. I think of a case where it would be easy, at first glance, to fault the borrower. In the situation described, a proprietor has taken many loans from his bank, over and over again assuring the bank of repayment but never doing so. As the case opens, the bank is weighing still another request for more credit. The situation is not one-sided. The account has become fairly promising; on the other hand, the proprietor has failed often to live up to his promises, and the banker might well feel that his chain has been jerked once too often.

Why, asked the instructor when the case was discussed, has the banker gone along with so many breaches of faith? Students began to see that the banker himself is a large part of the problem. One said, "His warnings to the proprietor about repayment didn't sound as if he really meant them." Another remarked, "He asked for 'seasonal cleanups' of the loan but his demands sounded weak." Others in the section noted that the banker's urgings to the proprietor to slow down his business's growth didn't have much of an edge to them.

However, many students were more sympathetic. They pointed out that if the banker tried to correct all these omissions right away and "straighten the proprietor out," he might well lose a good account, for it appeared that at this point the proprietor could turn to another bank, if necessary. Still, even the most sympathetic agreed that a great deal can be said for a bank officer's taking a firm but encouraging stance, setting terms in a "no kidding" fashion for the future relationship, yet staying flexible.

Instructors teach the importance of cash flow in analyzing the future needs and prospects of a firm. Cash flow isn't everything, of course, but it is one of the vital indicators, and students learn to emphasize it. From a cash flow projection, all sorts of implications may be seen. For instance, a decision about the most desirable financial structure for a firm may be influenced by factors such as sales increases or delays in collecting receivables that may cause a cash crisis for the company.

Instructors also teach students to pay a lot of attention to the particular conditions that may affect a company's strategy for obtaining cash. I have sat in on discussions showing that a company in a volatile industry should issue new equity to get the cash it needs, while a company in a stable industry should issue debt and gain the tax benefits of debt. The timing of a stock sale also depends on the company situation. In one case, students see that a firm that has been making many large investments might do well to borrow enough so that it can get by, hoping that the investments will create a better opportunity for selling stock a little later on. On the other hand, a company that has recently dazzled analysts with superb profits might well wish to strike while the iron is hot and float a new common stock issue right away.

COMPUTING RISK AND RETURN

Early in the first-year finance course, instructors teach students that the return on an investment should be commensurate with the risk. (The student shorthand for this "golden rule" is, return = risk.) In general, the reasoning is simple. If you put, say, $1,000 into a bank savings account and another $1,000 into a nuclear instruments company's stock, your chances of getting back your money plus interest from the savings account are very good; your chances of making a profit from the nuclear instruments investment are less good. The savings account is relatively risk-free, but the nuclear instruments investment is subject to quite a bit of risk—in fact, the firm may not even be around in a few years. To compensate, you expect the nuclear instruments investment to pay you a lot more money (if it works out) than the savings account will.

This concept of risk and return runs throughout the numbers courses. As instructors teach, it is not always an easy concept to apply, nor do people in practice always apply it well.

One example is investment proposals, a common problem for top executives. When a division in a sizable company proposes a substantial investment, it shows what the income from the new equipment or facility will be over a period of five, ten, fifteen, or some other period of years. But, as indicated before, a dollar of income to be received ten years out should be valued less than a dollar received five years out, and a dollar to be received five years out should be valued less than a dollar received today.

The amount by which future dollars are discounted, in professors' opinion, should be the cost of capital—not the whole corporation's average cost of capital but the division's cost. And that cost of capital should mirror the risk involved in the division's business. The risk for a computer manufacturer may be much higher than the risk for a gravel producer.

However, this customized risk is not always easy to compute—at least, objectively and quickly. Professor David Mullins and others on the faculty argue that the capital asset pricing model—everybody at the B-school calls it CAPM—is useful here. While

CAPM may have huge limitations in market analysis, it can be adapted readily to management's needs when assessing company investments. As Mullins has told me, financial executives should not rely on CAPM as a precise measure of an organization's capital cost, but it offers a usable routine for translating risk into expected return.

But risk is a way of life in business, and for many executives most assessments of risk cannot be cranked into any model or algorithm. Much of one first-year course at HBS—Managerial Economics—is devoted to risk analysis. The effort of the faculty is to show students that, although practically all decisions about the future involve uncertainty, there are rational ways of specifying that uncertainty—and these rational ways are usually better than rules-of-thumb and seat-of-the-pants decisions.

Generally speaking, rational prediction means collecting data from past experience. "The data won't answer your decision question for you," one instructor in the course emphasized to me, "but it'll give you patterns and averages, and you can get a feel for what might happen and the likely consequences. You still run risk but you know what the risk is—and that's better than being ignorant and trusting blindly to chance."

So students ponder data from past experience, try to assemble it in manageable ways, and argue over its validity. My impression from classes is that a surprisingly large number of situations can be turned from black holes into relatively predictable problems. In one class I attended, for instance, the case under discussion involved the head of a West Coast winery who had to decide whether to harvest right away or take a chance that a forecasted storm might destroy his grapes (if you like puns, you might entitle the case "The Grapes of Math"). In another class, a professional baseball club was wondering how best to sell seats in view of perplexing data on attendance. In still another, an oil company executive debated whether to bid on oil-drilling rights in an area that looked promising but hadn't been tested. In these and many other situations, the sections saw, rational risk analysis could improve a decision maker's prospects in the long run. Useful data was available—and more data *could* be found if wanted—on which to base a rational judgment.

At another stage of the course, instructors try to get students to improve their decisions by better understanding their own attitudes toward risk. The approach is called *preference theory*. Two people will look at the same data on the chances that, let us say, a research project will and won't produce a usable product. One of the two people will say that the data show a high prospect of success, the other will say that the data show a mediocre or poor chance of success. The difference lies in how the two people look at risk. Through an ingenious set of questions, students can convert the optimist's and pessimist's estimates into a more objective evaluation of the prospects for success and failure. In effect, they learn to do logically what many wise managers do intuitively—for instance, the marketing manager drawing up a budget who revises salespeople's projections up or down because they are known to be bullish or bearish.

Students also learn about the often-decisive role played by people's expectations. Suppose, Professor David Bell told a seminar, that your boss announces that he's delighted with your performance over the past year and is giving you a $5,000 bonus. Are you pleased? If you weren't expecting a bonus, naturally you would be delighted, but if you were counting on a $10,000 bonus, you would be disappointed. In other words, your satisfaction with the bonus will depend on your expectations beforehand, and the higher your expectations, the greater your probable disappointment. In organizations and markets there are countless parallels, from reactions to plant closings to responses to product warranties.

Students learn, too, about the often-decisive role of values in perceptions of a problem. At a B-school colloquium on decision analysis, I heard David Bell and Professor Howard Raiffa give this example:

A new strain of flu comes on the scene. According to reports in the media, it will probably kill 600 people this year. Worried about getting the disease, you find you have a choice of two vaccines. Vaccine X, according to public health experts, will save about 200 people. Vaccine Y, they say, has a one-third chance of saving all 600 people, and a two-thirds chance of saving no people. Which do you choose?

Now let us say that the question is presented to you in a different way. You are told that vaccine X will result in the deaths of about 400 people, while Y will create a one-third chance that none of them will die, and a two-thirds chance that all will die. Do you choose the same one this time?

Most people, reported the professors, reverse their decision. Because the problem is presented to them in terms of lives *lost* instead of lives *saved,* they go for vaccine X instead of Y the second time around, or Y instead of X. Yet the problem posed is *exactly the same.* The point, as students are quick to see, is that the response to a question often depends on how the question is presented. Intuitively, many managers know this—and smart professional communicators apply the knowledge continually. Managers are better off if they know exactly what is going on.

In managerial economics, instructors also talk about the subtle tricks our imaginations can play on us. Probability is a case in point. In one class I saw the instructor demonstrate that the probability of two things occurring at once is no greater than the probability of either one occurring alone. The discussion made it clear, however, that people tend to rate the probability of an earthquake and a flood occurring together as greater than the probability of a flood occurring alone. Why? Well, one student said, the conclusion may be logically unsound—but people imagine an earthquake leading to a flood (sometimes it happens). The instructor agreed. The error, he said, is called the "conjunction fallacy." Wise managers will look for this phenomenon, too, when analyzing communications and public opinion.

PRACTICAL CONFLICTS AND DILEMMAS

Beneath the veneer of professionalism, slick presentations, and facile manipulation of numbers, the experts who influence organizations often are torn between conflicting interests, and their know-how allows them to go either way. In all courses the faculty wants students to learn this, not for the sake of making judgments about financial interests but to appreciate the practical dilemmas

· these experts have to live with and the effect this may have on the management employing them. One professor gave me this example:

Suppose your company is a "glamour" company that needs funds from the market. How should the shares be priced? Now, textbooks make valuation of a firm a fairly straightforward task. You can estimate the value of the assets or what they can be sold for; you can compare market prices received for similar outfits; and/or you can capitalize the firm's earning power and estimate its dividend potential. What could be simpler?

In practice, however, the investment banker whom you entrust with floating the new stock issue may have to choose between extremes. Each approach contains numerous assumptions and predictions of the future, as indicated earlier; what is more, the investment banker may get quite different results depending on the valuation approach chosen. In the meantime, the banker sees two routes that can be taken, either of which can be supported but one of which may appeal more to him or her—or to the investment bank—for personal reasons. If the stock is offered at a high price, ownership and earnings will be diluted as little as possible; if the offering is made at a low price, the probability is greater that the stock price will rise after the issue. Your investment banker may argue hard for one route or the other, but if he or she were completely objective, it could go either way. Be aware of this possibility.

For a second example, let me take you to a Control class I sat in on. The students discussed a case involving a certified public accountant who was auditing a company in financial difficulty. Despite smoke screens of conflicting data and testimony, the instructor skillfully led the section through the financial statements and verbiage to see a couple of things that were going on. Management was putting pressure on the CPA to show the company in the most favorable light within the limits of minimum acceptable accounting practices. The CPA was of two minds about how to report the situation, for he saw many problems. On the one hand, he felt an obligation to warn investors and lenders; on the other hand, he realized that if he was too strict in reporting, the company could be thrown into worse difficulty, perhaps even bankruptcy, and nobody wanted that to happen.

The company's head was screaming at the auditor and threatening to find another firm. As might be expected, the CPA yielded to this pressure. But nobody went scot-free. Later the company was sued and the auditor had to defend his statement.

Professors in Control tell me that this and other cases illustrate a couple of important things in the business world. One is the difference between auditing and other professions. In medicine, law, the ministry, and other fields, the professional's sole job is to help his or her client. Not so in accounting. In accounting, CPAs are responsible for protecting the *public* from their clients. However, management can use a lot of clout on auditors, since it pays their fees. In consequence, accountants usually do not hold their clients to more than the minimum standards required by the profession. In a large part of business, in fact, minimum acceptable accounting standards are the norm.

Some suggestions. Thus, students see a multitude of ways of treating figures and arguing for different points of view when there are conflicts to resolve. The faculty encourages no illusion that management is a pat art. It is therefore up to the would-be manager to argue potently and persuasively for the viewpoint he or she likes. One instructor told me that he makes these suggestions to students:

- Use your imagination in choosing among the alternatives that can be considered in a problem, but don't select so many that you bog down before you begin.
- Don't expect everyone to agree with your conclusion simply because you have supported it with carefully worked out figures. You still have to sell your conclusion to those who must act on it, and that may take a little thought.
- Be realistic about the margin of error in any calculation involving the future. No matter how thoughtfully you or others have made the calculation, it may be off the mark when events unfold.

- Many people tend to underestimate the cost of doing something new because they cannot foresee all the consequences. Assure them you have studied the possible consequences and demonstrate this in your presentation.
- Often you will find it easier to work with total costs than with unit costs. This is because unit costs are obtained by dividing the total cost by the number of units, and both figures are subject to variation.
- Don't let someone snow you with an overwhelming number of arguments. One of them may be more important than all the others. Some may be harebrained. In short, the sheer number of arguments or reasons may be irrelevant.

PHILOSOPHIES AND BIASES

Just as the management world has biases, so does the HBS faculty. In the finance, control, and managerial economics areas, five stand out in my mind. Depending on your viewpoint, these will either be heartwarming or worrisome.

Financial theory. Financial executives should know the theory of markets, valuation, and the rest, say professors, but more as a point of departure than as a provider of answers. The capital asset pricing model mentioned earlier is a good example. It has practical and theoretical uses, but the applications are limited. The model was spawned in the rarefied atmosphere of financial theory, professors tell me. It is based on unrealistic assumptions and an idealistic portrayal of how financial markets operate to price securities and determine expected returns on capital investments.

After October 19, 1987—"Black Monday" on Wall Street—a financial roundtable was held at HBS. If stock exchange prices accurately reflect stock values, wondered many, how could such a drastic and sudden drop in prices occur? David Mullins agreed. "One of the 'antiefficient markets' people," he remarked, "calls the efficient market hypothesis the most remarkable mistake in the history of economic thought." After lending his weight to the suspicion that markets tend to run away from real values, he said he suspected that not only the teaching of finance but the whole field would get a face-lifting in the years ahead.

Dividends. The finance faculty holds some strong views about dividends. It wants students to realize that corporations pay dividends for various reasons. For one thing, the board of directors represents the shareholders, and the board has a legal obligation to distribute earnings when it can. For another, dividends support a high market price for the stock, which discourages corporate raiders, gives the company more value in merger negotiations, and means more money for stockholders who have to sell their shares.

But how large should a dividend be? For some time the prevailing belief of finance instructors has been that you should look more to the forecasted *funds flow* of the business than to its forecasted earnings to determine the answer. You can then relate the dividend payments to the estimated earnings to derive a payout ratio, if that step is necessary.

What about stock dividends? Finance professors appear generally opposed to paying them with regularity. Their investigations lead them to conclude that few recipients of stock dividends sell them, which undermines the theoretical argument that a stock dividend gives shareholders something they can convert into cash. Also, stock dividends make for clerical problems, produce annoying details to resolve both within and without the company, and create confusion among small investors. Admittedly, stock dividends have information value for some shareholders— but these shareholders, one prof told me with a wink, are mostly people who don't read their annual reports carefully.

Unions. Most instructors I know in finance and control have a bias against unions (though they may not admit it publicly). They may admire unions' efforts to stand up for workers against excessive managerial demands in mining, textiles, meat packing, and other industries. On balance, however, they see unions as restricting and constricting management's freedom to manage as it sees best, with all that means for efficiency in global economic competition.

In part this bias may arise from personal beliefs and ideologies, but it also is empirical. For example, in one case on a unionized meat packer, analysis makes it clear that the company can get out of the predicament it is in only by lowering its labor costs and relocating its plant. For all intents and purposes, this would mean liquidating the existing business and starting over. If management does this, however, the company would have to make large termination payments to employees; also, it would face a hostile union that would surely try to crucify it for thinking of such an adventure. As a result, the company would start over again with two strikes against it vis-à-vis nonunion newcomers, a revelation that startles many students and confirms in others their dim views of unions.

Cases on companies in the U.S. steel industry also fortify the prejudice against unions. I remember one class where the consensus was clear that over the years unions have negotiated wage levels that far exceed the levels that would develop in a freely competitive marketplace. These high wages have to come out of the hide of capital because the steel companies compete against foreign producers and cannot simply pass their labor costs on. Nor can the U.S. companies flee the industry—their investments in plant and equipment are enormous and make them immobile.

Mergers and acquisitions. Professors are divided over the pluses and minuses of the takeover mania. There is a growing consensus, however, that many takeovers of the type we became familiar with in the 1980s won't do the economy any good. Naturally, this belief doesn't apply to takeovers of unhealthy and poorly managed firms that need new management but to assaults on the numerous corporations that are healthy or whose managements are working hard at putting their organizations on a better keel.

At one panel discussion I attended, Professor Joseph Auerbach railed at leveraged buyouts and other forms of hostile takeover on the grounds that they were financially driven and not good for society. He elaborated:

"Let's face something: There is not one hostile acquisition that is based upon the kind of analysis we teach in business schools. The hostile acquirer doesn't know what is behind the balance sheet. He doesn't know what causes the income statement to be the way it is, and 10Q's and annual reports are not reliable for this purpose. We've all been directors; we know the problems inside the corporation. The hostile acquirer never knows them. He merely is measuring what can be financially driven for his own personal benefits." Auerbach is now retired but a good many teachers share his view.

Accountability. Perhaps the majority of professors believe that, in practice if not in ideology, top management in most blue-chip companies does not work solely for the stockholders and is not beholden solely to the profit motive. This belief challenges one of the oldest mind-sets in capitalism.

The leading spokesman for the view is Professor Gordon Donaldson, who has studied many companies closely for years. His firsthand observation clearly shows, he tells me, that financial decision making is less wedded to theories that fascinate classic capitalists than most observers think; also, it is more sensitive to a variety of constituencies (banks, suppliers, employees, etc.) than theory suggests.

He finds that in established firms top executives tend to be driven by the desire to create and conserve corporate wealth, not shareholder wealth. What is more, they make themselves accountable to various groups who can, if dissatisfied, withhold money and commitments that management badly wants. They do this not necessarily because they want to but because they have to in order to further corporate interests. Competitors, too, finds Donaldson, impose limits on what a company can do and keep it from setting goals freely.

Note that this view of accountability is descriptive, not normative; that is, it is based on what professors see and hear managers doing, not on what they as teachers feel should be the norm.

PRODUCING MORE EXPERIENTIAL LEADERS

The unwritten assumption in finance, control, and managerial economics is that economic decisions are too often based on myth and irrationality rather than facts and objectivity. The common effort of these courses is to invite leaders-to-be to share in the delights of rational analysis as a basis for policies and practices.

For young men and women heading toward economic leadership, this is an important message. U.S. firms in world-class competition don't succeed because they do things in approved ways. What counts is *performance.* It does a financial manager no good to plead that his or her debt policy passes the test of expert approval if the policy gets the organization in trouble. It is no excuse for an executive to say that he or she computed risk in the approved way if that way leads to missed opportunities.

At the B-school and other good management schools, the quantitative courses have a chastening impact on almost every student. Their message, in effect, is that we are all victims of illogical motives and outdated mind-sets about risk, investment policy, valuation, financial ratios, and other aspects of efficiency. Whiz kids, stars, geniuses, magicians—all are the imperfect results of biased training. Not one of us can afford to feel superior to new and better ways of relating cause and effect and exploring relationships. The arrogance of the person who insists on factual analysis (if that can be called arrogance) may be excusable, but not that of the person who thinks that he or she "knows the answers."

Of course, discerning executives know this. Many of them, however, had to learn reality the hard way, after many years of trial and error and *un*learning rules of thumb they had acquired from books, seminars, or school. What the B-school can do for students is open their eyes to the value of inquiry so that they can absorb experience more skillfully and rapidly. What better preparation for the rough world of competing with the best from other areas?

If you look at the boards at the end of a class, you may get the illusion that B-school students learn esoteric techniques, and that it is the techniques that get them through. The boards may be full of numbers, decision trees, special notations, and even cryptic formulas. In truth, however, none of the number-crunching courses teaches any arcane knowledge. In fact, no math beyond simple algebra is required, and any cryptic notations you may see are the instructor's shorthand for a factual relationship expressed by a student or someone in the case.

One of the advantages of the quantitative courses is that they can do this. The simple fact that numerical relationships, not popular notions, are the crucible is what makes these courses as influential as they are. The boards and exhibits are a laboratory, so to speak. The numbers express the truth or nontruth of an idea, the essence of a relationship. One fact can pull the rug out from under a whole chart of facts. One set of facts can say more than a thousand pages of exposition.

But the relationships must be valid, and the situations symbolized must be real, and that is where the inquiring mind comes in. For an economic enterprise, reality never stops changing.

> ■ *There aren't many companies that can be complacent, and the past is less and less a measure of the future when you're lending, so the need to anticipate industry changes and changes within companies has become even greater.*
>
> —PROFESSOR CHARLES WILLIAMS

GUIDES FOR NEGOTIATORS AND DECISION MAKERS

Americans are good negotiators. This is one of our strengths. Perhaps we owe our skill to our freedom. Used to speaking out, bargaining at the drop of a hat, going freely from one organization to another, we begin practicing the art as soon as we can talk. At any rate, skill in negotiating is important to economic success—often, in fact, there is no success without it. The more adept our economic leaders are at making good deals, the more worthwhile our efforts to produce and market efficiently.

The Harvard Business School and other leading management schools stress the art of negotiation in many ways. It comes up repeatedly in first- and second-year courses. At strategic points in discussion, instructors ask students to role-play. They set up formal exercises in negotiation, often simulating the effects of actions by computer. Cases show negotiating styles and the impact of various negotiations on costs, prices, and freedom of action. In the second year at the B-school a whole course (an elective) is devoted to the subject.

What does the faculty teach about this fateful art? In this short space I can do little more than hint at the principles and techniques taught. Also, let me stress again that HBS emphasizes learning rather than regurgitation—students are expected to analyze facts and weigh evidence, but the interpretation of knowledge and experience is up to them, with no requirement that they agree with the professor. Given this latitude for understanding, however, some general ideas and approaches stand out in the courses and tell us a lot about what instructors try to do.

RECOGNIZE THE HUMANITY OF NEGOTIATIONS

In his prologue to *The Art and Science of Negotiation,* Howard Raiffa reflected as follows upon his experience as director of the International Institute for Applied Systems Analysis:

"I learned the need of others to feel that they are part of the inner circle. I learned that 'gentlemen's agreements' that are not documented are fragile; that a party may be sincere about such an agreement, but that they may not be able to withstand internal pressures from objectors at home; and that because negotiators are embarrassed when they have to back away from promises made, they often become more amenable to other compromises. I learned that the boisterous atmosphere of an Austrian tavern often does far more to establish a proper ambience for negotiations than does a sedate cocktail party or dinner."

My impression from watching and listening to HBS instructors talk about negotiation is that they pay a good deal of attention to human nature. At the B-school there are, to be sure, some exercises where negotiation is fairly economic—where, let us say, a student party to an exercise never sees his or her "opponent" but bids and acts on factual knowledge only. In talking about face-to-face dealing, however, instructors try to convey the significance of human foibles, pet peeves, and biases.

When Donald Straus '40 was a visiting fellow at the B-school early in the 1980s, working with Raiffa and others on teaching negotiation, he talked to a group of us and gave the example of environmentalists confronting spokespeople from the Northeast forest products industry. At the beginning, he said, the two parties appear to be in irrevocable conflict, with each having "non-negotiable" demands. For instance, the environmentalists say that their desire to preserve the wilderness is "non-negotiable," and the industrialists say that their right to exploit the wilderness is "non-negotiable." In fact, however, such statements overstate the opposition of the two sides. Most environmentalists use forest products, and most industrialists like to vacation in places having clean air and water.

"In such a case," Straus told us, "you try to make each side aware of its common interests with the other. You might remind the environmentalist that he or she lives in a wood-frame house, enjoys fireplace fires, and publishes books made of wood fiber paper. You might remind the forest-products executive that he or she enjoys hunting and fishing in the backcountry and works for an employer who depends on renewable natural resources."

Such appeals to human mutuality won't end the conflict, emphasized Straus, who had had a lot of experience in arbitrations (among other things, he was a past president of the American Arbitration Association). But they should produce the *beginnings* of progress toward a resolution.

WORK FOR WIN-WIN SITUATIONS

Generally speaking, B-school instructors try to show students the value of creating win-win situations, if possible, instead of win-lose situations or "zero-sum games"—that is, situations where one side gets what it wants and the other side loses. Can the size of the pie be increased so that everyone gets a bigger slice? Can some common objective be advanced so that all parties come out ahead?

Professor Quinn Mills told me that the United Auto Workers–General Motors agreement of 1984 was a good example of an agreement based on shared purposes. Rather than seek wage increases, as it traditionally had, the union focused on job security. It agreed to the unusual steps of accepting bonuses instead

of contractual wage increases—a Japanese practice—and com-
mitting itself to work with management to build up the company's business. Also, the union and company set up a $1 billion
fund to assist workers in retraining, relocating, and readjusting
to dislocations caused by fierce industry competition.

As an assistant professor, David Lax organized and taught the
negotiation course in the mid-1980s. He offers the example of a
small firm with a promising new product that is negotiating with
a prospective buyer, a venture capitalist. At the beginning, each
side is dead set on having majority control of the firm's equity;
it looks like a win-lose situation. During the course of negotiations, however, it turns out that the two parties are not as much
in conflict as at first thought. What the venture capitalist wants
most of all is profits; what the firm's owner-managers want most
of all is to retain control. The stalemate can be broken by creating
two classes of stock where there has been only one class before.
The owner-managers can get a majority of the new class-A stock
with voting control, while the venture capitalist gets a majority
of the new class-B stock with greater rights to profits.

Lax points out that either side would do better if it went for
all the marbles and succeeded. The trouble with such an aggressive approach is that it may create bitterness and ill will. Also,
the chances of winning are less than with a shared-purposes
approach.

Sometimes, says Lax, negotiation can be a test of a manager's
skill in communication and persuasion. For instance, suppose
that the manager wants the office staff to work straight through
a holiday weekend. The idea is onerous. But if the manager can
get the staff to see the job as a means of advancing a good cause—
perhaps by his or her own words, perhaps by bringing in someone who can inspire the staff to look beyond the immediate
task—the chances of the staff's agreeing cheerfully are much
better.

LEARN WHAT MAKES THE OTHER SIDE TICK

To find out as much as possible about the other side, Lax suggests looking into such things as the other party's:

- Past behavior in similar settings
- Training and professional affiliation (for instance, engineers and financial analysts tend to approach a potential conflict quite differently from lawyers and insurance adjusters)
- Organizational position and affiliation
- Objects of admiration, people sought for advice, etc.

If possible, learn the other party's *reservation value,* that is, the minimum it will settle for or, more precisely, the value it would get if no agreement were reached. If you can't get reasonably good information, it may be wise to let the other party make the initial offer when you sit down at the table to negotiate. This tactic is useful because it may give you valuable information about the other side's perceptions. Also, if you open without knowing the other side's reservation value, your initial offer may well be too high or too low.

In his book *Going for It!* Victor Kiam '51, who is head of Remington Products, known to millions for his TV commercials, and owner of the New England Patriots, talks mostly about negotiations. He describes his attempt to buy a man's business. The talks had come to a stalemate. Kiam, who believes in keeping his eyes open to all information about the other side's habits and interests, got to talking with the owner-manager's relatives and friends. He learned that the man was sick of business and wanted to sell his firm for a certain amount. Using this information, Kiam made a successful offer at the next negotiating session and completed the deal.

PUT YOURSELF IN THE OTHER SIDE'S SHOES

This idea, which is related to the one just described, is a favorite of many professors. Learning from experience, veteran negotiators take this step habitually and credit it with part of their success; students, on the other hand, tend to be self-centered and need to be thrust into the other side's position.

Laurie Leonard '77 told me how such an experience opened her eyes at HBS. The head of station WMTV in Madison, Wisconsin, recalled:

"I remember a second-year labor-relations class with about half the students MBAs and half union stewards attending another Harvard program, the Trade Union Program. They were heads of the meatcutters' union, boilermakers' union, and whatever. At one point in the class we conducted mock negotiations for a union contract. The faculty made it as real as possible, sending telegrams to our houses saying what the other side acknowledged, and so on. You had to get together with your team and decide what you were going to do.

"The interesting thing was that they made the MBA students be members of the union, in the negotiations, and the union people be management. We learned much about how and what the other side thinks because we had to *be* the other side. The exercise lasted several days."

SHAPE THE OTHER SIDE'S EXPECTATIONS ABOUT WHAT IT CAN GET FROM THE NEGOTIATIONS

This is relatively easy to do if you can exploit the media, as U.S. and Soviet negotiators often do before a meeting, staking out positions, "leaking" confidential information, and so on. It is not so easy in many private negotiations. Here you may need to turn to middlemen, skillful wording of letters, a few lines in a speech, and so on.

Lax gives the example of a company head who wants desperately to sell his company. A prospective buyer comes into view. Knowing the company head's desires, the buyer shows modest interest, even though he or she may be *very* interested. For instance, the buyer may feign indifference over the telephone, or nonchalantly defer for a month a meeting with the company head to discuss a sale. In so doing the buyer sends a message: You're going to have to interest me with a low price offer.

DON'T GET CAUGHT UP IN OUTRAGEOUS PROPOSALS

Although Henry Kissinger, a fine negotiator, once opined that the initial proposition should be outrageous (giving more leeway to compromise), Lax and other B-school instructors are wary of this tactic. They tell me it is risky in that it may sour the atmosphere or damage your credibility when you get down to brass tacks. "Your initial offer should be optimistic but realistic," one professor told me.

What if the other side buys Kissinger's advice and opens with what you consider to be an outrageous offer? "You can act offended or even a little insulted," I was told, "but don't overreact. Don't walk away from the table. Try to divert attention from it by making a more realistic counteroffer."

In sum, skill in negotiations demands ingenuity and innovativeness. For example, the resolution of the small-company sale by creating two classes of stock, as in Lax's example, calls on an aptitude for invention. But the most important requirement for negotiators may be something else: a willingness to put the game first. As one instructor put it to me, "You don't wear your feelings on your sleeve." You look coolly at the dictates of the situation (including your position) and the personalities of the parties, and only then do you formulate your strategy. This approach comes naturally to good negotiators but for many people it is painful, unnatural, and very difficult to practice successfully.

PERSONAL STRATEGIES AND TACTICS

To conclude this series of chapters on teaching, I want to offer some guides for decision making. All these rules have been offered at one time or another by professors. All are remembered by students and alums as rules that stuck with them and got them to thinking. Sometimes the principle was offered explicitly, sometimes it came out of class discussion and questioning as gratuitous advice.

I recognize, of course, that these rules seem inconsistent with my earlier description of the school's "golden rule": its belief that wisdom cannot be told and its insistence on making students think while not trying to tell them *what* to think. It should be stressed, therefore, that these decision rules have never, so far as I know, been the subject of class discussion. They have emerged from discussion as professorial observations and asides, but they have never figured prominently in class dialogue or in the analysis of a case, been debated, or figured in an exam. The professor says, in effect, "Take it or leave it, it's just an observation. . . ."

During my talks over the years with instructors, students, and alums, I have heard seven guides mentioned most often:

1. Don't make a decision until you have to. This may sound at first like an excuse to procrastinate. Also, it appears to fly in the face of the wisdom of the ages. Hesiod, the ancient Greek poet, warned that the procrastinator would struggle with ruin; and Benjamin Franklin had Poor Richard say, "Never leave that till tomorrow which you can do today."

But this rule isn't a justification for putting off a hard decision. It simply says that there may be a value in delay that should be weighed against the value of deciding now instead of later. It also says that it doesn't pay to make as many advance decisions as possible in order to get peace of mind. That's not a good way to relieve yourself of anxiety. Good decision makers are able to put up with the tension and uncertainty of not deciding something until they have to.

When do you have to make a decision? It all depends. Sometimes the time comes when further delay would mean paralyzing people who should be working. Sometimes it comes when delay would mean losing a great opportunity. Sometimes it comes when directors or investors get agitated about inaction—or when your boss gets upset. You have to weigh such consequences, I remember Professor Stephen Fuller once explaining, against the value of delay.

As for the value of delay, that, too, is a judgment call. If you can specify exactly what information you may be able to get and what difference it would make to your decision, and also specify where and when you think you can get the data, you can make a better judgment as to the value of delay. How much better might your decision be? The question is whether that betterness is worth waiting for. For example, if you hold off on deciding between accepting A's offer or B's, you may be able to gain information from certain friends about A or B that will change the complexion of the offers, and the delay will not be costly. On the other hand, you may not have the luxury of delaying a decision between the offers of C and D; it may be quite important to take one of them *now*.

2. Something worth doing isn't necessarily worth doing well. This rule practically crawls out of the woodwork at the B-school. Instructors mention it in subtle and not-so-subtle ways. Many feel deeply about it because they themselves have to practice it in their busy lives. The rule also appears in the cases—companies and executives, knowing they can't do everything as well as they might like, therefore try to focus their efforts and energies on doing a few things very well, the rest in a minimal sort of way. Yet we are brought up on the notion that "something worth doing is worth doing well," and, achievers of the HBS type being particularly gullible to that notion, it must be *un*learned at HBS.

Most students don't unlearn the fallacy by choice but by necessity. They find they can't get through otherwise—the work load forces them to set priorities. Lee Buechler '78 told me:

"Being an engineer by background, I had felt before HBS that it was always important to construct the elegant solution, which often meant giving a 110 percent effort to the last 2 percent of

the job to make sure that things turned out exactly right. One of
the most important things I learned at the school was the old
80–20 rule—that is, get 80 percent of the job done and you'll
probably make out just fine. Then go on to the next job."

3. Don't let anybody get control of you. This rule used to be
given by Professor Myles Mace when he taught at HBS; he would
mention it in the final class of the term, and many students were
impressed because it jibed with so much of the experience of the
cases. Some colleagues with whom I have discussed this rule find
it more applicable today than it ever was. It is most obviously
relevant to small-company managers, but it really applies across
the board in management life.

The rule means that you shouldn't let yourself get boxed in so
that you have to do what somebody else tells you to do. Don't put
yourself at the mercy of some boss, investor, creditor, or other
who can make you march to his or her tune. As former defense
secretary Robert McNamara '39 might say, keep your options
open so that you can change, if necessary, to some other course.

4. Don't be afraid to be wrong. This is another rule that seems
to come out of the woodwork at HBS. Instructors work hard at
getting students to stick their necks out. They have to succeed
or they won't have a lively class. "Don't worry about sticking
your necks out," Professor Robert Austin used to say, borrowing
a line from Austin Scott, the famous Harvard Law professor.
"The worst that can happen is that I'll cut them off." Professors
like Charles Williams have legendary skills at drawing students
out on limbs.

Marshall Cogan '62, chairman of Knoll International Holdings
in New York, remembers how hard it was for many of his section
mates to see the value of this rule. Until HBS, they had gotten
used to being right all the time. "The class discussions [in the first
six months] showed me that most people were reluctant to express their views because they were afraid to be wrong," he said
at his class's twenty-fifth reunion. By late winter or spring, however, they were getting used to the idea that it is not a sin to be
wrong, and were speaking more freely. Cogan thought this was

important training, that managers are likely to be more successful if they aren't afraid of trying new things and risking failure.

Gregory Copenhefer '86 told me that it was virtually impossible to go through the first and second years of the B-school without making a fool out of yourself at least once, and he cited the old adage that if you don't make at least ten mistakes a day, you're not doing anything. "If you're in an atmosphere which is supportive," he said, "you're not afraid of making the leaps that sometimes result in a fiasco."

Of course, that is the gimmick. Many of us find ourselves in situations from time to time where we are *not* supported in making mistakes, where, in fact, we are penalized for being wrong. In fact, managers often see that their best chance for leadership and control may be to keep their decision records untarnished—at least during a certain period. Even in such situations as these, however, most professors I know think the rule has validity. Maybe you can't talk about it or admit it, they say, but *in your own mind* you can be honest with yourself about ideas you once had that now seem wrong, or about a colleague's notions that now seem right. Willingness to revise one's thinking, they know, is crucial to creativity.

One of my favorite testimonials for this general viewpoint comes from Peter Drucker. Writing about Alfred Sloan, the famous head of General Motors, he related a crucial incident in the development of GM technology. When the decision was about to be made, Sloan asked his top lieutenants for their views. One by one, every executive at the table spoke in favor of going ahead. Sloan himself was known to favor the step. But he told the group the decision could not be made yet. Not until they could hear someone speak for the reasons on the other side, he said, would they be able to make up their minds wisely.

5. When you delegate, keep your hand in. This is one of the oldest rules in management, going back at least to Alexander the Great, but it is also one that each generation of managers must learn for itself. For too many managers, Professor Frank Tucker used to tell me, often with illustrations from his own business experience, delegation means, "Either I do it or you do it." That misses the point, said Tucker. Delegation means, "You do it, but I'm going to check in from time to time to be sure we're on track."

A good delegator almost always makes clear what he or she wants the delegatee to do, or what direction the subordinate is expected to move in. In fact, Professor Richard Hackman told us in a conference at the B-school a few years ago, you empower your assistant when you give him or her a clear mandate. Hackman was speaking against vague delegation. If you delegate well, you *should* say, "This is the mountain we're going to climb." What is depowering, in Hackman's opinion, is to waffle about which mountain you have in mind, or whether you want the person to climb at all. (It also is depowering to go to the other extreme and say, "Here's how I want you to cross this creek on the way to the mountain. . . .")

6. If you're wasting time, don't blame it on your boss. Don't say it's "their" fault or that "they" are in control. You—not they— are in control of what you do. "In most organizations," says a young instructor who mentions this rule to his sections, " 'they' aren't controlling your time, either."

This advice is in line with the B-school's emphasis on self-responsibility, as described earlier. If you don't have the authority you need, get it; don't ask for a paper from superiors granting you more scope. If you don't have enough able subordinates, get them—by hook or crook, if necessary. Similarly, if a stupid boss or bosses are leaving you idle or putting you on meaningless tasks, take charge and do something that *is* worthwhile.

Years ago Professor Georges Doriot, usually called General Doriot because of his career in the French army, spoke about how to avoid such frustrating experiences in the first place. The way to be successful, he told his classes, is to find a small group with whom you're compatible. Find a way of joining that group, he urged, and then do the things they really need to have done, even if it's just sweeping the floor better than it's ever been swept. Eventually, when the group is successful, you'll be successful, too.

7. *Listen to your inner voice.* This idea has become such an important part of faculty and student thinking that it is now incorporated into a second-year course that seeks to help students make better career choices. "The world is always organized to get people to do what it wants them to do," said Associate Professor Shoshana Zuboff, who taught the course in 1988, in an interview. "Self-understanding is one way to lean against all those demands." One student who took the course said that it freed him from the hang-up of thinking that he would have to go to work in Chicago, where his family lived. Paying more attention to his inner drives and interests, he decided to begin his career in a completely different section of the country.

My impression from knowing hundreds of instructors over the years is that most of them wouldn't have been teaching but for an inner voice that they listened to. On the basis of pure economics, they would have opted for careers in business. And virtually every instructor I have known has appreciated the very significant role of intuition and "sixth sense" in executives' decisions, whether they be marketers, entrepreneurs, general administrators, or something else. Often these people can't explain—at least, in logical terms—why they decided in a certain way against the evidence and advice of colleagues.

In sum, these rules for negotiation and decision making are conditional. They work for managers but not necessarily nonmanagers. They work for bright, committed people but not necessarily for dolts. They work if tempered by discernment and experience but not if applied blindly. The decision not to try to do everything well, for example, depends on deciding wisely what one's priorities are; likewise, the judgment to recognize personal interests in negotiations must not be carried imprudently far.

So what value are such rules? Who needs them? If you are a bright, committed manager with experience, won't you have devised better rules to rely on than anyone on the B-school faculty can suggest?

Guides are a way of organizing experience and making sense

of it. Of course they are fallible. Of course they carry no guarantees or warranties. But they are useful reminders. They may even serve as presumptions, as rules of thumb that you can apply to a problem *unless* intuition or evidence points in another direction.

One bellwether of the thinking of our economic leaders is the presumptions and rules of judgment they use. If, say, they habitually try to organize negotiations so that each side can come out ahead, or perceive with empathy what the other side's interests in a bargaining session are, or encourage pro and con views in discussing an important question, there is a good chance that they will advance the causes of their organizations. This is especially important for heads of U.S. organizations because the world looks on us as products of democracy. Other people's expectations of us are unique because of our unususal history in furthering freedom, liberty, and participation.

> ■ *These owner/presidents [members of an HBS executive program for entrepreneurs] have advanced to their present positions because of their underlying experience and judgment, not because of formal business education. The hope is that understanding of formal concepts may complement but never replace "street smarts."*
>
> —PROFESSOR PHILIP THURSTON

PART III

GOINGS-ON BACKSTAGE

THE GENTLE ART
OF TIGER-TAMING

Late in 1985 Andrall E. Pearson '47, president of PepsiCo and once described by *Fortune* magazine as "the quintessential professional manager," left the corporate suite and joined the HBS faculty. He described his appointment as being roughly equivalent to an invitation "to join the Church as a cardinal." He told a writer for the *HBS Bulletin* that he knew he would have to change many of his ways. "I'm going to have to convert myself from a directive environment to an indirective one. It's not something that can be achieved simply by willing yourself from one world to another overnight; it's something I'm going to have to work at."

Pearson realized how different the world of teaching is from the worlds taught about. Outsiders often don't appreciate this difference and its enormity. How many executives you hear saying that one day they will leave business, go to Harvard or Evanston or Stanford to teach, and pass on their hard-earned wisdom to aspiring students! It can't be done—not at HBS, not at other leading management schools. I don't mean that a career as an executive keeps one from being a good teacher, for that is not true. During my years at HBS I saw more than a dozen top executives forsake their careers in business and government, come to Boston, and succeed in the classroom. But these people succeeded not because of their track records in management but because of other qualities.

If life in the pit is different, so is life at committee meetings and in the office. Things just aren't organized as they are in business— the atmosphere is collegial, different cognitive skills are required, a different sort of parrying and responding is emphasized, there is some authority and sense of team discipline but nowhere near the extent usually found in business and government organizations.

And if life in the office and conference room is different from life in business, so is the kind of politics played. Politics is very much in evidence, and it is very important, sometimes altering, as we shall see, the academic structure as well as individual careers, but it is different in quality and degree from politics in organizations.

What are some of these differences, and how do they affect the ability of the B-school to mold economic leaders? In this chapter, we will focus on the professorial life. It is not what the public usually assumes it is.

HELL AND A HALF

Once at the faculty lunch table several professors were lamenting the perils of pedagogy. The man sitting next to me listened quietly for a while, then told of a student who had trudged into his office and wailed, "It's hell to be a student here, professor." Scarcely flicking an eyelid, the professor said, "I told him that if it's hell to be a student, it's hell and a half to be a professor!"

Facing a class at HBS can be a trying experience. You may be scared silly, no matter how many assurances you have received, no matter how carefully you have prepared. In a first-year section you face more than ninety bright people, all a step or more higher in the amphitheater than you, all looking down at you expectantly, and you can be sure that at least one of them knows more about the topic at hand than you do. What is more, they have an uncanny knack for seeing through pretenses, and a fiendish potential for booby-trapping an unwary instructor. In a second-year class there may be fewer people but the capacity to devastate may be even more terrifying.

What is more, many of those people looking down at you are more accomplished already in their young lives than you or your colleagues are. Olympic champions, ex-professional football players, successful entrepreneurs, superb mathematicians, inventors, erstwhile freedom fighters—you wonder why they bothered to come to the B-school! The faculty has some stars of its own, but its luster can't compare with that of the student body. On top of this, you can be sure that in a few short years—possibly sooner—most of those kids will be earning much higher salaries than you earn, even if you are a veteran and being paid near the maximum.

In truth, the B-school faculty as a body excels at only one thing, and that may be regarded with mild disdain by professors elsewhere. You can't bank it, you don't win trophies for it, it doesn't show in your *Who's Who*. That thing is teaching by the case method. I have known many instructors at HBS who couldn't manage, couldn't write, played no sport well, had no powerful friends on LaSalle Street or in Washington—but could they teach!

In the end, students come to appreciate this. They may not while agonizing over the midnight oil in the first year, but in the second year many wake up to the fact that their instruction has been superb, and out in the "real world" as alums *most* of them come to realize this fact. In the twenty-fifth reunion book of the class of 1961, one member wrote about HBS:

"I loved it,

"Unapologetically . . .

"Because it worried about how to teach

"And what was taught,

"And that was a first in my educational experience."

For most of the 185 professors at HBS, teaching is what it's all about. They devote their lives to it, they "work their asses off," as some of them put it, yet they learn never to take a class—any class—for granted. Teaching is endlessly rewarding for them, it is endlessly frustrating. It is happiness, it is despair. It is mastered, it is never mastered. It is a bouquet of violets, it is a hideous monster. It is triumph, it is defeat. It is leaving class on cloud nine, it is crawling away like a spineless worm.

Instructors study films on teaching. They analyze cases on teaching. They spend countless hours with each other discussing problems and techniques in the classroom. They ponder alone with their office or den doors locked. They go jogging in order to forget teaching, they go fishing to soliloquize about it, they sometimes rupture their home lives because of it. Whatever their faults, they don't fall into the slough that threatened to capture James Hilton's Mr. Chips: "that creeping dry rot of pedagogy which is the worst and ultimate pitfall of the profession: giving the same lessons year after year. . . ."

As soon as possible after class, instructors generally shut their office doors and scribble down a summary of the session just completed. What issues did they cover? What gaps did they leave that they hadn't intended to leave? What leads were suggested for the next class? Eventually, says Professor C. Roland Christenson, they will have a diary that they can use to critique themselves and the course.

Equally important, professors make notes on who spoke, for as we have seen, class participation is an important element of the grade (50 percent in some courses). Many instructors have an informal quota for the number of different voices they should have heard—30, in the case of one assistant professor I know, 15 or 20, in the case of another. Most professors know all students by sight after a week or so into the course—nearly 200 people for profs with two first-year sections, 30 to 100 or more people for profs teaching second-year classes. Some instructors are known for being able to commit every new name to memory before the first day of classes. Some are famous for being able to retain names and faces in mind for a long time after the event. Once at a football game I saw Professor Charles Williams recognize and call by name a student he hadn't laid eyes on for years.

A week or so before classes start, an instructor gets the stack of name cards for the students who will be in his or her section. Each card gives the student's name and some vital facts plus a photo. One young instructor told me with glee about a meeting with her section head shortly before classes were to start. (In the first year, a professor is put in charge of all who will teach a certain section.) "With a poker face he pulled the old drill on me. Did I know each student yet by heart? I told him no, I didn't—not all of them, anyway. I have trouble with names. He informed me demurely that he had memorized the names and faces of all ninety of his students the first night. Then he asked me how many Johns there were in the section. Without batting an eye I told him I wasn't sure—did he mean johns as down the hall or men's names? Men, he said. By chance I had grouped all the Johns in one pile the preceding evening, and I happened to know that there were 12 of them in the section—10 Johns, 1 Jon, and 1 Jonathan. So I answered, 12. No, that was wrong, he told me. There were 14. I told him I thought it was 12, and so we went through the list to check. When I proved that I was right, he was extremely impressed."

Once at a seminar on teaching I heard a young prof blurt out, "It makes me feel like a tiger-tamer in the circus down there. Last week they gave me a scare. I damn near lifted my chair to hold them off. . . .!"

Having heard about one prof's finesse in the pit, I attended one of his classes. It was a first-year class in finance, and when the night before I read the case assigned, my heart fell because it seemed so prosaic. In the classroom, however, I was astounded. For an hour and twenty minutes the professor ran the session with the consummate skill of a performing artist. In horn-rimmed glasses he flew back and forth between the rows and the boards. He called on people by their first names in all parts of the room, signaling to the raised hands like an orchestra conductor beckoning to instruments to play. Often there were bursts of laughter, often there was profundity. When he wanted to direct the discussion in a fresh direction, he would fire a question, and always after a question a dozen hands would shoot in the air. When a board was filled, he would run a clean one down over it or move to a side board, and when the class was ended, every bit of board space was filled as if by plan. Often he scribbled weird notations, curious abbreviations, strange polygons and cryptic numbers, but since he explained as he scribbled, the class knew what the words meant. Time after time his chalk broke, and after the class was over, I counted six broken pieces on the floor. A janitor hurried in to pick them up and wipe the boards clean for the next instructor.

Before the class began, the bespectacled professor laid out a dozen sheets of notes on his desk in the pit. I could tell that, although he had taught the case many times before, many of his notes were fresh. Some sheets contained diagrams, others had lists, still others looked like flow charts with circles, squares, and clock times. And back in his office, I knew, there were more scratch sheets with notes on the case, and at his home, still more.

In that particular session, I did not hear him once say the word *no,* nor did I see him frown. He looked constantly cheerful. He heard like a robin, never missing a voice, and he seemed to have eyes in the back of his head, for even when he went to the board to write something down, he appeared aware of what was going on behind him.

The case wasn't used the following year, which meant that all those notes would have to be filed away. What a shame! I thought. But a knowing friend of the instructor told me, "He would've made fresh notes anyway because the people and course change." Professors' offices and alcoves are crammed with files of cases no longer used, some quite successful but discarded for ones hoped to be more useful still.

Some professors are part-time acrobats. The late professor Charles Bliss became famous for a stunt of leaping up and *backward* onto the top of the table in the pit. Visiting the class of a young man I knew, I was startled to see him suddenly climb up the wall that the boards were on, clinging there like a cat with his feet on a small ledge for chalk so he could add a note to a board that had been raised rather than lower it and hide the board he was scribbling on. From the way the class tittered, I realized that he must have done this stunt several times before.

While there appears to be a little of the ham in every good instructor, not all are dramatic. In fact, some of the best are quite straightforward. They don't pace the room like tiger-tamers, their demeanor is not unusual, they don't point to raised hands like an orchestra conductor signaling instruments. Some of the profs that students like most, in fact, are not acrobatic or charismatic.

The hours of preparation required, many spent in conference with other section instructors and course heads, never cease to cause groaning and teeth gnashing at times, even though instructors know the sessions are necessary and useful. Cracks about meetings as "the favorite indoor sport around here" are common.

PERSPIRATION IN THE PIT

Once Professor Benson Shapiro told me that the one task that every good instructor at the B-school must work at is making sure that students "own" the discussion. The dialogue is theirs, not the instructor's. The responsibility for making the class go is theirs, not the instructor's. The instructor's task is to moderate, to lead. Most of the time, in his experience, the students were willing to accept that responsibility, and when they did it well, the results were wonderful to behold.

As every discerning B-school instructor knows, however, a power struggle is always going on between the pit and the rows. It is ferocious because of student "ownership" of the discussion and the classroom. In the case of Shapiro and other good instructors, this power struggle may not be in clear evidence to the outside observer visiting for the first time, but even with the most proficient teachers, it always lies beneath the surface. Looked at in adversarial terms, the instructors have such powers as cold calls, grades, better preparation for the case (thanks to section conferences, case notes, and so forth), and humor, while students have such powers as sheer numbers, mass note sharing, "strategic looping," unpreparedness, visible lack of interest, and humor. At issue, fundamentally, is who has control and authority in the classroom—and the outcome is never a foregone conclusion.

Even in the doctoral seminars I taught on written communication, where there were only ten to twenty students, all of whom were practically motivated, I was aware of gamesmanship. Most of the classes went well and were fun, but I recall one that was sludgy and apathetic. Halfway through the soporific discussion, I interrupted to ask, "What's going on here? How come nobody seems interested today?" After an awkward silence, one of the students answered, "You act as if we oughtta know more." We spent the rest of the time discussing how our mutual expectations conflicted, and what they thought I was doing that they didn't like and vice versa. I went away from that meeting properly chastened and wiser for the experience.

In the first year, when sufficiently bored or irritated, students may sail paper airplanes or throw paper balls. They may squirt each other with water pistols. They may throw doughnuts or cookies. Such childish tricks from executives-to-be! New instructors may shake their heads in consternation; veteran instructors just purse their lips. One time a student told me that, because of his seat position, he passed notes each way when students felt antipathetic to the case discussion. "I felt degraded to the rank of Western Union courier," the student said.

Sometimes students play "learning curve" games to see how many buzzwords, such as *product life cycle, strategic planning,* and *suboptimization,* they can insert into a discussion of a point. The buzzwords are likely to bear little relevance to the issue, and many a new instructor has been sorely puzzled.

One of first-year students' favorite tricks, if they can find a willing and accomplished electrician in the section, is to rewire the boards so that when the professor pushes the "up" button, a board comes down, and when he pushes the "down" button, it goes up. When and how someone accomplishes the feat is mind-boggling, but when pulled off, it invariably creates great pleasure among the students and profound consternation in the perspiring instructor.

Occasionally a student with movie film know-how will be inspired to doctor a film scheduled to be shown for class. Once a short pornographic sequence was inserted into a serious film on production methods. While the section burst into an uproar, the humiliated professor had a fit. But afterward, the prof told me, the section settled down into an exceptionally good discussion of the case.

Sometimes students pull off unusual stunts in class. At the opening of a class on a motorcycle manufacturer, two students wearing black leather jackets and dark glasses thundered into the room on a Harley-Davidson—how they got the heavy motorcycle up to the second floor of Aldrich is still a moot question. Once as a class on Federal Express opened, two students were delivered to the front of the classroom in the familiar package. Another time, to celebrate the forthcoming wedding of the professor, the students in a second-year class arranged for a belly dancer to come in and perform around the startled man.

Then there is the venerable game of "Turkey Bingo." An enterprising student distributes sheets showing the names of the leading class talkers, displayed in columns and rows as on a bingo card. Each sheet shows the names in different order. Students who buy the sheets—the charge is likely to be something like a quarter—take them into class and, as the discussion begins, check off the names of talkers. The pot goes to the first student whose checked names occur on a straight diagonal and who announces this fact in class with the coded expression (found on the sheet). The coded expression usually is something ridiculous that can have no bearing on the case discussion.

Once I attended a first-year class in which, unbeknownst to the instructor and me, Turkey Bingo was being played. At the climactic moment in the game (which also happened to be, to the instructor's chagrin, a critical point in the case discussion), a student raised his arm and fluttered it wildly. "Yes, Norma," said the instructor, expecting a breakthrough in the case discussion. She said, *"Even though Napoleon's guns were silenced at Waterloo,* professor, I believe that production line one-oh-four in this case should be . . ." Although the instructor was baffled, the students knew what was going on. They greeted the announcement with cheers, groans, and balling up their sheets and hurling them at the winner.

Once a young professor I knew was bemused by the event staged in his class. What was going on? Turkey Bingo was unknown to him and hadn't yet become part of the lore that new teachers are told. From a student he learned the answer and was told how the game was played. Ah! he thought. Not wishing to have the incident repeated, he drew up a sheet of frequent talkers before the next class and, when he had a diagonal formed, shouted "Bingo!" at the startled class. When he told them what he had done, they gave him a laughing ovation—and didn't play the game again.

There are many other stories about imaginative professorial responses to student unrest. According to legend, Professor Thomas Raymond was disturbed by negative student reaction to a new course he was teaching. Only a couple of weeks had passed, yet students were lambasting the course from every angle and at every opportunity. So the wily Raymond put his thinking cap on. Opening the next class with some announcements, before the discussion of the case began, he said poker-faced that he now had the students' grades for the course if any wished to see them. Silence. One puzzled student asked, "How can you give us grades for the course after only a half-dozen classes?" Raymond replied, "Well, you people have graded the course after only a half-dozen cases."

In her book on her MBA years, *Toughing It Out at Harvard,* Fran Henry describes how she went to one professor's office and berated him for his toughness on certain members of her section. "Why do you have to be so tough with us? You made us feel like you were some kind of dictator." The instructor replied, "Well, I appreciate your opinion, and all I can say is that it's damn hard to be trying to control all of you."

Lest I give the impression that power struggling is a constant way of life in the HBS classroom, let me stress that many instructors can give heartwarming examples of just the opposite: student-professorial cooperation. These examples bear out Shapiro's earlier-quoted statement about "ownership," showing how students can and do assume responsibility for classroom operations. R. Lee Buechler told me about this experience in his second year:

"I can't remember the name of the case, but it involved an entrepreneur, and the professor came to class with a very sore throat. He called on a volunteer from class to lead the discussion, while he sat to one side. The volunteer came down into the pit to lead the class, but nobody seemed ready to talk. I'd figured the case out before class, so I began answering the questions that the student instructor posed. We established a tremendous dialogue over the course of the class. Every so often I glanced at the professor to see how he thought things were going, and he looked pleased as punch. It was fun and a very rewarding experience for me to have such an in-depth discussion and pull the fat out of the fire for the professor. After class I got congratulations from many students. The professor came over to me and said, 'You figured that case out well and picked up all the points in it.' Those kinds of strokes don't happen very often!"

ONWARD AND UPWARD OR OUTWARD

It is almost impossible to tell a good teacher in advance. One or more duds or lemons in the pit turn up almost every year, often confounding the sweet expectations of senior professors who had lured them to Boston.

It is astonishing how fast the word gets around that so-and-so's classes are great or grisly. The instructor who doesn't measure up doesn't teach again—up or out is the rule. In most cases this happens with assistant and associate professors, who don't have tenure, so they simply can be let go, but if by any chance a professor with tenure turns sour, he or she can be switched to research.

What happens if a tenured professor becomes more interested in outside consulting than in teaching, or offends the faculty and administration with egregious acts? In such event, the dean can counsel the offender behind closed doors, suggesting that it would be better if the person resigned and left with dignity. If not, the dean can make life miserable for him or her—lousy assignments, wretched secretarial help, refusal of routine requests to travel, and so forth. In more than one case I know of, deans have quietly forced resignations in such a manner.

If instructors show promise, how are they promoted? Generally speaking, there are three criteria. The most important two over the years have been teaching ability and written work, which includes research output and course development. On at least one of these yardsticks the school wants excellence; on the other, superior performance. If you are privy to the process, however, you soon realize that decisions aren't mechanical. The faculty and administration want a candidate to demonstrate excellence, but the particular mix of proofs varies from person to person. For instance, one person may be just a "good" teacher in the classroom but may have developed superb cases or developed a new course with outstanding prowess, while another may be less strong at case or course development but a genius in the classroom. Both may be rated "excellent" by peers and observers.

The third criterion is congeniality and "fit" in the instructor's area, which can mean what the faculty wants it to mean. In general, this criterion has to do with the fact that professors serve long hours on many committees, and ask each other for help in numerous ways, so they want this part of their life to be constructive and creative as well as friendly.

Two of the three professorial levels, assistant professor and associate professor, are nontenured; only full professors are tenured. Generally speaking, in perhaps the majority of cases new instructors begin at the assistant professor level with a three-year appointment. After the person has worked at HBS for a year or two, the department decides to continue him or her for a second three-year term if the person has demonstrated superior teaching and/or research skill and has managed to keep any real black marks from the record.

In the second term, a subcommittee is appointed to assess the candidate's record, and that subcommittee makes a recommendation to the faculty to promote or not promote to associate professor. The recommendation is given at a closed meeting of full professors that is likely to be held on a Saturday morning in some well-guarded classroom of Aldrich.

As a general rule, if the candidate survives this vetting and goes on to an associate professorship, where the normal term is five years, the same basic process recurs near the end of the term, only this time the scrutiny and arguments are more intensive and time-consuming; since the issue is full professorship and tenure, the act is irrevocable. The scrutiny and argument are not as exhaustive as for a person nominated to the U.S. Supreme Court, perhaps, but they are the next thing to it.

Increasingly, full professors come not from the pool of associate professors but from executives and academics at other institutions. Thus, nearly one-third of twenty tenure awards in the 1986–1989 period came from outside.

"Of each year's heavily screened pool of new hires," reported Alane Bertsche '90 in a recent issue of *The Harbus News,* after talks with Professors Dwight Crane and Ronald Fox, "half will make it to the associate professor level, and a quarter will become full professors with tenure."

In all cases, the promotion process begins with a faculty committee—one full professor from the candidate's area, three professors from other areas, and the dean for faculty development. These people review the candidate's credentials and organize a group of experts both inside and outside Harvard to rate the person's written work.

Recommendations for promotion to the top go to the university president and corporation, which is a five-person body with ultimate power at the university, roughly analogous to a board of directors. Harvard is the oldest corporation in America.

An interesting wrinkle in the process is that the dean is not necessarily bound by the vote of the faculty. He can, if he wants, turn down a recommendation—or recommend to the president and corporation that a person not voted for by the faculty but supported, say, by the examining subcommittee and/or a strong department chairman *be* appointed full professor.

The president and corporation habitually accept the recommendations of the dean, but always they can, if they see best, reject a recommendation. This is one of the few important powers that the president and corporation hold over a dean, and it is a compelling reason why deans, despite their independence and autonomy, always smile at the president when they pass him in Harvard Yard.

BREAKING OUT OF THE CAGE

To be sure, this procedure is fraught with shoals, shallows, Scyllae, and Charybdi. On the other hand, it is clear and visible. Harvard is as subject as any university to petty and not-so-petty politics, but at least there is clear accountability for promotion, and this is not always the case in academe. "Would that it were that way here" is a lament that I have heard uttered many times by deans and professors of other institutions.

For a nine-month year (September through May) a full prof at the B-school can get up to $105,000. Although this isn't comparable to what a good person can get in top management in industry, it is a lot better than things used to be at HBS. In 1910 the starting salary was $2,144; the highest, somewhere around $5,000. In the mid-1920s the maximum pay for a full professor rocketed to a breathtaking $8,000, at least after fifteen or more years of service. In those days the school must have taken to heart Ralph Waldo Emerson's maxim that "money often costs too much."

As a general rule, professors at all levels supplement their income handsomely from consulting, workshop teaching, directorships, and special posts. "Anytime that I don't earn twice as much as my salary from outside work," confided one tenured prof I know, "something is wrong." For most instructors this overstates the case, but the point remains that consulting is not pin money for the HBS faculty, it is fairly big bucks. A professor who lives on his or her salary is as rare as a Swiss admiral.

In setting fees for consulting and speaking, the majority of professors operate in a reasonable range for a prestigious institution, but some ask (and get) fees that border on the obscene— $25,000 for a banquet address, a six-figure sum for a retainer. As one professorial friend quipped, "Ivan Boesky is alive and well and living at HBS."

Another distinguishing feature of the B-school faculty is that fewer than half of the 200 or so professors have tenure. (In other graduate management schools the proportion is usually much larger.) Moreover, the odds on any one new instructor's gaining tenure are lengthening. A quarter of a century ago, those odds weren't bad; today they are not favorable.

The best-read information in faculty circles—at least those concerned with the second year—is not the *Harvard Business Review*, memos from the dean, or some economic forecast, but the annual student ratings of second-year courses that appear in *The Harbus News*. "In the old days they had the rack," a professor once grumbled to me. "Now they have the student ratings." After a course is over, students rank their professor on a five-point scale for close to a dozen criteria—preparation, skill in developing class participation, and so on. The results are fed into a computer and published on a spread of the newspaper in small enough print so that all course ratings can be displayed, even if blindness is caused in readers. Contrary to a common impression, *Harbus* only publishes the data; the evaluation forms and data-processing are taken care of by the administration.

The ostensible purpose of the ratings is to help the next crop of second-years select courses (most second-year courses are elective), but the faculty also is served, for the evaluations tell it how the teachers are perceived. When a person is up for tenure, many things are considered besides his or her student ratings, but the latter are a factor. However, no professor on a selection committee can blame a wayward judgment on the ratings, for committee members value their own opinions of one's teaching ability over popularity ratings.

Thus, promotion is a traumatic experience for assistant and associate professors. They are continually under observation and are conscious of it. They work amazingly long hours, prepare with extra diligence for class, spill their cerebral cortexes on research projects, struggle to publish, turn up punctually and conscientiously prepared for countless committee meetings, lie awake at night worrying about gaffes and possible gaffes committed, make every effort to please their seniors, and worry about worrying. Often you can see the strain they are under—bags under their eyes, shaky hands, family stress.

But the pit and the promotion arena are not the only places at HBS where the temperature often runs high. The continual questioning and challenging that go on—admissions policies, courses, the work load, facilities, case development, and so on—embroil everyone in controversy. In the past decade alone the curricula for both the first and second years have been changed several times, student work loads have been reduced, field studies have been enlarged, computers have become required hardware for students, hundreds of cases have been computerized, living halls have been altered and renovated, a new building has gone up (and the name of another has been changed—from Anderson House to Loeb, after Robert B. Anderson was convicted of tax fraud), and other major moves have been made.

In the words of Dean John McArthur, the aim has been to do more than "repot"; it has been to "break out of our traditional intellectual cages." All this has added excitement and stimulation, but at the same time many profs have found themselves suddenly fighting for their courses and careers. As Harvard university president Derek Bok noted in 1979, in his annual report, no part of the university practices the relentless self-scrutiny it preaches like the B-school does.

Withal, there are compensations. One is the faculty club. On the second floor of Kresge Hall, it is a large and cheerful area with spacious windows overlooking the Charles River. Tables are wood, with pretty place mats and flowers. People take trays and stand in line for their food, and there are both hot- and cold-food counters. Between the dining area and the stairs are two spacious lounges with fireplaces. The first has a handsome clock over the mantel, an enormous oriental carpet, leather chairs and sofas, ornate brass chandeliers overhead, a silver coffee urn, and a bowl of colored candies. For up to an hour after lunch, this lounge is generally filled with groups discussing matters of mutual interest or with professors poring over newspapers.

Faculty meetings are usually lively. They are held in one of the seventeen classrooms in Aldrich. The dean sits at the table in the pit, the faculty sits at the row desks where students sit. The dean

is addressed simply as "John," when someone wants to speak—
not with the pompous "Mr. Dean," plus a clearing of throat, that
characterized the beginnings of remarks in years gone by. Seat-
ing is on a first-come-first-served basis; I could take a seat in the
front or back rows, depending on preference, or at the side or
middle. Occasionally at faculty meetings I would find the president sitting at a second table beside the dean. (At Harvard, when
you use the word *president* you mean the head of the university,
not the man in the White House.)

ADMITTING STUDENTS

The Admissions Department has the power to make or break the
school. If it were to admit the wrong people, class discussions
would fail, the case method would be a bust, the section system
would sputter, and alums wouldn't bring credit (and money) to
the school. Not surprisingly, therefore, the Admissions Department has a continuing dialogue with teachers and is monitored
as closely as any function of the administration. Sometimes to
accomplish these purposes the director of Admissions even
comes from the teaching faculty. Back in the 1970s, for instance,
Professor Anthony Athos headed the department. As a general
rule, however, the director is a nontenured administrator.

About one applicant in eight is admitted. What does Admissions look for in that person's application?

First and most obviously, it looks for intellectual capacity. You
don't have to be a genius to get in, but you have to be able to read
and digest large quantities of reading material, understand many
types of cases, and hold your own with the rest of your section.
Admissions also looks for the kind of person who will contribute
to class discussions. For example, a bright, outgoing person will
get the nod over a reticent intellectual with a dazzling IQ. Another quality is demonstrated interest in management. Many
bright applicants are solo performers who lack the aptitude or
interest to manage and control; they don't get in. Still another
thing Admissions looks for is the likelihood of bringing credit to
the school as an alum. A person may have all the other qualities

needed but if something in his or her record suggests a tendency to unethical conduct, the application will go into the reject pile.

The Admissions Department also looks for a balance of backgrounds in a class. It doesn't want too many students from some particular region or even from the United States (in each section, as mentioned earlier, there will be some people from foreign countries). It doesn't want too many to be ex-athletes or social activists or engineers. It doesn't want too many of one sex.

How does the department decide? The application, with its many essay-type questions, is an extremely valuable indicator; it has been been revised hundreds of times over the years and will be retuned many times again in years to come. Applicants may grind their teeth because it takes so long to fill out and write the essays required—but it is the rare person who gets admitted without working long and hard on the form.

An applicant's college and work record (all but a few people admitted have worked at least several years since college) are relevant. Also, the interview is becoming increasingly important. As of this writing, not all students are interviewed, but the school sees a day not far off when almost all applicants are interviewed.

Note that the once-famous GMATs (general management aptitude tests) are no longer part of the admissions procedure. This test was dropped in 1985, beginning with the class entering in the fall of 1986. The announcement received quite a bit of publicity, created consternation in many quarters, and caused ripples throughout management education, for HBS was the first graduate management school to drop the test.

Why did the administration discontinue the GMATs? For one thing, it found a poor relationship between test scores and performance in the MBA program; it also found little or no relation between test scores and managerial performance after graduation. During the period Admissions was debating the move, it decided on applications without considering the GMAT scores, then went back to the test scores to see if they would have made a difference. It found that only a handful of decisions would have been changed—and it was by no means sure that the changes would have been good.

To some people it is ironic that the interview was once a criterion and was discontinued. Until the mid-1950s it was part of the procedure for most applicants; at one time, in fact, the Admissions Department encouraged many of us on the faculty who didn't generally work with students to interview applicants at their place of work. Admissions discontinued the interview because it didn't feel its time and expense were justified. In the 1980s, however, the pool of applicants became older, more diverse, and harder to assess. The school wanted diversity and maturity but couldn't get at it well enough on the basis of documents alone. Therefore it resuscitated the interview.

What the school wants, Dean John McArthur told the student newspaper, are "emotionally healthy people, honest people, people who have lots of energy and get along well with others, who like to help other people and are creative." Such applicants, the school feels, are more apt to become leaders and managers. As the dean pointed out, the GMAT test scores and grade-point averages measure important qualities, but the things measured are "not the ball game in terms of what seems to be associated with people who do well in life." Rather, they are more apt to correlate with ability to do well in the quantitative courses in college.

Also, educators at HBS and other graduate management schools are concerned that applicants can prep for GMATs and make themselves look better than they really are. Preparation courses have sprouted up all over in recent years; they promise to improve applicants' test scores—and often do. Further, educators at HBS and other schools object to the fact that such courses usually are expensive and unfairly benefit applicants from well-to-do families.

ROCK OF SAGES

How does faculty life affect the B-school's mission?

For one thing, it keeps HBS from becoming a research institution and makes the school's primary purpose teaching. Research is vital, and the administration spends plenty of money on it—but the classroom comes first. That means not only class-handling but case and course development.

So what alumni *do* with their training really is the main test of the school. Graduates are the professors' surrogates in the management world, accomplishing what the teachers might accomplish if they had opted to become practitioners. Not the length of an instructor's bibliography, not the work he or she has done for prominent corporations, but the person's demonstrated ability to help students learn is what the faculty and administration value most.

For another thing, the faculty's approach gives a particular meaning to student power. We are used to thinking of student power in terms of the demonstrations at Berkeley in the 1960s or in Beijing in 1989. At the B-school, this is not the form student power takes. It is less conspicuous—but extremely potent. It shows itself every day in every class. The students in a classroom literally have the power to make the class grind to a halt if they want to. To use Shapiro's term again, they "own" the place, and they can make it or break it. The case method surely has accounted for many a miserable moment, in the rows as well as in the pit, and it exposes instructors and makes them vulnerable in a way that could not possibly happen otherwise, but at HBS it is to student power what wheels are to an automobile.

While at Harvard, thus, students taste responsibility as adults, and this experience has a profound effect. It not only speeds maturation but it opens their eyes to their possibilities as heads and members of teams. To the extent that alums succeed as entrepreneurs and executives in sizable organizations, at least a small part of the credit must go to the unique experience of power sharing in B-school classrooms.

Still another implication of faculty life is the model of responsiveness that students get used to. The men and women in the pit don't think of themselves as behavior models, but they are. The fact that they are in front of students so much and so actively makes this unavoidable. As models, they set examples of listening, attention to facts, willingness to listen to heresy, and interest in problem solving that students rarely have seen before—and will not often see again. Almost every talk I have had with alums attests to this influence. Students see, hear, remember, and are moved. They may or may not become successful emulators, or even want to be, but the images stay with them for a long time.

THE SHORT, HAPPY LIFE OF *HBR*

For a dramatic example showing the school's commitment to teaching, consider the case of the *Harvard Business Review.* While various newspapers have reported fragments of the true story, until now *HBR* and the administration have managed generally to stonewall reporters. This is unfortunate, because the *HBR* story dramatizes not ineptitude, as many believe, but a careful decision of the administration to put down an organization that was threatening to eclipse the school as a teaching institution. By cutting *HBR* off at the knees, the administration has showed the world what its top priorities are: the classroom, teaching, and case development.

As many business people know, *HBR* is published by the school, and its editorial board is composed mostly of faculty members. All board members are appointed by the dean. Most of *HBR*'s subscribers, readers, and reprint buyers are non-Harvard people, hence the magazine represents an important extension of the school's influence. The magazine is, in fact, an educational program of the school.

From 1922, when it was started, until 1947, *HBR* stumbled along as a little gray magazine with several thousand hard-core subscribers. In 1947 Dean Donald David, a gifted entrepreneur and talented executive, decided with Edward Bursk, then editor, that *HBR* might amount to something if properly pushed and promoted. In 1948 Bursk began hiring several full-time staff people in addition to himself and Virginia Fales, the managing editor: a business manager, a circulation manager, and a space salesman. In 1949 he hired me as assistant editor. In succeeding years the staff grew steadily as the magazine grew.

In 1971 Bursk left, following many disputes with the administration. He was replaced by Ralph Lewis '41, until then a partner in Arthur Young & Company; in 1980 Lewis died and was replaced by Professor Kenneth Andrews, a distinguished teacher at HBS; and near the end of 1985 the dean pulled Andrews out and replaced him with Professor Ted Levitt.

Here are a few salient facts about the stunning growth of *HBR* from 1948 to the end of 1985:

- From a paid circulation of about 10,000 in 1947, paid circulation rose to more than 243,000 in 1985. These numbers are published Audit Bureau of Circulation (ABC) numbers. In the magazine industry, ABC is generally regarded as the objective, independent authority for advertisers, readers, and analysts to rely on.

- From 1950 to 1985, the all-important renewal rate was always above 60 percent, and in the early 1980s it rose to between 65 percent and 70 percent. This unusually high renewal rate was a measure of strong readership and the importance that subscribers attached to the magazine. It also showed how effectively the business department was managing direct mail promotion (the mainstay of circulation growth).

- In 1947 *HBR* sold a thousand or so reprints of articles; in 1985 it sold about 2.5 million reprints. Reprints were a very profitable arm of the magazine; also, they extended the magazine's editorial reach much farther than the regular issues could. From a teaching standpoint, reprints were important because they were used in every first-year course as background reading, and they were sold in large numbers to management schools and training programs around the world.

- In 1947 *HBR* ran a few pages of advertising, many of them drab black-and-white "tombstone" ads. In 1985 the magazine carried 433 pages of advertising, the majority of them printed in color. From 1975 to 1985 alone the number of ad pages was up 90 percent.

- In 1947 *HBR* represented an annual deficit to the school of several thousand dollars—since 1922 it had been a constant deficit. In 1949 the B-school loaned *HBR* $100,000—a whopping sum in academe in those days. This sum was paid back by 1953, and after that *HBR* stayed handsomely in the black. From 1980 to 1985, *HBR* produced an average annual net income for the school of $2 million (the net ranged from $2.4 million in 1980 to $1.6 million in 1983).

- In 1947 *HBR* had little influence on the management world. By 1985 it had become a major force in management thinking, read more closely and seriously than ever by its growing executive circulation. The magazine's editorial influence ranged from pioneering in the explanation of such specialized techniques as discounted cash flow to philosophies such as participative management, from exploring such perennial issues as business ethics to new issues (at the time) such as equal employment opportunity, and from such venerable topics as sales management to new problems (at the time) such as U.S. failures in manufacturing.

- In 1947 the staff was amateurish and tiny—several people who, though extremely capable, weren't altogether sure of what they were doing. By 1985 the staff was strong, well integrated, and many times larger—nearly twenty editors plus more than a dozen savvy full-time people in the Business Department.

- From about 1960 to 1985, *HBR* pioneered in the frequency and techniques of editorial research—in-depth psychological studies, readership audits of particular issues, unusual subscriber questionnaires, and other approaches.

In 1985 the staff was working on half a dozen important extensions of *HBR*'s editorial reach. All signs pointed to an increasing market share, an ABC circulation of 300,000 by the end of the century or before, and a net income of $3 million. What it didn't realize, however, was that the administration had other ideas.

The administration had become very concerned about *HBR*—not its lack of success but its prodigal success. The magazine was becoming *too* influential. What had started out as a tail on the dog was now wagging the dog, or, at least, threatening to wag the dog in some areas.

Obviously, thought the administration, it was time to call a halt—to stuff the genie back in the bottle before it was too late. *HBR* was not classroom education, it was not case method education, and, worst of all, it was not closely controlled by the administration and faculty.

In the fall of 1985, therefore, the administration moved with lightning speed to alter *HBR* drastically. It changed editors. It made the head of the Business Department accountable not to the editor, as in the past, but to the dean. In turn, the new business head transferred the reprint manager, who had been physically close to the editors and almost as valuable to them as to the business staff, to another location, where he worked but part-time for *HBR* and reported instead to several administrators. As for the new editor, he forced several key members of the staff to leave.

Five actors played the main roles in this "takeover." Four of them were Harvard MBAs. None of them was new to the school.

In terms of editorial leadership, the results began showing almost immediately. For instance:

- Paid circulation dropped. As of this writing, Standard Rate and Data report the ABC figure as a tad above 200,000, but the actual current figure is supposed to be lower. (In contrast, *Fortune* and *Forbes*, perhaps the nearest magazines to *HBR* in editorial aim, were increasing their worldwide circulation during the 1985–1989 period by 6 percent and 1 percent respectively.)
- By 1989 the renewal rate had fallen to between 50 percent and 55 percent, with severe consequences for readership quality, editorial reach, and finances (each percentage point represented upward of $40,000 in circulation income).

- By 1988 the number of reprints sold had fallen from the 2.5 million sold in 1985 to 1.2 million, a drop of more than 50 percent.
- Advertising pages plummeted in 1986 and stayed miserably low in 1987 and 1988. Not until 1989 did this dismal picture begin improving. Ad revenues, according to *The New York Times,* went down substantially.
- Overall editorial influence waned. Despite expensive changes in paper quality, color printing in reprints, and artwork, and despite some fine editing, a large part of the magazine's influence evaporated.

Not surprisingly, late in 1989 a new editor, Professor Rosabeth Kanter, was appointed by the dean.

Although *HBR* has been effectively neutered as a competitor to the classroom, its net revenues apparently have been maintained. (I have to hedge on this conclusion because it is now almost impossible to get a clear financial reading—*HBR* costs and sales are buried in figures for other activities). The school accomplished this feat by making enormous price increases. The U.S. subscription price rose precipitously, from $28 a year in 1985 to $55 in 1988 to more than $60 today; reprint prices also were jacked up drastically; and advertising rates soared like a space shot at Cape Canaveral. Because of the close relationship between readership and pricing, these increases caused part of the magazine's editorial fall.

Although often regarded as an example of the old maxim that those who can, do, while those who can't, teach, the *HBR* story actually documents just the opposite: an adroit bit of maneuvering to adjust priorities. *HBR* was—and is—a piano player in a marching band. It is printed teaching, more like a lecture form than oral case-method learning in the classroom. The B-school believes in spreading its educational message by the acts and attitudes of alums, not by written communications.

The story also tells us something about HBS's financial

strength. Few schools can risk damaging a cash machine such as *HBR* had become—more than $2 million of net income annually, and rising, to say nothing of the public relations value. In fact, not too many years ago the B-school itself couldn't afford to jeopardize *HBR*; "don't fix it if it ain't broke" was the administration's attitude toward its troublesome but successful child. Today, however, the school is so affluent and has so many robust sources of income that it can curb one of its most successful enterprises.

> ▪ *If all else fails, fame can be assured by spectacular error.*
>
> —JOHN KENNETH GALBRAITH

WRITING CASES
FOR TEACHING

Sometimes people react to descriptions of the case method by saying, "In other words, instructors don't tell students anything." The implication is that teachers contribute nothing substantive to students.

In an important sense, as we have seen, that reaction is correct. In another sense, however, it is wrong. The faculty tells students quite a bit by its choice of cases to develop and teach. Each time a class studies a case and discusses it for an hour and twenty minutes it gets a glimpse of the world. Some professor or professors are telling the class, in effect, "This is what it's about out there."

In short, the faculty influences student perceptions of management in a major way. One time I was talking with a student in his room. He was about to graduate, and in the various corners of his bedroom he had stacks of cases—800 or 900, he told me, almost every one he had ever studied. As we sat there talking, it occurred to me all of a sudden that those cases were like 800 snapshots of the management world, a collage of reality as seen from HBS. The cases did not purport to reflect reality; in fact, each had a line at the bottom of the front page disclaiming any purpose but teaching. Yet the unspoken message was loud and clear.

But reality is not the only faculty consideration in case development. If it were, the cases stacked in that student's room would have been quite different. Professors have another criterion, and it influences their choices continually: stimulation. As Professor David Hawkins once pointed out to a group of us, "The students are quick to tell you if you are not challenging them." So those who design courses are ever mindful of a case's potential to catch and hold student attention, to provide them with the feeling of moving forward and covering new ground. Instructors also imagine themselves teaching the case. "Will the class find it a dog, so that I've got to practically whip them?" a finance professor told me. "Or will they enjoy talking about it and make my job easy?"

In practice the two criteria—reality and stimulation—are not always consistent. One result is that there is always a quiet tug-of-war going on between what different instructors think should be taught in a course. Another result is the amount and quality of impact that the school has on managers-to-be.

FROM CONCEPTION TO GESTATION

When you first look at a B-school case, printed single-spaced on plain white paper, you may be unimpressed with its physical appearance. But if cases could talk, they might echo Dolly Parton's words and tell the student, "You would be amazed to know how much it costs to make me look this cheap."

Some cases don't cost much over $1,000, in today's currency, even when overhead is allocated. However, many cost 15 or 20 times that much or more, a sobering fact when one remembers that several hundred may be developed in a year. (In the academic year of 1986–1987, for instance, 314 field-based cases were developed by the faculty and staff.) Moreover, some never get taught after being produced, others get taught once or twice and are then discarded, and still others have to be revised because of shortcomings discovered in class.

Students don't see such trials and errors, nor do they see the enormous amount of time and effort that go into the making of a typical case and preparations for teaching it. They would be stupefied if they did. For students, a case has a life of one day and then gets tossed into a cardboard box in the corner. In a moment of irritation, one student muttered to me, "They don't even make good toilet paper."

How is a case made? Cases A and B on Chaparral Steel illustrate many of the principles (though the exact processes necessary to develop cases vary widely).

A few years ago Karen Freeze, a researcher and case writer at HBS, wrote a case—actually, a pair of cases—on Chaparral Steel Company. She wrote under the supervision of Professor Kim Clark, an energetic young man who teaches Production and Operations Management with a sense of mission, and the cases were intended originally for teaching in his first-year course.

Recalling the experience in an article in the *HBS Bulletin,* Freeze says it began when Clark told her one day, "We've got a great case on a minimill down in Texas. Chaparral Steel near Dallas." Freeze asked, "Dallas?" She had never been near Texas, and stereotypes began flashing through her mind—swaggering cowboys, decadence, nouveaux-riches socialites, and so on. Clark answered, "Midlothian, actually." When Freeze asked, "Mid-what?" Clark explained, "That's the town where they're located. I visited them last year, and found them to be some of the craziest and most innovative people around. You'll have a great time doing the cases."

Clark had gotten to know Gordon Forward, chief executive of the company, and wangled an invitation to start the case project. He thought the company situation would challenge students as well as show them that U.S. steel companies, while not doing well collectively as an industry, *could* compete with the best in the world.

So Freeze unfroze, learned something about the steel industry, studied materials sent by Chaparral, and went to the company site in Midlothian. She interviewed many employees at length, watched many processes over and over, and wrote copious notes—thirty-three single-spaced pages. In the heat of the mill she began to see the light for the classroom. The notes were full of questions to herself such as "I don't really understand this" and "What's that?"

Back in Boston, she drafted an A case, which described Chaparral's operations and secrets of high productivity, and a B case, which looked at the company's markets and customers and asked the question whether, if productive capacity were doubled, buyers could be found for the extra steel. She gave the drafts to Clark. Going over them with a fine-tooth comb, he would scribble in the margins such lighthearted comments as "What in the world do you mean by this?" or "We need more data on this operation."

After many amendments and alterations, the cases were sent to Texas for approval. In her account Freeze notes, "This [the time when release is sought] is always a tense moment for the case writer. Weeks, even months, of work rest on the company's willingness to release the case. At HBS a whole department of watchdogs very strictly monitors confidentiality and will not let us, under any circumstances, distribute a case to students without written permission from the appropriate company executive." (Once I wrote a case that couldn't be released, so that all my work on it went down the drain. Many HBS faculty people know the experience well.)

Approval was first given, then withdrawn; Forward decided he didn't want to be in the limelight yet, therefore thought that the cases should be disguised. A loud groan arose in Boston. "Already in my post-case recovery mode, exhausted, I could hardly face the idea," says Freeze in her reminiscence. "I had never disguised a case before (and never since), and didn't know where I would find the imagination and energy to do so." But she did, with some noble assists from Clark and others. *Texas* was changed to *Oklahoma*, pseudonyms were invented for the names of people in the case, the company became *Red River Steel*, and so on.

Off by mail to Midlothian again. Finally approval came, the cases were printed, teaching notes were added, sessions with instructors were hastily scheduled, and both A and B finally saw the light of classrooms. Ironically, Chaparral's CEO immediately broke the disguise by visiting and talking in several classes. He also wrote an article that was published happily in the *Harvard Business Review.*

The cases have been taught with great success in the MBA program, a couple of executive programs at HBS, and in schools and training programs elsewhere. In the latest revision, the disguises have been dropped and the cases appear under Chaparral's name.

PITFALLS AND PRATFALLS

The B-school's ability to commit resources lavishly in the manner described is one of its great strategic advantages in management education. A few years ago the first-year course on business and government in the international economy spent months to develop materials on Chinese economic planning—and the materials were used for but one class. That is unusual, of course, but it shows what the faculty is willing and able to do if the occasion demands.

In view of the uncertainties of release, professors and case writers carefully review with the appropriate executives what they plan to write and what they expect the company or other organization to do when the draft is ready. Even with the most careful groundwork, however, things can go awry—and for unanticipated reasons.

For example, early in the 1980s Professor Quinn Mills was teaching a second-year personnel course with an assistant named James Medoff. Searching for a case to plug a certain gap in the course, Mills spoke to about fifty people and called a number of companies. "I was fishing," he told a reporter for *The Wall Street Journal.* "I had a lot of lines out." Medoff, who also was fishing, finally got the bite: The Norton Company had developed an interesting incentive pay system that had the right elements for a case.

So Mills and Medoff went to work. They made numerous plant visits, got reams of data from Norton, procured details on the plan, and so on. In the end they produced a thirty-page write-up and sent it to Norton for release. In due time the write-up came back to them, approved with minor changes. Mills might have celebrated, he told me, but for a hitch: Norton released the case for teaching in Medoff's section only, not in Mills's (the course had two sections). The reason Norton gave was that thirty trade union officials sat in Mills's class. The company's top executives felt that the union officials might distort the case and report the pay system unfairly to other union people. "We wanted the discussion to fairly represent the company," said one Norton executive.

"Had there been more time," said Mills, "I would have invited Norton officials to a class. I would have tried to convince them that the union officials wouldn't use the material outside of class." But there wasn't time, so Mills had to swallow hard and use another case for his section while Medoff happily taught the new case to his group.

Sometimes a new case looks good on paper but wilts in use. One B-school professor told me about an executive-program experience that he fervently hopes will not reoccur:

"The new case was about an elaborate manpower scheduling plan that the headquarters staff of a large company was going to require the heads of operating divisions to complete. I thought the case was going to be okay. Well, in my first class the first person who spoke started off with an elaborate speech about what a bunch of crap the case was and the ridiculousness of the school assigning it for discussion. He spoke for several minutes (it seemed a lot longer to me). To tell the truth, I found his arguments compelling. I didn't know what to do. In an effort to buy time to think, I told a joke that I had reserved for possible use at the end of the class. Then I asked if there wasn't someone in the room who would be willing to argue for the manpower plan. One student made a halfhearted attempt to do so. It was a long hour and twenty minutes, let me tell you!"

"PROFESSORS CAN DO ANYTHING"

The B-school currently has close to ten thousand cases in inventory. (Early in the 1980s it reportedly threw out many thousands believed to be unsuitable for teaching anymore.) In the majority of instances a teaching note is made available for instructors teaching the case. For the instructor, a teaching note is like a map for a traveler in a strange city.

The document is produced when the case is released for teaching. While nobody stamps teaching notes Top Secret or Confidential, they rarely get beyond the eyes of the faculty. Students tell me they know such things exist but don't seem to give them much thought. Teachers, on the other hand, give them a lot of thought.

Teaching notes succor instructors. In some instances that I know of, the notes have been academic salvation, enlightenment, a steadying hand in the dark. If you are the man or woman who will go into the pit in front of a bunch of bright and potentially captious students who would love to trip you up on something, a good preview of the case is well worth having. Thus, a teaching note can be a pit dog's best friend. Also, when you are reading a case for the first time, the teaching note may make the difference between the situation opening itself up to you as live, human, and interesting or settling in your mind like a tank of cement.

For example, the teaching note for "Mitek Corporation," a case referred to earlier, outlines the purposes of the case (such as getting students to think about how specific a growing company's goals should be), picks out highlights of the situation (such as the entrepreneur's facile ability to talk like a professional manager but not act like one), points up issues that will probably arise in class (such as thoughts about short product life cycles in the industry), suggests some questions that the instructor might want to organize the class discussion around (such as how the entrepreneur should respond to the criticisms of the goals statement he circulated), and predicts various reactions that an HBS class might have (such as opining that the entrepreneur acts as if he were God Almighty).

Again, the teaching note for a famous pricing case used in the Control course tells us to expect some students to say that the company should have no trouble concealing a certain pricing arrangement made with an important customer. The note tells us why such an opinion is unrealistic—because of the way the grapevine works among salespeople. (The instructor won't respond so bluntly, of course, but he or she is given the material for countering gracefully by putting a question to the student or beckoning another student to counter the opinion.) To take still another example, the teaching note for a well-known accounting case suggests what issues the instructor might write on the board and how he or she might want to have the class discuss the issues raised, in what order and with what results.

Almost always the note walks the instructor through the purposes of the case, including, in many instances, a candid reflection on why the course head or professor chose it, the main questions and issues posed, and some thoughts on teaching strategy. I have before me some case teaching notes that are only a couple of pages long; but others have extended comments, figures, diagrams, and other material running to ten or twelve pages.

Some teaching notes are as cold as a fish, but I have others in my file that are warm and human. A few, in fact, even interject a humorous note now and then. Before me is a teaching note for the case on Deere and Company, which suggests at one point that the instructor take the class back fifteen years for background, adding tongue-in-cheek, "Tell them professors are powerful and can do anything."

From the broader standpoint of the school, teaching notes are crucial to quality control. In the first year there are nine sections, and in some courses that means nine instructors (sometimes one or more instructors teach two sections, reducing the size of the teaching group for that course). In the second year you may have two or more sections for a course. Either way, you want students in different sections to cover the same main questions in a case discussion. Although you don't want to regiment the instructors and try to make them teach alike, you do want them to see the case as raising the same issues; after all, students in all sections of the course will get the same examination at the end. Also, if the case has some potholes to avoid, you want all instructors to know what to watch out for, and if experience points to some useful tricks in handling the case, you want instructors to have the benefit of that knowledge, too.

Teaching notes, other information, and instructors' views and questions after reading the case are hashed over in private sessions before the case is taught. Almost every week a calendar is distributed to faculty and staff offices with the scheduled meetings of teaching groups, and in any given week you are likely to find several such meetings listed. The meetings last from two to four hours.

VISITING CZARS AND CZARDINES

Sometimes the professor will invite the main character or characters in the case to attend the class. The instructor's motive is usually to make the case come more alive and give students a chance to hear a flesh-and-blood explanation of an action or policy. As for the visiting executives, they may be motivated by interest in outsiders' reactions, simple curiosity, vanity, or a missionary desire to recruit.

The late John Donnelly, a would-be priest who brilliantly headed the Donnelly Corporation for many years, sat in on several classes about his company in the hope of gaining useful insights about operations. A modest and unostentatious man whose company ways appealed greatly to students, he fielded many questions after the case discussions and spoke candidly about several dilemmas on his mind. "It was like a consulting experience," he told me afterward. Not all visitors impress students as much as Donnelly did, but the success of his appearance is typical. Most professors have had positive experiences with visitors.

Occasionally, however, both professor and students can't usher the visitor to the exit fast enough. This was the case a few years ago when an associate professor invited a corporate head to attend his business policy class and comment on the discussion. Instead of adding a fillip to discussion, the visiting czar turned off everyone as soon as he opened his mouth. His language was needlessly coarse, he said sarcastically that he wouldn't need any B-school "superstars" to consult at *his* plants, and he exhibited a chip-on-the-shoulder attitude toward Harvard while flaunting his own degree from a lesser-known college. "I wanted to crawl out of sight," the chagrined professor told me. A fine teacher, he explained that he had talked to the man at his company and gained no premonition that he would bomb in class. (With his usual aplomb, the professor managed a rebound the next day by asking the class to reflect on the disastrous episode and discuss the qualities of corporate leadership.)

On some memorable occasions, students have blundered onto a bad limb in the visitor's presence. When a foreign face shows up in class, professors always introduce the person to the students, but sometimes the latter pay little attention, and at other times the names of the guests don't jibe with the names in the case because the latter have been fictionalized, in which case the guests' names mean nothing to anyone but the professor.

Several years ago students told me about one of their number who had got aroused about what, in his mind, was an egregious style of the top executive in a case. In class the student denounced the executive at great length, ranking him with Attila the Hun and Adolf Hitler in terms of human decency, and in general questioning his place in the human race. With a poker face the prof listened to the beginnings of this virulent tirade, then interrupted to say, "Since 'Mr. Hubbard' [disguised name for the executive] is sitting a short distance from you as our guest today, perhaps you would be willing to explain your feelings in more detail to him." The astounded student turned to where "Mr. Hubbard" sat at one end of the room, smiling grimly.

Sometimes students themselves will invite a leading character in a case to the school. Not long ago a number of first-years became fascinated with the approach of a maverick moviemaker, Suzanne de Passe, who was the subject of a case entitled "Suzanne de Passe at Motown Productions." About ninety students turned out on a busy weekday to hear, question, and meet her. I attended the session, which was held one late afternoon in a room reserved for the purpose in Aldrich Hall. After talking at some length about her management style and career, de Passe answered questions about her philosophy of involving people creatively in operations.

MAKING CASES COME ALIVE

Professors don't point at a potential case situation and say, "It happens to turn me on, so let's write it up." Most likely, they look first at a course they are teaching, pick out some places they would like to shore up or modernize, and seek a case or cases that will do the job. For this purpose they use leads from colleagues, research, consulting experiences, and magazines, books, and newspapers. (The claim of some uninformed critics that cases are used as bait for consulting, or vice versa, is 99.9 percent nonsense.) If the professor happens to be working on a new course, the chances are good that some of the case material can be drawn from the school's inventory but that there are gaps.

For instance, Quinn Mills explains that a course should do several things. It should give students an overall conceptual framework for the material that's being presented, such as, in the case of the course on human resources management, showing how many employees turn out widgets and how they are organized. The course also should be reasonably comprehensive, hitting all major topics and not covering the ground in hit-or-miss fashion. In addition, says Mills, the course has to be entertaining. "It has to grasp the students—and not just grasp their intellectual or academic attention, but their managerial and operational attention as well. They have to believe that the material is going to be important in their careers, that they are learning something practical."

Once you begin to work out a course with these purposes in mind, significant gaps begin to appear. One gap can be an important topic for which you have no material. "So you go out and get the material," says Mills. Another gap can be an important topic for which you do have material—"but it may be the world's most boring material, so you go out and get cases that are more engaging." As an example of a gap, Mills cited the lack of cases at first in the human resources course on corporate culture—the personality of an organization, its values and ways of doing things. When the course heads agreed on the need to fill the gap, they set out to develop some useful cases.

Usually the case writer tries to feature certain elements of the situation so that a kind of game plan can be used by the instructor in the classroom. A common game plan is to guide the class through three stages of discussion:

1. In the first stage, the instructor encourages students to sort out the relevant facts and develop logical conclusions. In this stage they tend to treat the case as somebody else's problem.

2. In the second stage the instructor tries to get students to project themselves into the situation with such questions as "What do you think Hampstead was trying to do?" or, "Why do you think Heath let himself get into this predicament?" In this stage students are led to see the situation not as external observers but through the eyes of the characters in the case, as if it were a story.

3. Finally, the instructor tries to get students to imagine themselves personally in the situation—"Suppose *you* were Hampstead. What would you do?" In this stage students talk about the case not as an abstraction but as a real-life situation in which they individually are involved.

Professors have all sorts of ways of leading students into this last, important stage. I recall one class where the instructor kept trying to get students to put themselves in the seat of the main character in the case, who was pondering a tough management problem as he drove to a management retreat. Up and down and around the classroom the instructor went, firing questions and holding his hands up in front of him as if they were on a steering wheel. "What're you going to do if you're this guy?" he kept asking. "You're driving your car, and in an hour you'll get there."

Once when I was teaching a doctoral seminar I saw that the students weren't catching on to the subtle politics of the problem under discussion. They were so caught up in questions of tricky

methodology that they were overlooking some issues of communication and acceptance that happened to be crucial to the outcome. So I asked the group to role-play, appointing three of them
to be members of a certain judging committee, another to be the
presenter of the proposal, and so forth. Once they made this leap,
they were able to see the situation as if it were *their* problem.

Until you work on case development yourself it is difficult to
appreciate the work required. Such appreciation came a few
years ago to a group of HBS alumni who sought to help the
Phoenix Symphony Orchestra. To broaden community concern
and heighten awareness of the symphony's situation, they decided to develop a case. They knew it would take a lot of work—
but just how much work would be needed they didn't realize
until after the twenty-seven-page document was completed and
taught.

The case writers began with many conversations with the orchestra members and directors. Background, finances, organization, marketing, a glimpse of other arts organizations in
Phoenix—all these were included. Then, Dorothy Wilmot '81,
vice president of a real estate group, told the *HBS Bulletin,* "We
talked to fund-raising people, and we contacted the American
Symphony Orchestra League. We talked to all kinds of people.
I must have spent twenty hours on the telephone talking to
marketing directors at other symphonies. . . ." Wilmot thinks she
wrote a couple of dozen drafts before the case was deemed ready
for teaching. Douglas Young '77, head of Sunbelt Holdings, William Gresser '78, head of American Greyhound Racing, and others were closely involved.

The case was taught to a group of seventy-one executives,
more than half of them chief executive officers or senior partners
in law or accounting firms. The HBS Club of Arizona hired an
assistant professor at HBS, John Whitney, to teach the case. The
session was a great success—"People are still talking about it,"
says Young, and the club is now considering developing more
cases on other topics. The word has gotten around, however, that
cases don't come easily. "We didn't realize at the time the unbe-
lievable amount of work required to write a case and plan for a
case discussion," adds Young.

DIFFERENT ROADS

In sum, the choice of cases to develop and teach at HBS has a far-reaching impact on student minds. It prepares them—or doesn't prepare them—for the management problems they will experience as entrepreneurs and executives. Pictures and images are created in students' minds that may be there for a long time. What is it like to run a factory in Omaha? What do you have to do to sell computers on the world market? Why do employees in the "back offices" of banks get alienated?

As a result, the faculty have great leverage on the mind-sets of leaders. They gain this leverage before they ever walk into the pit—because students have had to read and ponder the cases the night before. The leverage is increased because of the intense quality control exercised by each course faculty—the endless meetings over course and case development, teaching notes, needed revisions in case facts, and so on. To the extent that instructors use videos, the leverage is increased still further.

If a case is developed in an appealing way, copies of it may swell the 2.5 million or so copies that the B-school sells annually to other management schools and training programs. In the new setting it may have a similar influence.

To be sure, cases have significant limitations. Being cognitive, they have no smell or "feel." Nor can they capture the chemistry between people. Moreover, since the majority appear to students only in written form, they are seen only in the mind's eye. And they focus on decisions to be made, whereas managers spend the greater part of their time not on decision making but on implementation. Nevertheless, they become the glasses through which students see the world of management during two impressionable years, and it is a rare alum from Harvard Business School, Chapel Hill, or California whose perceptions of this world are not permanently influenced as a result.

In addition to their effect on perception, cases tell students another thing: to manage effectively, you must read. Company reports, memos, financial statements. Industry data, trade figures, commercial statements. News stories, written analyses. As a result, our economic leaders are growing farther apart from Americans who get most of their information from television and the grapevine. Managers are using their minds to perceive as well as their eyes and ears. And when they make up their minds, they do so on the basis of information that is to others invisible.

Inevitably and inexorably we are heading toward a new kind of two-culture society. There are the elite who rely on written data as well as on visceral sensing, and all the rest who do not. In terms of numbers, the latter have it all over the former—but the former control the levers of understanding and power. This division is going to grow wider and deeper, until what is now a rift becomes a chasm.

Since similar trends are occurring in other economically advanced countries, this fact has stark practical implications. Today and even more so in the future, our economic leaders must come increasingly from leading management schools. If not, we stand little chance to build world-class organizations and compete head-to-head in the world market, with all that means for domestic programs and social well-being.

- *I wrote so many drafts of that damn case that I "hit the wall."*

—Weary case writer to author

14

ETHICS—
RARE, MEDIUM,
OR WELL DONE?

In a remarkable address at a B-school faculty meeting in April 1987, Professor Thomas Piper, who was also senior associate dean for educational programs, raised the question of whether ethics can be taught at a place like Harvard. He concluded that it could be—and should. He said:

"Students scrutinize us carefully as we make our decisions about what to talk about and what not to talk about, and about what to bring into our courses and what not to bring into our courses. Bob Coles, a colleague and an outstanding child psychiatrist, once admonished me that there is no such thing as education without values. Through our decisions and through our actions, we signal our values. If we decline to talk about ethics, responsibility, and leadership, we implicitly convey that these issues are not a priority. Worse, we take an eraser to whatever progress other people have made in this critical area."

Piper wasn't talking off the cuff. He was articulating a position that the administration was going to push with all its muscle and know-how. The issue was a sensitive one in faculty circles—it had been debated off and on for years.

Why bother about ethics at a time when U.S. business is losing in global economic warfare? Won't things like research, production, marketing, and strategy take every ounce of energy we can muster? After all, taking time from first-year courses—that was what the administration was after—meant sacrificing some of the material that would otherwise go into the basics. Moreover, a "righteous" position on ethics could cost many companies doing business abroad a lot of business—the last thing we need at this critical juncture.

The answer is basic: Rightly or wrongly, ethical behavior and misbehavior is a decisive issue in American management. The stance taken by top executives not only influences morale down the line but also colors what U.S. business stands for in international commerce.

I don't propose in this chapter to judge the pros and cons of the debate, only to report on a major innovation in HBS teaching. Like the general management point of view described in an earlier chapter, ethics teaching at the B-school now cuts across all departmental and functional lines. That is why it is important to this book. While the faculty ranges all over the map in its thinking about many specific questions, as I know all too well from firsthand experience, its general views on teaching the subject reveal a great deal about the quality of leadership that HBS is trying to produce for the economy.

ETHICS FOR ALL

At about the same time Piper was talking to the faculty, Dean John McArthur was announcing a $20 million megagift by John Shad '49 for the teaching of ethics at the school. This gift did not come out of the blue but as a result of a long dialogue between McArthur and Shad. In 1981, shortly after McArthur became dean and before Shad left New York for Washington to become chairman of the Securities and Exchange Commission, the two began talking about the need to pay more attention to ethical issues in business. Six years and many talks later Shad made his gift to finance a "program of unprecedented scope and scale." McArthur is aiming for a program funded by more than $30 million.

At the beginning of their talks, according to my sources, the two men felt that an endowment of perhaps $1 million would be enough. The more Shad looked about him, however, the more he came to believe that a more ambitious program was necessary. An investment banker before going to the SEC—among other things he was vice chairman of E. F. Hutton—he saw that there must be more than greed motivating some members of the financial community to play loose with the rules. What led bright, well-educated people with the world at their feet to engage in illegal and unethical activities? For instance, two of the men implicated in insider trading abuses were able graduates of the school, one of the class of 1971, the other of the class of 1981. Money didn't seem like an adequate explanation, for these people already had large bank accounts.

Haunted by such questions, Shad and McArthur began to lift their sights concerning the scope of program necessary to illuminate the problem. McArthur says:

"John and I had begun to talk back in 1981, before his tour as head of the SEC. And as he got, week after week, a bellyful of the abuses and illegalities that naturally crossed his desk, he became more and more adamant that the school do something to deal with value issues. When he realized how widespread unethical behavior was, his support grew, along with his concern. And what started out as a few small awards grew into a comprehensive program."

The announcement of the Shad gift in April 1987 was greeted with a surprising amount of cynicism in some quarters. The *Boston Globe* ran a headline, "Can Harvard Buy Ethics?" There was publicity about three untenured faculty members with strong commitments to ethics teaching and research who had just been released from the school—what kind of commitment to ethics did this represent?—and a doleful quote about the dismissals was attributed to a tenured professor. The press suddenly remembered a call in 1979 for more ethics in the HBS curriculum by university president Derek Bok in his annual report, and it was intimated that the faculty and administration had turned a cold shoulder on this exhortation. *Business Week* quoted an unidentified junior faculty member as saying that most professors on the south side of the Charles thought the subject of ethics was "garbage."

B-school students got into the act. In *The Harbus News* Mark Contreras '88 referred to one school of thought that believed it was futile to teach MBAs ethics. The contrary Contreras quoted a student as saying, "If your mother hasn't taught you what's right and what's wrong by the time you get here, it's too late."

One time when I was visiting a finance class, several students objected to a certain course of action on the grounds that it was unethical. One exasperated fellow sitting in the wormdeck blurted, "Look, this company isn't in the business of ethics, it's in the food business!" Many appeared to agree with him.

To support their case, skeptics often asked rhetorically what amount of ethics teaching might have prevented the egregious scandals on Wall Street that were currently on the front pages of newspapers and news magazines. In rebuttal, McArthur was quick to point out that the new program was not designed to save souls. "This program is not aimed at trying to take twenty-six- or twenty-seven-year-old moral cripples and trying to deal with that," he told Loy Sheflott '88 of the student newspaper in an interview. "What we can do is help people who want to do the right thing learn from other people and gain practice in these dilemmas." As a onetime professional football player—he had once played for the Winnipeg Blue Bombers as a middle linebacker and tackle—the dean saw nothing wrong in hard blocking but abhorred clipping.

Undeterred by skeptics' blitzes and zone defenses, the administration pushed ahead. A module was designed to be taught in the first year. But when? As we saw earlier, anxiety runs very high in the first year. No time looked good. Piper, who was calling most of the plays, asked the school psychiatrist's opinion on when the module should be introduced; he was told to hold it off until the second semester, when there was a little less trauma than in the first. But Piper decided against the psychiatrist's advice, reasoning that the earlier students saw that the school took the problem seriously, the more they would figure it into their own game plans.

In the fall of 1988 the new program became visible to students. Highly visible, in fact. In the first month of the first semester of the first year, students began a module of seven classes devoted to ethical problems. The cases were varied. They came from general management, organizational behavior, marketing, production, finance, and control. The module was taught by some of the most senior professors. Although students might elect to remain silent in discussions of ethical issues in classes to come later on, and although they might skip several second-year offerings on ethics, there was no electing about the module: every first-year got it.

A somewhat controversial feature of the module is that it is not graded. While just about everything else in first-year classes is graded, the ethics sessions are not. This is because the faculty wants ethical thinking to become part of a student's approach to management in general, not segregated in the way of finance or marketing. Also, as one student lugubriously told me, "Can you imagine the poor guy who failed the ethics course?"

Thus, these are crucial years from the standpoint of ethics teaching—not just for HBS but for academe and the business community, for all eyes are on the B-school's controversial effort. Student questionnaires on the value of the module, focus group interviews, and other forms of feedback are being used to evaluate what is being done, and as usual, the faculty will soul-search itself over and over—ethically, no doubt, but relentlessly.

YANKING THE B-SCHOOL CHAIN

Before describing how ethics is taught and showing a few things we can learn from this material, let me offer a short passacaglia on the background of HBS's brave new venture. There seems to be much more darkness than light on the past. Also, a notion is going about town that the school is getting its feet wet for the first time in teaching ethics. Not so. The school is not innocent in this area—neither to the difficulties of teaching ethics nor to close-to-home reminders that the subject demands attention.

When Piper addressed the faculty meeting in 1987, more than one hundred cases on ethics and corporate responsibility were listed in the current case catalogs. How many cases had been collected on the subject since 1908 but were not listed is anyone's guess—certainly many more than appeared in print in 1987. In his remarks, Piper also noted that twenty-four courses on ethics and corporate responsibility had been introduced into the MBA curriculum since the school began.

One of these courses was an ill-fated elective taught by the legendary Professor Carl F. Taeusch. For seven years, starting in 1928, the torch-bearing Taeusch directed and taught the course, which was a second-year offering. Although he possessed many advantages, not the least of which was Dean Wallace Donham's wholehearted support, the faculty dropped the course after seven grim years. As some recall, the substance was too theoretical to grab students. Also, many students thought the course too closely resembled Sunday-school talk.

The school also tried its hand at the awards game with less than stimulating results. In 1926, Edward Bok, retired editor of the *Ladies' Home Journal* and grandfather of university president Derek Bok, funded an annual advertising award to encourage more truthful advertising. Unfortunately, that award was discontinued after two years, though whether for lack of interest or simple despair over trying to reform the ways of snake-oil peddlers, we don't know.

In their books, professors lucubrated about ethics questions from time to time, but it was not until the 1980s that they really focused on the subject. In 1984 a scholarly text and casebook, *Policies and Persons—A Casebook in Business Ethics,* was published by Professors John Matthews, Kenneth Goodpaster, and Laura Nash. In 1986 Assistant Professor Barbara Toffler produced *Tough Choices,* based on a remarkable set of interviews with managers who had experienced ethical dilemmas.

In the meantime the *Harvard Business Review* repeatedly was raising ethical questions, sometimes in expositional articles, sometimes in case-and-discussion formats, sometimes in other forms. Piper counted 111 *HBR* articles on ethics and corporate responsibility just since the middle 1950s. A number of these pieces had won much acclaim for *HBR*.

At the same time, critics could point to a checkered history in the B-school's own ethical behavior. For instance:

In 1986, a second-year student was indicted for filing false federal tax returns related to securities trading while employed in a prominent New York investment firm. For a while the administration withheld judgment, but when the wayward student pleaded guilty, the administration threw him out of the school.

In the same year occurred a troublesome violation involving a sporadic student publication. In most first-year sections students were writing and distributing occasional photocopied newsletters called generically *Skydeck News.* Typically issues were filled with parodies, gossip, and inside jokes. In some sections the authors were anonymous, in some they were not. In most sections the publications were funded from general section funds or contributions. Until the spring of 1986, at any rate, the content was generally harmless.

Unfortunately, one section's *Skydeck News* came out with some racist, homophobic humor. Indignant, the section called on the authors to step forward and identify themselves. This they did, and they apologized to the section for their conduct. Unplacated, the administration investigated and placed the students on probation. Piper sent a long memorandum to the staff and students about trust, stress, and caring.

The incident worried many people at the B-school. In a stinging editorial, *The Harbus News* fumed about what was going on:

"It would be nice to think we are belaboring the obvious. The evidence suggests that we are not. Very few people here think of themselves as racists. The people now on probation for their roles in producing that *Skydeck News* do not consider themselves to be racists. Their section mates are not racists either. Nevertheless, over the course of the year, they allowed a culture to develop in their section in which insensitivity was greeted without censure and treated as a matter of course."

In the spring of 1982 occurred an imbroglio involving the annual Business Game played by first-years. The exercise had

ETHICS—RARE, MEDIUM, OR WELL-DONE? 241

become an annual rite. Students took a week of spring to play a computer simulation that pitted six teams in a section against each other in a fiercely competitive situation. Each team used all it knew about business to try to come out ahead, appointing its members to play the roles of chief executive, financial executive, marketing head, research director, and so on. The game was one of the emotional highs for first-years, and to this day graduates regale friends and associates with tales of their prowess in that grueling week. (Today the Business Game is no more, having been replaced by another computer simulation with the judicious acronym of WISE.)

The imbroglio was happily described by *Fortune,* which rarely misses a chance to tweak the HBS nose. Briefly, one team got—no outsider is quite sure how—a rival team's confidential computer password. Without thinking much about the ethics of the situation, the first team exploited its find, using the password in every advantageous way it could think of. "We never had a meeting over whether it was right or wrong to use the password," said one member afterward. "In the context of the game, once you have access to information, it would not make sense not to use it." Some took the attitude that the Business Game was supposed to be a simulation of the real world, and in the real world you use every bit of intelligence you can get.

Obtaining simultaneous printouts as the victim team typed its decisions into the computer, the first team knew exactly what its rival planned to do, whether to try to get more market share by lowering prices, spend funds on a new technology, or something else. Gleefully it charged its "snoop reports" to the victim. The "snoop reports" were market studies and other data sheets; they cost a bundle. No matter what the victim team did, its actions got it into deeper and deeper trouble, and when the exercise ended, it was deeper in debt than Eastern Airlines, while the first team was holding violets.

At the debriefing after the game, a party replete with chilled champagne and huge plates of goodies, the first team confessed to the secret of its success. The victims were furious. Demanding meetings with classmates and faculty people, they claimed that they had been done in unfairly and unconscionably, and they placed part of the blame on the lack of emphasis on ethics at the school. "What upset the Team 6 [victim] students," *Fortune* happily noted, "was that the competitive atmosphere of the B-school, in which they participated as much as anyone, seemed to suspend ethical considerations in the game."

In the mid-1970s a front-page article appeared in *The Wall Street Journal* alleging that the game rules in managerial economics, a first-year course, allowed students to cheat. Tsk, tsk, the article said. Fie on the faculty for allowing such a thing! Although other professors saw that the article was absurd—the aim of the exercises was just the opposite from what the reporter inferred—the course chairman, generally considered one of the best teachers at the school, was upset. He was so perturbed that when some of his jocular colleagues "pulled his chain," as one of them put it, they learned quickly how deeply he felt. The dean, too, was upset.

Some oil was spread on the troubled academic waters when, reportedly, one of the Rockefellers heard about the course head's trauma and called him up. "Look, we know how you feel. How about coming down to our place for the weekend? We'll send a plane up to get you." The course head went.

STUDENT IDEALISM

Events and episodes like the foregoing have been hard for many professors and students to take. The fact that business is essentially materialistic makes them sensitive to criticisms and innuendos. Does greed so permeate business that teaching ethics is hopeless from the start? The majority answer is a loud "No!" What is more, cynical behavior runs counter to a certain amount of idealism on campus. At times, to be sure, the idealism seems swamped by materialism, ambition, and ad nauseam references to the bottom line, but it is there—very much there.

One of my interviews with alums was with Russell Amick '65, president and owner of Floy Tag in Seattle, an international fishery tag and research firm. Amick told me about an incident in Boston that brought a bunch of students, including him, head-to-head with a police sergeant who apparently saw himself as the Ferdinand Marcos of law enforcement:

"We arranged for a party on park property, property under the supervision of the Metropolitan District Commission. Two sections were in on the deal. A guy from a midwestern state was in charge. He made a deal with a local sergeant of the Boston police to stage the party in the park. One policeman would show up and monitor the door. We would pay the policeman $25.

"The party went fine for a while. However, at about eleven the sergeant calls the party. 'How's everything going?' he asks. The student chairman answers, 'Everything's great, no problems.' The sergeant says, 'Tell you what. I've got another guy that I'm gonna send down there. It'll be another $25.' The student says no. "We agreed there'd be one guy for $25, and that's it. That's all you're gonna get.' The sergeant says, 'I think you'd better pay this other guy $25. He'll be there in a couple of minutes.' The student says no and hangs up.

"About five minutes later the second policeman shows up and asks, 'Where's my $25?' The chairman says, 'No, we've already paid $25, and a deal's a deal.' The policeman says, 'Well, it's going to be your problem.' A few minutes later a bunch of Boston policemen show up with a paddy wagon and the whole deal. You'd think we were the Mafia or something, the way they all came up. They busted our party. They all came into the dance hall and pulled the plug on the music and started hustling us out. Some of our guys started making wise comments to the police, and a couple got lippy enough so that the cops threw them in the paddy wagon and took them downtown. The guys spent the night in the slammer. The next day everyone from the dean on down got involved, meeting with the mayor and the city council and the police department."

The students who went to jail resumed classes the next day, Harvard officials diplomatically told the police they were off base, and the event ended. The police proceeded more judiciously with the next group of HBS partiers.

After he graduated and went to Seattle, Amick says, he joined a local task force whose mission was to clean up the police department in that city. The task force was very successful. One thing that motivated him, Amick told me, was the memory of the students' confrontation with the police.

One more insight about the HBS student body, this one from a nonbusiness observer: Several years ago Robert Coles, the child psychiatrist and author who teaches at Harvard University, began running a seminar at HBS on what can be learned about business morality from fiction writers. In a *New York Times* piece in 1987 enticingly entitled "Gatsby at the B School," Coles wrote:

"For me those two years of teaching 'across the river,' as it is often put on the occasionally self-important Cambridge side, were both edifying and gratifying. I was not only impressed with, but surprised by the idealism and decency of many of the students I met, with the yearning they had to join with Binx [character in Walker Percy's novel *The Moviegoer,* discussed in the seminar] in his moral search, to link arms with Johnny Hake [character in John Cheever's story "The Housebreaker of Shady Hill," also discussed] as he shook his world upside down in such a dramatic and unsettling way. I had acquired over the years all sorts of stereotypes about those students—quite wrongheaded notions, I slowly realized. Once, sitting and listening to a wonderfully alert, sensitive discussion of Cheever's stories, I remembered—perhaps to let my patronizing self off the hook—a comment of the cranky Dr. Williams, expressed through a rhetorical question: 'Who the hell is without some kind of prejudice, I ask you?' "

GAUGES AND GUIDELINES

Not surprisingly, the faculty believes in teaching ethics by the case method. Cases range from Dow Corning Corporation's lusty efforts to enforce a global code of conduct prohibiting the giving of bribes, even in countries where this is common practice, to H. J. Heinz's confrontation with an accounting practice of over-reporting earnings. What do professors hope to teach? Although generalizations are difficult, I think that the following are fair answers:

1. You can steer clear of a lot of trouble by taking some simple precautions. One course note (a kind of essay by a professor on some topic covered in the course) in marketing offers a list of suggestions to "help the ethical manager stay that way and nurture his or her standards." One suggestion is to have "walking dollars" and low fixed costs relative to your income so that you feel free to leave a job rather than compromise your standards. Another is to avoid giving the appearance that your ethical standards can be compromised so that you won't give others the wrong idea. Another is to choose your associates well, as "it is impossible to walk through a swamp without getting mud on your clothes."

2. Good intentions will not keep you out of all ethical morasses. One of Barbara Toffler's favorite lines in *Tough Choices,* she told me, comes from a manager who says, "You know, nobody *sets out* to make a car with a gas tank that explodes."

In a *Harvard Business Review* article, Professor Paul Lawrence and Associate Professor Jeffrey Sonnenfeld quote a frustrated top executive in a company convicted of conspiracy:

"We've tried hard to stress that collusion is illegal. We point out that anticompetitive practices hurt the company's ethical standards, public image, internal morale, and earnings. Yet we wind up in trouble continually. When we try to find out why employees get involved, they have the gall to say that they 'were only looking out for the best interests of the company.' They seem to think that the company message is for everyone else but them. . . ."

In this company as in others studied by the authors, the sincerity and integrity of top management was beyond question. Their failure, one of the authors told me, was to acknowledge that dire ethical difficulties often result from choices that originally seemed insignificant.

3. Top management's example can make a lot of difference if it is communicated widely. In the Lawrence-Sonnenfeld study, one company appeared to have succeeded in keeping its hands

clean because, according to the authors, "this company's executives are making an old-fashioned distinction between clean, earned profits and rigged, dirty profits." By its everyday deeds and actions, not speeches, this management had succeeded in infusing its attitude through the corporation.

4. "Close-up" views of ethical problems are likely to be misleading. Associate Professor Kenneth Goodpaster once told an *HBS Bulletin* editor that ethics often has a "nested" quality. He explained:

"Looking at an ethical problem is a lot like looking at an Escher print. If you approach it thinking that there is only one image, you're probably not looking at it right. Likewise, if you just look at the individual and his or her ethical dilemma, you're likely to miss the organizational environment around the individual; and if you look at the organization character or ethic, you'll probably miss seeing the larger 'system ethic' that's pressuring the organization to act in a certain way."

5. Ethics and enlightened self-interest are often in conflict; the two do not, as we might wish, coincide happily. Forest Reinhardt '87, now a doctoral student, explained to me:

"If economic self-interest and your ideas about what constitutes ethical behavior tell you to do the same thing, then the question isn't really one of ethics: it's just a matter of pursuing your interests. Only when economic interest and notions of ethics lead to different answers about how you ought to behave does the question become interesting. This means that in any genuine ethical dilemma, being ethical is going to cost you money. I am not saying you shouldn't behave ethically. But people tend to confuse 'ethics' with 'enlightened self-interest,' and they're not the same thing at all."

6. You can't decide most ethical questions in the abstract. A good deal usually depends on the time, actors, surrounding events, prevailing mood, and other parts of the situation. For an example, let's visit a class:

The case that is up for discussion involves a salesman for a large manufacturer of children's clothes. The salesman becomes troubled. Shortly after being assigned to his first sales territory, he is asked for a bribe by the buyer of an important customer. We hear a brisk argument over whether the seller or buyer is at fault; the discussion gets heated. "Pay the bribe—it's well worth the money," some argue. "Don't pay the bribe under any circumstances," insist others. "Either tell the buyer that bluntly, or pretend he's joking, or stall him." Another group urges, "Check to see if the salesman's predecessor paid the bribe. If he did, do the same." Still another faction says, "Stall and think about it," while others argue that the salesman should quit the job and seek another employer.

After a while, we see the professor draw a continuum on the board. At the far left she scribbles "cup of coffee," and next to that, "lunch." Moving to the right, she captions more serious gestures such as "dinner," "dinner and theater tickets," "weekend at a nice resort," "color TV," "$1,000," "women" (if the buyer is a man), "$10,000." Most students agree that "cup of coffee" at the far left is not a bribe but that "$10,000" to the far right is. However, that leaves a big gray middle area, which is where most questions arise. Where is the dividing line between a harmless social gesture and an unethical bribe? We see it dawning on the class that you can't draw that line in the abstract like a painter dividing a canvas.

7. Don't underestimate management power to head off ethical difficulties. It can head off some simply by instituting clear policies and directives.

I think of a lively class discussion of a newspaper that had been running advertisements for a South African coin. With South Africa in the news as it was at the time of the case, there was dissension on the newspaper staff about running the ads. Before long, the unpleasantness was compounded as community pressure groups protested the ads and threatened a boycott. Emotions ran high in the class. Some insisted that the newspaper should keep on running the ads. They argued that the newspaper had a contract with the advertiser, that advertising revenues were needed (the exhibits made this clear), that dropping the ads was a form of censorship, and so on. Yet many other students saw the ads as an outrage. They said that the ads were offensive to the many blacks in the area, that they were inconsistent with the newspaper's human rights stand in the editorial pages, as shown in the case, that they implied an endorsement of South African racial policies, and so on.

Instead of arbitrating and trying to show which side was right, the professor nudged the class (after a while) to focus on the management questions. To what constituencies was the newspaper responsible? Were some more important than others? What were the newspaper's responsibilities to each? What process or procedure should management establish for dealing with questions like this one?

What the professor wanted the class to see was that, from a managerial standpoint, procedures for resolving ethical conflicts and questions of accountability may solve part of the potential problem. By avoiding murk and uncertainty, clear procedures can render a dispute unnecessary.

Another case makes a similar point. A company engages in improper income transfer prices (prices charged one division of a company by another division from which it buys products or services). At first, students are inclined to see the issue as one of goodies and baddies, but the instructor has another goal in mind: management itself is partly to blame. Students begin to see the case in a new light. One student notes that management has created an atmosphere in this company where not meeting annual profit goals is seen by employees as a mortal sin, so that naturally ethical implications take a backseat to financial performance. Another student points out that management has created an environment in which employees find it easy to look the other way when questions of dishonesty come up.

In sum, to many observers, ethics seems like a "soft" subject, not "hard" like accounting or finance or manufacturing. Nevertheless, Americans are a moral people. The media bombard us continually with accounts of fraud, extortion, negligence, and murder, but the reason such items make news is that most of us don't countenance them. The employees in U.S. organizations grow up in this climate. If they hear that their organizations are engaged in shady practices, or if they personally encounter questionable practices, they are troubled. Morale suffers. The organization loses in effectiveness.

No one yet knows whether the B-school's start in making ethics a required part of the curriculum is the best possible one. What does seem sure is that some such effort is important to U.S. competitiveness. Being the kind of people we are, most of us simply won't give our all to organizations that seem unethical.

Moreover, as many professors and cases make clear, ethics is partly a management responsibility. Top executives can't wash their hands of ethical lapses by employees, saying that they're the fault of the educational system, the media, or some other force in society. It may well be that nonmanagement forces are partly to blame for the sins of commission and omission, but that does not relieve leaders of their responsibility. If anything, it increases it. By their personal example as well as by policies and regulations, managers can influence the tone and standards of employee behavior.

■ *I calculate that 25 percent of the students already agree with the ethics considerations [posed in HBS's new ethics course] and another 25 percent disagree and won't change. We're aiming for the middle 50 percent who could go either way.*

—PROFESSOR MICHAEL BEER, quoted in *The New York Times*

■ *People of the same trade seldom meet together, even for merriment and diversion, but the conversation ends in a conspiracy against the public, or in some contrivance to raise prices.*

—ADAM SMITH in *The Wealth of Nations*

15

MATING GAMES
(CORPORATE STYLE)

For many students, one of the most memorable learning experiences at the B-school occurs out of the classroom. It happens in the carrels of Aldrich, where recruiters interview, at noisy cocktail parties in Cambridge and Boston sponsored by interested companies, on the telephone with offices in distant places, in soul-searching with friends. I refer, of course, to job hunting.

Good jobs are supposed to be the payoff for attending the school. Most of the time they are. But they often are not the easy, automatic payoff that many students naïvely expected when they signed up at HBS. I have talked with many students and alums about their experiences with corporate recruiters, and read hundreds of opinions about the process in the student newspaper, and I never cease to be amazed at the intensity—sometimes vehemence—of student response. They have known for some time how important the job search is. From Day One on at the B-school, they have seen how seriously the administration takes recruiting, corporate relations, and alumni relations. They understand the rules for recruiting, which have been clarified and discussed many times. They know exactly when the recruiters will arrive.

Yet the experience often catches them by surprise. To their credit, they usually react by learning fast and well. "I guess I made every mistake in the book," one alum told me, reflecting back on his job-hunting experience. "I paid through the nose—I must have been one of the last in my class to get placed. But I learned a lot that I won't forget—not just up here [pointing to his head] but also down here [tapping his stomach]."

The company-student mating season is interesting to watch and very visible. When the recruiters roll into town in late winter, the complexion of HBS changes. No longer does the place look informal, given over to teaching. Suddenly the outside world barges in. Nattily dressed men and women swarm over the campus. Special areas are given over to interviewing. The attitude of second-year students changes. For a year and a half they have put knowledge, understanding, and grades first. They have pondered cases and argued who in the case situations should push what buttons of power to get what desired results. Now it is *their* turn to get going and push their own buttons.

I have watched this subtle transition many times. To their credit, most students most of the time quickly get in stride with the changed pace. But not all do—sometimes, in fact, quite a few don't. Dr. Jekylls turn into Mr. Hydes. Friendly types become grasping, humorless, and materialistic. The effect is not flattering to the student body or the B-school.

Students may blame this unhappy transition on recruiters. It is true that many headhunters are pushy and devious and by their crude tactics exacerbate the problem. But I wonder if it's fair to hold the recruiters wholly to blame. Most of my faculty colleagues don't think so. In the words of the old saying, It takes two to tango. "Dennis always was a bastard," I was told by an instructor as we discussed one particularly odious case (the student name is fictional).

For most students this first step back into organizational life—this reentry into the "real world"—will have an important bearing on where, how, and with what speed they rise to positions of

power and influence. The school knows that. Its institutional ego
is at stake as well as the individual aspirations of the grads. If
students do not get good jobs, not only will its prospects of large
future donations be diminished but, just as bad, it will be frustrated in achieving its driving ambition, which is to influence the
economy and make an ever larger and ever more indelible mark
on the world.

The upshot of all this is that some policies and practices have
a profound impact on the role of the B-school and its grads. What
we see here is an institution-wide willingness to face the facts and
learn from experience—as pragmatically and unidealistically as
possible. I will focus here on a few impressions that stand out in
my mind.

THE PLACEMENT MACHINE

By making placement as conspicuous and prestigious as it does—
by not tucking it out of sight under some pretense that the
school's only mission is learning—the administration sends an
important message to employers, alums, and students: We want
and expect the best for these young people.

Let's begin with the setting. During recruiting season close to
half of the second floor of Kresge Hall is taken over at lunchtime
by recruiters. The tables are set festively. The atmosphere is
congenial. As for Aldrich, the main classroom building, during
mornings and afternoons the corridors that gird the classrooms
are busy with recruiters and student applicants sitting on the
window seats in the carrels with the pleated plastic doors closed.
Interviews generally run for about half an hour.

In the placement office in the Career Development Center,
one of eight small stucco buildings on campus, there is a long
counter for students, a wall-size bulletin board crammed with
notices, piles of schedules and reports, and an efficient office
squad. Across the common ("Baker Beach") in a similar building
are the *HBS Bulletin* offices. In Sherman House, another building
just like it on the west end of the campus, one floor is devoted
to alumni relations, another to the HBS fund. In an identical

building on the east side of the campus, Glass Hall, the corporate relations offices are located. These four buildings form an east-to-west axis through the middle of the campus.

Right inside the massive front doors of Baker Library, to the left, you will find the Cole Room, a large space converted from an auditorium to house a compact library of annual reports from prestigious corporations, slick promotional films, brochures, booklets, computerized listings, and computer banks, complete with reference librarians, colored cubicles, and terminals. As you flip through the brochures, your eye may be caught by one from Brown Brothers Harriman & Co., printed in an elegant typeface on glossy paper, its pages graced with photos of bankers in three-piece suits posing in front of great buildings in New York, London, Zurich, and other famous cities. If you're interested in marketing, you may seek out the literature from Procter & Gamble, one of the world's most skillful marketers—Pampers, Tide, Duncan Hines cake mixes, Citrus Hill orange juice, to name but a few. The Cole Room is a virtual candy store of information about employers, and students cannot be blamed if their job-seeking eyes get bigger than their stomachs.

The implicit message of all this space and staff to students is: *We want you to do well.* To corporate recruiters, the message is: *Your top hopes can be found here.* To ease the pain of coming and looking, the school shows off its plant to recruiters. In trade jargon, it pursues its most visible strategic advantage—its campus. *No business school has the space and facilities that we have.* In a low-key but unmistakable way, the administration reminds recruiters who happen to be B-school alumni themselves that they can be proud they went here.

During late winter and spring, several hundred corporate recruiters throng to the school to hold many thousands of interviews. In 1989, for instance, 265 employers conducted more than six thousand interviews. Another 400 or more organizations send letters or brochures describing job openings. The heavy recruiting is for second-years seeking permanent positions; less ambitious—but still earnest—recruiting is for first-years desiring summer jobs.

The placement office is the hub of activity, scheduling interviews and staying in touch with any company that interviews on campus or sends in written information about an opening. Early in the year placement sends a staple-bound "book" to faculty members listing scheduled recruiters alphabetically and chronologically. In a recent listing the employers began with A. G. Edwards & Sons, a financial firm, and ended with Young & Rubicam, the advertising agency, with several hundred other companies sandwiched in between. (A 1987 listing appears in the Appendix.)

Generally speaking, placement does not spend time beating the bushes for prospective employers. That sort of probing is done by another office, the corporate relations department, as well as by faculty, alumni, and students.

When HBS opens its doors to a corporate recruiter, it gives the company certain rules to abide by. For instance, interviews are not to be scheduled during class hours, and the company should allow students a reasonable time to consider job offers (the current guideline calls for two weeks). Unfortunately, these rules and guidelines are not always observed. Who are the perpetrators? More often than not, the very companies that are first in line when recruiting season starts.

SCRAMBLING FOR POSITION

Students learn that, even with their unique schooling, and even with the HBS placement juggernaut supporting them, job searching is not an armchair task. They have to work as furiously at it as at any course. In the words of one student I talked with, "You can't take *anything* for granted."

So students rely on the same basic procedure that has gotten them through their courses—dialoguing with each other. In an article in *Manhattan* magazine, Robert Massie, Jr., '86, an Episcopal priest who entered the HBS doctoral program after his first year, reminisced about the experience:

"At no period is the emphasis on individual success and achievement more evident than in the frenzied winter mating season when recruiters arrive on campus. Throughout the fall students rewrite and edit their résumés, join organizations such as the Finance Club, the Marketing Club, the Investment Banking Club, and the Venture Capital Club (in part to get their names included in special club books), and pore over annual reports and lists of alumni in the Career Research Center. Then the recruiters arrive and the students begin a swirling dance of first- second-, and third-round interviews and callbacks that lasts for three weeks. Attention is paid to the most minute details of performance and appearance. 'I was going out the door to an interview,' recounted one friend, 'and my roommate stopped me and asked with alarm, "What are you doing?" I didn't know what he was talking about. "You can't go to an interview with a bank wearing brown shoes!" He made me change them.' "

If you visit a class during recruiting season you will see the majority of students dressed in casual clothes as usual but a half dozen or so dressed in spiffy gray or navy blue suits and shiny shoes. They stand out like slick *New Yorker* ads slipped into a pulp magazine. These are the students who are rushing to job interviews after class. Being a priest, Massie was spared the need to interview for a summer job, but occasionally he did come to class dressed in a business suit because of an appointment he had to go to in town. When this happened, he told me, friends would playfully inquire if he had given in to the urge to talk with a recruiter from Goldman, Sachs or McKinsey.

Students acquire a lexicon for recruiting. For instance, a *bullet* is a letter of rejection from a prospective employer. *Getting dinged* is another way of saying that you got a bullet from a recruiter. (Getting dinged should not be confused with *getting donged,* which means getting drunk. Example: "Charley got dinged by Amex, then went to Harvard Square and got donged.")

The Harbus News often is stocked like a resort fishing pool with ads for recruiting companies. Sometimes the companies will invite all interested students to cocktails in a swank hotel with drinks, egg rolls, and shrimp. Students have told me that during the recruiting season, they could have survived, if necessary, on the free handouts offered at receptions by fat-cat recruiters.

In all courses professors operate under strict rules about what they can and cannot divulge about students, but some of their phones ring incessantly with calls from interested companies. Because job hunting is such a big thing for second-years, there are no Friday classes for them from January on; this frees them to use the long weekends for interviews, trips, and calls.

THE MUNIFICENT OBSESSION

Students improve the results of job searching by talking frankly about money. "You don't go for the big fish," one told me, "by baiting your hook with worms." Even those with an idealistic bent learn to feel no embarrassment about money talk.

Sitting in the student dining hall and listening to the conversations around, especially during the recruiting season, I have been struck with the frequency of talk about money. "Yeah?" somebody asks at the next table. "How much did they offer him?" "How much does she make on that job?" asks someone at another table. "You better figure out how much those stock options are gonna be worth," advises someone at another table. Several years ago, I am told, the big news in the dining hall was that a graduate the previous spring had broken the "100 K barrier" by landing a job in an investment bank that paid a six-figure salary. (Today breaking the "100 K barrier" isn't news anymore, though still unusual.)

Dollar signs float in the air like seed pods in spring, especially during recruiting season. Money! Many students have a love-hate relationship with it, loving its power, hating their dependence on it. How can they help but think in terms of it, however, when for two years they have learned that money = power = a club at the top = personal contacts with prime movers and newsmakers? The message has seeped constantly into their minds like an intravenous drug dripping into a hospital patient's arm—in incidental lines in cases ("At a breakfast at Tiffany's, he told the deputy assistant secretary of state . . ."), in the words of visiting speakers ("I always fly first-class and make it a point to know who my cabin mates are. . . ."), in professors' talk ("I'll put you in touch with John Jones, who organized the senator's campaign chest. . . ."), in the press ("The two played golf at the Beverly Hills Country Club . . .").

How does this attitude toward money affect students' job hunting? For one thing, it sets a mood for recruiting companies. They learn fast via the grapevine or experience that they better not try HBS at all unless they are prepared to offer high starting salaries. For another, it makes it easier for students to negotiate. They don't swallow hard before asking what their starting salary would be, thus giving themselves away. Money talk is almost as easy and natural for them as breathing.

Let's get down to statistics. What pay do students get when they start out after graduation? This year the average starting salary is about $60,000, with some students (typically those choosing investment banking or consulting) starting at close to or above $100,000. About two-fifths of the grads opt for careers in consulting (one-quarter) and investment banking (one-eighth). McKinsey & Company, the giant New York consulting firm, hired fifty-three members of the class of 1989. Many fewer students go into the automotive industry, despite the need, partly because it offers starting salaries far below the average (a median salary of $47,300 in 1988 versus $65,100 for consulting).

For many students the choice of a high-paying job is dictated partly by economic necessity: they have high debts to pay off. Around two-thirds of a class are likely to borrow about $30,000 from HBS to get through the two years. Lawrence Fouraker, dean during the 1970s, probably went too far when he told a reporter of *The Boston Globe* in the fall of 1989 that Harvard MBAs "take the hot jobs that pay the most money, live out of a suitcase for five years, and pay off their debt," but certainly that is true of a great many.

Nor do salaries plateau after graduation. Judging from averages compiled by William Sihler, secretary of the class of 1962, a B-school grad can expect income of about $160,000 after twenty-five years (in 1987 dollars), and his or her net worth will come close to $2 million. It may be significant that on the occasion of its twenty-fifth reunion at Harvard, Sihler's class gave $4.5 million to the school, a record gift at the time.

■ ■ ■

In short, the B-school doesn't blush when its obsession with money, power, and placement is brought up. It is proud of its track record; people in the placement juggernaut are esteemed. How does an institution of learning rationalize this phenomenon?

The search for power, faculty friends remind me, begins with money. In fact, money *is* power. It is the power to live in a nice suburb with affluent neighbors, vacation in fashionable resort spots in Europe, contribute to political campaign chests and get rewarded, entertain important people and call them by their first names. It is a major credit card in the world of economic and political policymaking. It's usually not enough by itself to put you on the governor's blue-ribbon commission or get you an invitation to the presidential ball, but it will take you a long way if you have half a brain and don't have bad breath.

Many people might wish otherwise, but that's the way the world is, say the faculty. The B-school is, above all, a realistic and pragmatic place.

■ *Captain John Smith sailed out of Jamestown . . . in 1614 to explore the largely unknown coastline to the north. His report on the Shawmut peninsula—later to become Boston—was succinct: only money, he said, would ever draw people there.*

—JEFFREY L. CRUIKSHANK,
A Delicate Experiment: The Harvard Business School, 1908–1945

PART IV

CONCLUSION

WHAT CAN
THE B-SCHOOL DO
FOR AMERICA?

The B-school wants to change the world. It wants the country to look to it for economic leadership just as the country looks to the service academies for military leadership. It knows that it cannot do the job alone, but it believes that it and other top management schools together can do the job. It is driven by a missionary desire to save economic souls, taking a backseat to no church or other institution in faith and fervor. When one or more of its alums fail, it is dismayed but undeterred; it keeps plowing ahead in the steadfast belief that it is right.

How does the B-school try to accomplish its mission? Not by research or the propagation of ideas but by turning out students equipped to lead. Its ability to transform young men and women is astonishing.

Earlier I mentioned a student in the class of 1989 whom I referred to as "Charley Shedd." What happened to Charley in his two years at HBS is typical of most men and women in his and other graduating classes over the years.

When Charley entered in September 1987, he was a bright, energetic, talented young man. The Admissions Department had selected him as the one in eight whom it considered to be the cream of the crop of applicants. But as I remember him on a warm day after his arrival, he was fairly sophomoric in his attitudes about management and ignorant about himself. His skill in decision making was primitive even though he had excelled as a supervisor in the oil fields.

When Charley graduated two years later, in June 1989, he still looked the same as in 1987 but between the ears he was dramatically different. In discernment about management he was quite sophisticated. He had gained a "feel" for management that would have taken him years to develop if he had not gone to HBS or one of the other schools he applied to. He knew a lot about management functions and different industries. He knew a great deal more about himself—what he could do, what he was good at, his endurance—than he had when he entered. In two years he developed aptitudes and insights that generally take many years to develop.

In short, his transformation was practically miraculous. Although he was unaware of the changes as they happened, he was able to tell me that he could remember nothing in his education that had changed him as the B-school had. In these respects he was fairly typical of more than seven hundred classmates. Yet academically he was only average in his class—if anything, a little below average.

The change that amazed me most in Charley, from watching him in class and hearing him talk, was his slowly acquired ability to put his arms around a complex management problem. Let me give you an example. I attended one of Charley's first-year classes in Production and Operations Management. The case for discussion involved a complicated logistics problem. Unions, conflicting interests, conflicting work traditions, difficult economies of scale, confusing management efforts—all these and many more complications frustrated one's efforts to analyze the case and decide what to do. But I had had a good many years of work experience and thought I would be pretty good at understanding the problem.

I read the case twice before class. The more I thought about it, the more baffled I became. Yet after twenty-five minutes of intense discussion the section had a good handle on the situation and was debating what courses of action to take. Charley made a strong contribution to that discussion.

Michael Maguire '85, marketing vice president at SGI in Warwick, Rhode Island, tells me:

"The trouble that so many people have is that they don't know how to approach a situation in a systematic, creative way. The case method taught me that while there is no right answer, there is a process for analyzing problems and planning action, and you can take that process in many different directions. The marketing concept, participative management, and so on—these concepts may or may not work in a situation. Besides, you can learn them on your own. What you get from the school that is so useful is a way of looking at the picture, seeing that a piece of the puzzle doesn't fit, and picking out a good way to fix what's wrong."

I have read the best written presentations on how to analyze and solve a complex management problem, and I respect their authors' fine efforts. Yet I know that reading can't come close to the value of learning *by doing,* as the students learn—hashing the situation over and over and over again with peers, both in study groups and in class, now being wrong, now being right, putting yourself in the situation of the manager and trying to figure out, What would I do if I were in his or her shoes?

If Charley Shedd and other alums can deal with complex management problems effectively, we can forgive them if some of their number aren't likable. Warm, gracious, charming people are the ones you want for a dinner party, but if you're having a heart operation, you don't care how disagreeable and steely-eyed the surgeon is if he or she is top-notch in competence. So with our country as it seeks to become more competitive.

I was also struck by Charley's learned ability to grapple with tough choices. He learned at HBS that there often is no way of wishing yourself out of nasty situations. Despite the best intentions, managers get into them again and again. They find there is no way out of them without hurting someone. Whether the problem is a web of commitments to the "push" or "pull" side

CONCLUSION

of marketing or a series of questionable loans to valued clients, management may have to choose one course over another, and the flak is going to fly. Charley learned this by trial and error, vicariously, to be sure, but memorably. He came to realize that often he would have to say no and make himself unpopular with employees and outsiders.

Another strong impression I gained is that Charley no longer thought much of easy rules of thumb about management, magic formulas, appealing shortcuts, and so on. Once again his feelings seem to have been shared by almost all classmates, as they have been by B-school grads before and since his class. In addition, he knew there were no arcane secrets in the special notations, cryptic equations, and formulas that filled many a board at the end of class. "Everybody thinks we learn secrets at the B-school," he told me, "but they're wrong." He recognized all too clearly that no matter how astute an executive is, there is no substitute for hard work and often painstaking analysis before deciding about a problem.

Charley learned that he could work a lot harder than he had thought he could. "I don't think I'll ever be a nine-to-five worker," he told me. "I don't want to be, it's no fun." At the same time, he looked forward to relaxing with a family, and I think he may be in for a jolt here, finding that there is no way he can be a really able executive and also satisfy the time demands of a wife and children. If so, he will not be the first HBS grad to discover this dilemma.

Numerous alums have confirmed the importance of the self-knowledge gained at the school. "I found that I thrived on the intensity of the first year," I was told by Thomas Fontana '83, head of Acme Visible Records in Crozet, Virginia, at the time of our interview. "It was a real self-discovery process for me." A great many, too, say they learned about likes, dislikes, strengths, and weaknesses that they never had known they possessed—an antipathy to certain kinds of situations, a feeling about how best to prepare for a negotiation, a bent for marketing or finance or production. "I learned to avoid some things I did that turned off people," one of my doctoral students told me, reflecting on her

MBA experience. "I learned that I talk better in small groups than large."

In these and other ways students try to explain how the B-school transformed them. Hardly ever do they think it was the knowledge of concepts or techniques that changed them, important as they were, but the ability to grasp and think through difficult problems, work under pressure, participate in groups, and discover their strengths and weaknesses—all things that a person must discover for himself or herself. It's as if they see their own sets of talents like fingerprints, different from anyone else's in the world.

This know-how gives them a running start when they return to management. It accounts for much of the extraordinary success of HBS alums, for management is not a formula or computer operation—it is more like playing baseball than chess. The secret of the B-school is not what it teaches students but what it enables them to learn.

One of the most important things learned is the interdependency of activities in an organization. Production is seen as being dependent on marketing, and marketing on finance, and finance on industrial relations, and so on—and then it is seen that each function is dependent not just on one or two others but on *all* others. In the student mind, an organization is a giant cobweb with every part connected with every other part.

R. Lee Buechler '78, president of Phamis, put it to me this way in an interview:

"Maybe the most important thing I picked out of HBS was the concept of the market as a whole, of a business as an entity, a whole thing. Like an army on a battlefield where so many different pieces come together to create the whole unit. If you have well-thought-out strategies and tactics to achieve the goals, it makes a difference. The people in the organization are what make it all work. Prior to coming to HBS I had never, ever thought of a business organization as operating that way."

As a natural extension of this approach, a great many students develop a mind-set about an organization's relationship to society, seeing the enterprise not as successful or unsuccessful in and of itself but as part of a community of effort. The educational level of employees, the church, the family, the role of government—these and many other elements come to be seen as important background affecting what a firm can do. I don't want to push this point too far, for alumni become preoccupied with their organizations and from time to time are as blind to social conditions as anyone, but in the backs of their minds is an awareness of a bigger picture than the organization's, often poorly articulated but always there.

It should not be surprising that numerous alums have been acutely conscious of their social responsibilities as executives. Thus, James Burke '49, for many years head of Johnson & Johnson (he retired in 1989), took charge within hours of the public response when cyanide-poisoned bottles of Tylenol began turning up in 1982; Robert Haas '68, head of Levi Straus, is going around the country promoting the idea that AIDS is a business problem as well as a social problem; Robert Rosenberg '63, chief executive of Dunkin' Donuts, serves as the head of the board of trustees for a small Vermont school for dyslexic boys (one of his children is dyslexic), as fund-raising chairman for the Retarded Citizens Association, and as an overseer of the Museum of Fine Arts; and Reuben Mark '63, chief executive of Colgate-Palmolive Company, actively supports his company's emphasis on youth education and sports in community relations, one such activity being the annual Colgate Women's Games in New York, which allow 30,000 inner-city young women to compete in season-long track and field events. There are literally thousands of such examples.

GETTING ITS ACT TOGETHER

How does the B-school motivate students? What enables it to influence and transform them with such awe-inspiring success?

The most important way, of course, is a well-balanced class of bright, energetic, managers-to-be. The feeling that you are with the best is the fuse that drives case discussions and the section system. The desire to hold your own in this elite group keeps you going through periods of setback and discouragement.

But there are other ways, and in combination with the magic wrought by the Admissions Department, they are very important. Since we have said little about them yet, let me mention a few specifics.

MESSAGE OF THE CAMPUS

The campus is one of the most significant things about the school. It is tangible, visual, dramatic. Without any words it delivers a stunning first impression to the arriving student or first-time visitor. The message is: Management is important. This place is important. *You* are important.

Now, this was not always so at the B-school. From 1908 until 1925, the school was an orphan, looked down on and even despised by many professors and students at Harvard. It began shakily in three borrowed rooms in Harvard Yard. However, when George Baker came along in the early 1920s with his $5 million gift enabling the B-school to leave the yard and cross the river, the administration in Massachusetts Hall was willing and able.

Lady Luck was kind to Harvard's Cinderella school. Although it began with no hoopla, no lavish public relations programs, it had such ardent champions as university president Charles Eliot, about to complete an illustrious forty-year-reign when the B-school was conceived, and Lawrence Lowell, one of the great renaissance men of this century, who succeeded Eliot in 1909 and collaborated with him in naming the new school. Lowell supported the fledgling for many years and played a key role in its building.

HBS has also been blessed by having great deans. Its first dean, Edward Gay, set the pace by giving the enterprise his all. "No gardener," he wrote in a report quoted by Jeffrey Cruikshank in *A Delicate Experiment*, "ever tended a fragile plant more carefully than I did, to keep an eye on all the details of our infant School." Although suffering a painful appendicitis attack in September 1908, Gay was so committed that he postponed surgery until after the school opened on October 1.

After Gay came Wallace Donham, Donald David, Stanley Teele, George Baker, Lawrence Fouraker, and John McArthur—all named by the Harvard Corporation, a lineup of educators that would be hard to beat.

"It took guts for Harvard to establish the school," Professor C. Roland Christensen told the HBS Club of Detroit a few years ago. "Imagine how the bricks in University Hall were shifting when Professor William James Cunningham, a lecturer in railroad operation whose formal education apparently consisted of enrollment in a correspondence school, was named to a chaired professorship." Academic skeptics abounded everywhere. A Harvard professor of literature is reputed to have asked rhetorically, on hearing HBS's name mentioned in conversation, "What? Sully the robes of Chaucer and Shakespeare with seekers of gold?"

After Baker's gift of the main campus and buildings the administration kept working. Small and large buildings were added. Money was plowed into making the campus more beautiful. Every year the school spends many millions on maintenance and renovation—close to $10 million per year between 1984 and 1988, much more than that in 1990.

With ecclesiastical finesse, Robert Massie, Jr., '86, who came to HBS from Grace Church in New York City, where he had been a minister, made biblical comparisons when he described the school for *Manhattan* magazine:

"The first time I walked around the Harvard Graduate School of Business Administration and looked at its massive and elegant buildings, its manicured lawns and pampered flora, I thought of Moses. According to the third chapter of the book of Exodus, as Moses stood on Mount Sinai before the burning bush, he heard a voice that said: 'Come no nearer, take off your shoes; the place you are standing on is holy ground.' "

When I see Baker Library, the original center of the campus with its wide steps, six Ionic columns, heavy black Georgian lanterns dangling on thick chains, and a white-and-gold cupola high overhead, I think of it as a symbol of several things. First of all, it symbolizes the importance of management by virtue of its collection of business literature, reportedly the largest in the world. Second, it symbolizes the relatedness of management to other professions. For instance, from the main reading room you can ascend stairs to a visible collection of law books. Third, it symbolizes that management is not a "nice guy" activity. When you enter the lobby, an enormous and rather formidable vault as big as a bus station's, you see the intimidating bust of Henry Clay Frick scowling at passersby, and at the top of the stairs to the reading room you see a large sullen portrait of George Baker glaring at climbers.

The library also symbolizes the B-school's relation to the university and non-HBS Harvard alumni. Inside its gleaming cupola is housed a huge bronze bell. Half a century ago, a Harvard College grad named Charles Crane, a diplomat and authority on Russian bells, heard that the Kremlin planned to melt down some old bells into armaments; in the nick of time he contacted government leaders in the USSR, purchased the bells, and gave a set to the university. The university in turn gave one bell from the carillon to the B-school. That bell rings at MBAs' graduation.

Under the roof peak of Baker is a large blue medallion, which is frequently painted and always looks fresh. Though somewhat individualized in style and contour, the medallion features the university motto, *Veritas,* and is shaped like the Harvard shield. Another symbol of HBS's connection lies a stone's throw away in the dean's office in Morgan Hall—a fine old oval table, known as the Eliot table, which was used for Harvard College faculty meetings in the latter half of the nineteenth century.

PROGRAMS AND ACTIVITIES

But the campus is not the only visual impact on students and visitors, and visual impact is not the only way the school gets its message across. HBS is a fantastic example of an organization that knows its purpose and works with uncanny skill at fitting each activity into that purpose. For instance:

Executive education. The B-school runs four programs on campus for executives. Altogether, these four programs account for more than 20 percent of HBS alums. During the past four years, more than half of the major U.S. corporations have sent executives to these programs; so have about a quarter of their counterparts abroad. Graduates range from Arthur Brashear, chairman of Tex-O-Cal Hardwoods in Temple, Texas, and Donald Platten, chairman of the executive committee at Chemical Bank in New York, to Herbert Barton, managing director of Zimbabwe Bata Shoe Company in Zimbabwe, and Alfred Mulder, managing director of Transmark Holding in the Netherlands.

The oldest and most famous program is the Advanced Management Program (AMP), a brainchild of Dean Donald David in 1943. It lasts for eleven weeks, runs three times a year, and counts about eleven thousand graduates. Two members in five come from foreign countries. These people have policymaking management jobs and are destined for higher ones. At HBS they live in comfortable but spartan single rooms, with a separate discussion or "can" room, complete with refrigerator and TV, for every six bedrooms. All cases used are tailored for AMP, including an eight-hundred-page-or-so Goliath typically used near the end of a session. In the words of one member I know, the participants "work their asses off."

Professor Hugo Uyterhoeven calls AMP "a fantastic quality-control device" because it forces professors to talk to experienced executives, not just to ambitious MBAs. Visually, AMPers give young people a close-up look at what they themselves are supposed to become someday. Alums open many doors for case writers, often let second-year students in to conduct field studies, induce their organizations to give generously to HBS fund drives, hire numerous MBAs, and, last but not least from the faculty standpoint, have helped many a professor to a generous consulting agreement.

The Program for Management Development (PMD) was started in 1961. It caters to managers with fifteen or so years of experience working in organizations. As with the other executive programs, applicants must be fully sponsored by their employing organizations, which generally means that they are slated for promotion. Typically around 125 middle managers make up a PMD session; about half of the members to date have been U.S. citizens and the rest have come from nearly thirty nations abroad.

The Owner-President Management (OPM) Program, started in 1972 as the Smaller Company Management Program, is for entrepreneurs and heads of companies with $1 million to $100 million sales. The program is unusual in that it is divided into three three-week sessions spanning three years. One of the aims of OPM is to acquaint entrepreneurs with general management problems, including the challenges that occur at different stages of growth and top management's role in the organization. A great practical value is enabling executives with different backgrounds to rub elbows with one another. As Professor Martin Marshall once observed, "When you're running one of these businesses, you're often lonely."

The International Senior Management Program was started in 1973. For many years it was headquartered in Switzerland, but in 1984 it came to the HBS campus. The program runs for eight weeks, boasts many illustrious alumni, and in a typical year is likely to draw members from a couple of dozen countries. "When I was at the program," said Peter Miller, from Great Britain's United Transport International Group, a couple of years ago, "I didn't know what country I was in."

Research. The school spends many millions every year on research. In addition to its obvious purposes of giving instructors a break from teaching and providing leads to good cases, research opens windows into new worlds and keeps the faculty, staff, and students in touch with what is going on. Competitiveness, ethics, financial techniques, human resources, employee dispute resolution—these and many other topics are covered. Perhaps the most conspicuous example in today's news is a remarkable research project just completed by a team of experts under the codirection of Professor Paul Lawrence. For months Lawrence and colleagues studied management practices in the USSR in four industries. (A Soviet team did the same thing in this country.)

This was the first time that American researchers were allowed to observe firsthand Russian operations. In the fall of 1990, four Soviet managers will begin the MBA program.

Professorial consulting. Even the school's policy of allowing professors up to one-fifth of their time for management consulting fits into the mosaic. For instance, early in the 1970s Professor Louis Wells went to Indonesia to gather material for a case on joint ventures. After he got the case, the Indonesian minister of manpower interested him in a consulting assignment on why foreign firms sometimes choose capital-intensive technology in a country where labor is inexpensive. After completing this assignment, Wells saw the possibilities for a large research project on corporate choices of technology, negotiated at home and abroad, and got the project under way at the B-school.

EDUCATIONAL POLICIES

As we saw early on, the case method has a profound influence on students, forcing them to take responsibility for decisions. In view of the agony this causes, especially when students have to wrestle with more cases than seems humanly possible, it may seem strange to call the approach a motivator, but it is that—and a powerful one. The reason is that the case method is empowering; it opens students' eyes to the fact that they don't have to be geniuses to improve management, that they can step in and make matters better without waiting years and years for everyday experience to soak in, without long apprenticeships in the mastery of local custom and detail. Professor Howard Stevenson put it this way to a group of us:

"The case method works on the idea that you can't have perfection, and I think this has been a very important element of our graduates' success. One of the things we do best is to show, in the classroom, in case discussion, that the perfect is often the enemy of the better. Students learn that if they are always trying to find perfection, they may never make those incremental improvements that really *will* improve the lot of everyone around. I think the case method gets at this problem directly. If you simply lecture to people, you create an entirely different attitude. Students are waiting for you to give 'the answer.' There's a built-in bias against action. What we say with the case method is: 'Look, I know you don't have enough information—but given the information you *do* have, what are you going to do?' "

In a word, the case method satisfies the *activism* in students. Especially for young men and women, it is a powerful motivator.

In my early years at the B-school I talked with many of the "greats" who developed this approach—professors such as Charles Gragg, Melvin Copeland, and Fritz Roethlisberger, administrators such as Dr. Andrew Towl. From these conversations I got no inkling that the fathers of the approach foresaw how deeply it would affect students. It was not until students became alums and started reporting back to the faculty that the school realized what a good thing it was on to.

The school's commitment to quality control of instructors is another policy that connects closely with the case method, section system, and the general impact of the school on students. Enormous amounts of time, energy, and money are spent on getting, instructing, and coaching the best teachers whom the school can get into the classrooms. Case method teaching is fraught with pitfalls and potholes; not everyone by any means can do well in the pit. Quality control of teaching acts as both carrot and stick in stimulating learning.

Finally, let me mention the no-mothering policies of the administration. They are another strand in the web that makes the B-school what it is, sooner or later affecting most students. Donald Brophy '47, chairman of the board of trustees of Hahnemann University in Philadelphia, tells of a time shortly after World War II when *The Harbus News* was in dire financial straits. He and four others on the staff approached an assistant dean. Could the school give some funds to help? The assistant dean told them, "Gentlemen, you are now at the Harvard Graduate School of Business Administration. You go out and find your own capital." Fortunately, Brophy and colleagues were able to do that, and they kept *Harbus* going during that difficult period. Today it thrives.

Now, I have told this story to outsiders, and often their reaction (especially before the final outcome is added) is one of dismay. "How could the assistant dean be so heartless?" What they over-look is that the kind of student admitted to HBS is a capable sort who can perform all sorts of wizardry—if he or she *has* to. One of the secrets of the school is how hard it tries in every possible way to see that such an effort is made.

In sum, HBS motivates because its incentives reinforce each other and are synergistic. However, let us not lose sight of the purpose of all this. The real test of the school is what its graduates do—not how well its faculty and staff perform but how its *alums* perform. If they help this country become more competitive in the global economy, they and the school measure up; if they fail, the synergy and symbiosis are misdirected.

So far, the tests are positive. A majority of B-school alumni are in top management, and a majority of the organizations they serve appear to thrive in the global economy. When other lead-ing management schools are factored in, the impact seems very great indeed. The result bodes well for America, for no other country in the world is blessed with such education and training.

CAPITALIZING ON AMERICANA

But in the long run the most important thing about the B-school may be its relationship with traditional American attitudes to-ward individualism, open inquiry, and human dignity. In the past we have tended to think of such attitudes as precious but expen-sive. What the B-school demonstrates is that they can be prodi-gious assets, too, hastening a process of maturing and broadening that is accomplished clumsily if at all under traditional forms of education.

How is this done? Reflect for a moment on some of the pro-cesses described:

- In class and on exams there are no "right" answers. Students must reason and show they know the subject, but they can score as well disagreeing with the professor or the majority as agreeing with them.

- Case discussions are open to almost any heresy or line of inquiry so long as it is relevant and factual.
- Students, not instructors, "own" the discussion.
- Instructors do enforce certain classroom procedures, however. For example, students must speak in turn, and they must listen respectfully. The genius from Princeton must listen to—and sometimes be humbled by—the drawling farm boy from Oklahoma, and vice versa.
- Instructors also are role models of the attitudes they want students to adopt. They listen attentively, respect heretical arguments, encourage diversity.
- Classes destroy the myth of the "giant brain," that is, the illusion that one person can come up with all the right answers. In any section or class, the brightest people are continually reminded by others that they don't have a monopoly on insight and judgment. In management, at least, the group has it over individuals, even though some one person must make the final decision.

I don't mean to suggest that all Harvard MBAs are open-minded and democratic. That is not so. Many are heavy-handed; many operate in totalitarian ways. But while at the B-school they learn as much as they do in such a short time because of, not in spite of, democracy in the classroom. And it is because of the democratic case method, continually invested in and updated, that they are well prepared for the "real world" and can get off to fast starts.

In 1802 the country established a military academy at West Point in order to provide a steady supply of trained army officers to meet the threat of military warfare. (The other military academies were established later.) Congress and public officials realized the folly of trusting to luck for plenty of future George Washingtons to lead the troops. Today it is not military warfare but economic struggle that we must prepare better for, and a striking parallel can be seen between the two. There is as much folly in trusting to hit-or-miss luck for corporate leadership as for military leadership. While our economic "academies" don't need to supply all the economic leaders, they guarantee the development of a hard core so that we don't have to count completely on self-made managers trained in the "school of hard knocks."

Global economic rivalries are, of course, less vivid and spectacular than shooting and bombing, and their effects take longer to become manifest. But in the end their consequences are far-reaching—standard of living, public programs, control over our destiny, pride. Foreign nations can defeat us more convincingly in economic warfare than in military action. As we are learning to our sorrow, the economic casualties inflicted can be severe.

The B-school is a thoroughly American institution that succeeds on the basis of democratic attitudes. This is an important test; with an economy's increasing ability to affect society, we want our economic organizations to be true to the traditions this country stands for. The implicit message of the B-school is that humanism, respect for the individual, and diversity are more than ideals for living. They also have great practical value in educating future managers.

> ▪ *Several years ago, in a burst of admiration,* The New York Times *called the Harvard Graduate School of Business Administration master's degree the 'Golden Passport.' It was not hyperbole. . . .*
>
> —PAUL SOLMAN AND THOMAS FRIEDMAN
> in *Life and Death on the Corporate Battlefield* (1982)

SELECTED
BIBLIOGRAPHY

Bennett, John B., and E. L. Felton, Jr. *Managerial Decision Making.* Columbus, Ohio: Grid, Inc., 1974.

Christensen, C. Roland, and Abby J. Hansen. *Teaching and the Case Method.* Boston: Harvard Business School Press, 1987.

Cohen, Peter. *The Gospel According to the Harvard Business School.* New York: Doubleday, 1973.

Copeland, Melvin T. *And Mark an Era: The Story of the Harvard Business School.* Boston: Little, Brown, 1958.

Course Development and Research Profile. Boston: Harvard Business School.

Harbus News, The. Boston: Harvard Business School.

Harvard Business Review. Boston: Harvard Business School,

Harvard Business School Bulletin, The. Boston: Harvard Business School.

Henry, Fran Worden. *Toughing It Out at Harvard.* New York: Putnam, 1983.

Kelly, Francis J., and Heather Mayfield Kelly. *What They* Really *Teach You at the Harvard Business School.* New York: Warner, 1986.

Mark, J. Paul. *The Empire Builders: Power, Money and Ethics Inside the Harvard Business School.* New York: Morrow, 1987.

Massie, Robert K., Jr. "Prophets to Profits." *Manhattan, Inc.,* August 1985.

McCormack, Mark H. *What They Don't Teach You at Harvard Business School.* New York: Bantam, 1984.

————. *What They Still Don't Teach You at Harvard Business School.* New York: Bantam, 1989.

Orth, Charles D. III. *Social Structure and Learning Climate: The First Year at the Harvard Business School.* Boston: Harvard Business School Division of Research, 1963.

Shames, Laurence. *The Big Time: The Harvard Business School's Most Successful Class and How It Shaped America.* New York: Harper & Row, 1986.

Solman, Paul, and Thomas Friedman. *Life and Death on the Corporate Battlefield.* New York: Simon & Schuster, 1982.

LIST OF EMPLOYERS INTERVIEWING AT HARVARD BUSINESS SCHOOL JANUARY–MARCH 1987

Subsidiary companies are listed under the name of the parent company.

A.T. Kearney, Inc.
AEtna Life & Casualty
AMR Corporation
  American Airlines
AT&T
  AT&T Eastern
    Region—Business Markets
    Group
  AT&T International
  AT&T–Headquarters, Business
    Research Organization
Advanced Micro Devices
Air Products & Chemicals
Alex Brown & Sons, Inc.
Alliance Consulting Group
American Cyanamid Company
American Express Company
  Shearson Lehman Brothers
  Travel Related Services
    Company

American International Group
American Medical International,
  Inc.
American Ventures Corporation
Amoco Corporation
Apple Computer, Inc.
Applied Energy Services, Inc.
Applied Materials
Arthur D. Little
Arthur Young & Company
Atlanta Sosnoff Capital
  Corporation
Atlantic Richfield Company
Ayers, Whitmore & Company
BOC Group PLC
  The BOC Group (Airco Gases)
  The BOC Group (Ohmeda
    Life Support)
  The BOC Group, Inc.
Bain & Company, Inc.

Balis & Zorn, Inc.
Banc One Corporation
  Bank One Columbus
Bank Paribas
  Consultronics
Bank of Boston
Bank of Montreal
Bank of New England
    Corporation
  BNE Associates
  Bank of New England
BankAmerica Corporation
  Bank of America
Bankers Trust Company
Baxter Travenol
  Travenol Laboratories
BayBanks, Inc.
Bear Stearns & Company,
    Inc.
Beecham Group PLC
  Beecham Products
Boise Cascade Corporation
Bowles Hollowell Conner &
    Company
Brian M. Freeman & Company,
    Inc.
Bristol-Myers Company
Broadview Associates
Brown Brothers Harriman &
    Company
Burlington Industries, Inc.
Burns, Fry, Ltd.
  Burns, Fry, Timmins, Inc.
Burroughs Corporation
CIGNA Corporation
CSX Transportation
  CSX Distribution Services
Cambridge Associates, Inc.
Cambridge Management Group
Capital Group, Inc.
  Capital Research Company

Carter Hawley Hale Stores, Inc.
  Carter Hawley Hale Corporate
    Emporium Capwell
    Neiman Marcus
Castle & Cooke, Inc.
  Dole Fresh Foods
  Dole Packaged Foods
Chase Manhattan Bank
Chemical New York Corporation
  Chemical Bank
Chevron Corporation
Chrysler Corporation
Ciba-Geigy Ltd.
  Ciba-Geigy
Circuit City Stores Inc.
Citicorp
  Citibank
Clayton Williams & Sherwood
Clorox
Coca-Cola Company
  Columbia Pictures
  Columbia Pictures Industries,
    Inc.
Colgate-Palmolive Company
Conrail
Cookson America, Inc.
Cooper Industries
Corning Glass Works
Creditanstalt-Bankverein
Cummins Engine Company
Data General Corporation
Data Translation
Dayton Hudson Corporation
  Dayton-Hudson Department
    Store
Decision Focus, Inc.
Digital Equipment Corporation
Dominion Securities Pitfield
    Limited
Duff & Phelps
E. & J. Gallo Winery

E.F. Hutton & Company, Inc.
E.I. du Pont de Nemours &
    Company, Inc.
  Conoco, Inc.
ENG, Inc.
Eastdil Realty
Edison Brothers Stores, Inc.
Eli Lilly & Company
  Eli Lilly & Company
  Eli Lilly International
    Corporation
Emerson Electric Company
  Copeland Corporation
  Emerson Electric Company
Equitable Financial Services
Equitable Life Assurance
    Company
  Donaldson, Lufkin & Jenrette
Ernst & Whinney
Exxon Corporation
FMC Corporation
FMR Corporation
  Fidelity Management &
    Research Company
FN Burt
Faxon Company, Inc.
Federated Dept. Stores
  Bloomingdale's
First Boston Corporation
First Empire State Corporation
  Manufacturers and Traders
    Trust Co.
First Wachovia Corporation
Ford Motor Company
GAF Corporation
General Electric Company
  Kidder, Peabody & Company,
    Inc.
General Mills
General Motors Corporation
  Hughes Aircraft Company

Gerald D. Hines Interests
Gillette Company
  Gillette Company
Golder Thoma & Cressey
Goldman, Sachs & Company
Gordon Capital Corporation
Grey Advertising
H.B. Oppenheimer & Associates
Hambrecht & Quist
  Incorporated
Hammond Company
Hartford National Corporation
  Connecticut National Bank
Helene Curtis
Henley Group
  Signal Capital Corporation
Hewlett-Packard Company
Honeywell, Inc.
Hong Kong Shanghai Banking
  Corporation
  Marine Midland Bank
Houlihan, Lokey, Howard & Zukin
ICF Incorporated
Indivers, N.V.
Information Resources
International Financial Markets
    Trading Limited
International Business Machines
  Corp.
  Rolm Corporation
Ivy Fund
J.P. Morgan & Company, Inc.
  Morgan Guaranty Trust
    Company
J.P. Stevens & Company
J.W. O'Connor & Company, Inc.
JMB Realty Corporation
Jefferson Smurfit Corporation
Johnson & Johnson
  Johnson & Johnson
    International

Johnson & Johnson (*cont.*)
  McNeil Consumer Products
  Personal Products
Julien J. Studley, Inc.
KLA Instruments Corp.
Kaempfer Company
Keith-Stevens, Inc.
Kohler Company
Krupp Companies
Kurt Salmon Associates
L.F. Rothschild, Unterberg,
    Towbin, Inc.
LTV Corporation
  LTV Aerospace & Defense
    Company
LaSalle Partners
Lazard Frères and Company
Liberty Mutual Insurance Co.
  Stein Roe & Farnham
Lithonia Lighting
Lotus Development Corporation
MAC Group
MBI, Inc.
MID
Maguire/Thomas Partners
Manufacturers Hanover
Marakon Associates
Mark Twain Bancshares
Mars & Company
Marsh & McLennan Companies,
    Inc.
  Putnam Management
    Company, Inc.
Maryland National Bank
Massachusetts Financial Services
May Department Stores
    Company
McCain Foods Ltd.
McCown De Leeuw & Company
McDonnell Douglas Corporation
  McDonnell Douglas Network
    Systems Company–TYMNET

Mead Corporation
Mellon Bank Corporation
  Mellon Bank
Merchants National Bank
Merrill Lynch & Company, Inc.
  Merrill Lynch Canada Inc.
  Merrill Lynch Capital Markets
Metropolitan Life Insurance
    Company
  State Street Research &
    Management
Microsoft Corporation
Milestone Properties
    Corporation
Morgan Stanley & Company,
    Inc.
  Morgan Stanley Realty
Motorola, Inc.
  Codex Corporation
NCNB Corporation
Narragansett Capital
    Corporation
Nature Conservancy
    International
Nesbitt Thomson Bongard
New Seabury Corporation
New York Life Insurance
    Company, Inc.
  New York Life Securities, Inc.
Nomura Securities International,
    Inc.
Norton Company
O'Connor & Associates
Oliver Carr Company
Onex Capital Corporation
Oppenheimer & Company,
    Inc.
Oracle Corporation
Owens-Illinois, Inc.
PA Consulting
  PA Computers &
    Telecommunications

PPG Industries, Inc.
Pacific Investment Management
Pacific Mutual Life Insurance
Pacific Realty Corporation
Pacific Telesis
  PacTel
  PacTel Services
PaineWebber Group, Inc.
  PaineWebber Capital Markets
  PaineWebber Development
    Corporation
  PaineWebber Incorporated
Palladian Software
Peat, Marwick, Mitchell &
  Company
PepsiCo, Inc.
  Frito-Lay, Inc.
  Pepsi Cola Company
  Taco Bell Corporation
Perkin-Elmer Corporation
Pfizer, Inc.
Philip Morris Companies, Inc.
  General Foods
  Philip Morris Credit Corp.
  Philip Morris USA
Pillsbury Company
Pittiglio, Rabin, Todd &
  McGrath
Price Waterhouse
  Strategic Management
    Consulting
Principal Group, Ltd.
Private Satellite Network,
  Inc.
Procter & Gamble Company
Progressive Corporation
  Progressive Casualty Insurance
    Company
Progressive Corporation
Prudential Insurance Company
  Prudential Asset Management
    Co.

Prudential Realty Group
Prudential Venture Capital
  Management, Inc.
Prudential-Bache Securities
  Inc.
Quadrex Securities
  Corporation
Quaker Oats Company
R. J. Financial Corporation
  Raymond James & Associates,
    Inc.
R.H. Development Company
Reuters North America
Richard Ellis
Rockefeller Group, Inc.
  Cushman and Wakefield, Inc.
Rohm & Haas Company
Russell Reynolds Associates
S.C. Johnson & Son, Inc.
  Johnson Wax
SIAR Planning A.B. Sweden
  SIAR, Inc.
Saatchi & Saatchi
  Hay Group, Inc.
Salomon Brothers Inc.
Sandoz
Sanford C. Bernstein &
  Company
Schroder Ventures/Schroder
  Group
Scientific Atlanta
Sears, Roebuck and Company
  Dean Witter Real Estate
  Dean Witter Reynolds Inc.
  Harbridge House, Inc.
Security Pacific Corporation
  Security Pacific National
    Bank
Smith Barney, Harris Upham &
  Company
Sonnenblick Goldman
  Corporation

Spaulding & Slye Company
Springs Industries, Inc.
Squibb Corporation
    Squibb Operating Group
Standard Oil Company
State Street Bank and Trust
    Company
Sun Microsystems
Swiss Bank Corporation
Swiss Colony
T. Rowe Price Associates
Techint Organization
Temple, Barker & Sloane,
    Inc.
Teradyne, Inc.
Theodore Barry & Associates
Thomson McKinnon Securities,
    Inc.
Time Inc.
Timken Company
Tishman Realty & Construction
    Co.
    Tishman Realty Corporation
Toronto Dominion Bank
Touche Ross & Company
    Braxton Associates
Towers, Perrin, Forster &
    Crosby
    Cresap, McCormick & Paget
Trammell Crow Company

Travelers Companies
    Dillon, Read & Company
Trust Company Bank
UAL, Inc.
    United Airlines
US Environmental Protection
    Agency
United Technologies
    Otis Elevator Company
VLSI Technology, Inc.
Vita Plus Industries, Inc.
WMB Consulting Inc.
Walt Disney Company
Warner-Lambert Company
Washington Post Company
    Washington Post
Weiss, Peck & Greer
Wellington Management
Wertheim & Company
Westchase Development
    Corporation
Westvaco Corporation
Weyerhaeuser Company
William Blair & Company
Windward Management
    Company Inc.
    J. Bildner & Sons
Wood Gundy, Inc.
Xerox Corporation
Young & Rubicam

INDEX